LIFE AMONG THE APACHES

LIFE
AMONG THE APACHES:

The Classic History of Native American Life on the Plains

BY

JOHN C. CREMONY

Skyhorse Publishing

First published in 1868
First Skyhorse Publishing edition 2015

Skyhorse Publishing books may be purchased in bulk at special discounts for sales promotion, corporate gifts, fund-raising, or educational purposes. Special editions can also be created to specifications. For details, contact the Special Sales Department, Skyhorse Publishing, 307 West 36th Street, 11th Floor, New York, NY 10018 or info@skyhorsepublishing.com.

www.skyhorsepublishing.com

10 9 8 7 6 5 4 3

Library of Congress Cataloging-in-Publication Data is available on file.

Cover design by Anthony Morais
Cover photo credit: Alfred Jacob Miller

Print ISBN: 978-1-62914-370-5
Ebook ISBN: 978-1-63220-023-5

Printed in the United States of America

TO THE PIONEER AND LIBERAL PUBLISHER,

Anton Roman,

THE ZEALOUS AND ENTERPRISING FRIEND OF LITERATURE ON
THE PACIFIC COAST, THIS UNPRETENDING VOLUME IS
RESPECTFULLY DEDICATED AS A TRIBUTE
OF THE AUTHOR'S ESTEEM.

CONTENTS OF THE VOLUME.

1*

CHAPTER VI.

CHAPTER VII.

CHAPTER VIII.

CHAPTER IX.

CHAPTER X.

CHAPTER XI.

CHAPTER XII.

CHAPTER XIII.

CHAPTER XIV.

CHAPTER XV.

CHAPTER XVI.

CHAPTER XVII.

CHAPTER XVIII.

CHAPTER XIX.

CHAPTER XX.

CHAPTER XXI.

CHAPTER XXII.

CHAPTER XXIII.

CHAPTER XXIV.

CHAPTER XXV.

CHAPTER XXVI.

CHAPTER XXVII.

PREFACE.

Those who may favor the succeeding pages with their perusal, must not expect any attempt at fine writing or glowing description. The author's intention is, to furnish a plain, unvarnished tale of actual occurrences and facts illustrative of the various tribes of Indians occupying that vast region which extends from the Colorado river on the west, to the settlements of Texas on the east, and from Taos in New Mexico to Durango in the Mexican Republic.

In the front rank of the tribes, occupying the region included within the limits mentioned, stands the great Apache race, and next are the Comanches. The former of these will engage most of the author's attention for very many and obvious reasons. It is believed that the book will contain a large amount of valuable information, to be derived from no other source extant, and it will be the author's endeavor to place it before his readers in a manner which will engage their attention. Nothing not strictly true will be admitted into its pages, and if some of the incidents narrated be found of a thrilling character, the reader will experience satisfaction in knowing that they are not the results of imaginative picturing. Whenever a personal adventure is narrated, it will be found to illustrate some particular phase of character; none are recounted which do not convey information.

Our Government has expended millions of dollars, in driblets, since the acquisition of California, in efforts to reduce the Apaches and Navajoes, who occupy that extensive belt of country which forms the highway for overland migration from the East to the West; but we are as far from success to-day as we were twenty years ago. The reason is obvious. We have never striven to make ourselves intelligently acquainted with those tribes. Nearly all that relates to them is quite as uncertain and indefinite to our comprehension as that which obtains in the center of Africa. Those who were the best informed on the matter, and had given it the closest attention, were, at the same time—most unfortunately—the least capable of imparting their information; while those who were almost ignorant of the subject have been the most forward to give the results of their fragmentary gleanings. If this volume shall have the effect of bettering our present deplorable Indian policy, by letting in some light, it will accomplish the author's object.

SAN FRANCISCO, August, 1868.   J. C. C.

CHAPTER I.

My first business acquaintance with "Lo" occurred
in the year 1847. A band of about one hundred Comanche warriors, led by a chief named Janamata, or the
"Red Buffalo," taking advantage of the subdued and
defenceless condition of the Mexicans, crossed the Rio
Grande, about seventy miles below Old Reynosa, and
commenced a series of depredations. Information was
immediately given to the American officer commanding
at that post, and the writer was detailed, with a force of
fifty men, to drive off the invaders, with orders not to
engage in hostilities, unless the Indians proved refrac-
tory and deaf to all other appeals.

After marching fifty miles, which was accomplished in
two days, we arrived at the scene of operations, meeting
the Comanches on the highway. Our force was immediately disposed to the best advantage, and placing a
white handkerchief on the point of my sabre, I advanced
alone toward the chief, who, leaving his warriors, rode
forward to meet me. He spoke Spanish fluently, having
evidently acquired it in his many marauding excursions
into Mexico. Having met, I offered him a cigarito, which
was accepted with Indian stoicism. We smoked in perfect silence for half a minute, when the cigaritos having
been consumed the following dialogue took place:

Officer.—"I am sent to tell you, that you must recross

2

the Rio Grande with your warriors, and come here no more to molest these people while we remain in the country."

Indian.—"I hear your words. They are not pleasant. These Mexicans are our natural enemies; we have warred against them for many years. They are also your enemies. You are killing them in their own country, the same as I am. The Comanches are friends to the Americans. Why do you prevent your friends from hunting your enemies and theirs?"

Officer.—"Red man, you mistake. These people were our enemies, but they have yielded, and all who have submitted are under our protection. We have ceased from doing them harm, and if we permit you to injure them after we have disarmed them, it would be the same as if we did so ourselves."

Indian.—"But your revenge is for yourselves. It does not satisfy us for the blood of Comanches slain by Mexicans. You made war upon them without our consent or knowledge. We do the same. A wise warrior takes advantage of his enemy's weakness. It is now our opportunity."

Officer.—"These people are our captives, and cannot continue to be your enemies while in that condition. Suppose you had a dozen Apache captives, would you permit the Kaddos to come into your camp and kill them; take their property and go off without resistance?"

Indian.—"White man, your tongue is double, like a woman's; but the Comanche does not feel to war against his American brothers. I and my people will recross the Rio Grande, but will not promise never to come back. Good-by."

Our colloquy ended—we smoked another cigarito; he waved his hand to his warriors, and without another word directed his course to the river, which was soon waded, and Janamata, with his followers, stood on American soil. This little interview imparted the knowledge that the American savages are rather keen logicians, from their own uncivilized stand-point, as they are incapable of appreciating the moral and religious sensibilities of enlightened races.

Janamata was a good type of his tribe, in point of physical development. He was about five feet ten inches in height, with well proportioned shoulders, very deep chest, and long, thin, but muscular arms. His forehead was very broad and moderately high, his mouth enormous, and garnished with strong white teeth. His nose was of the Roman order, broad and with much expanded nostrils, which appeared to pulsate with every emotion; but his countenance was rigid and immovable as bronze. His arms consisted of a bow and quiver full of arrows, a long lance, a long sharp knife, worn in the top of his moccasin boot, and a very good Colt's revolver. A strong shield of triple buffalo hide, ornamented with brass studs, hung from his saddle bow, and his dress was composed of buckskin and buffalo hide well tanned and flexible, but wholly free from ornament. I afterwards learned from a Texas Ranger that he was called Janamata, or the "Red Buffalo," from a desperate encounter he once had with one of those animals, which had ripped up his horse, and attacked him on foot. In this encounter Janamata had only his knife to depend on, as he had lost lance and bow when unhorsed. It is related that as the buffalo charged upon him, he sprang over the animal's lowered front, and landing on his back, plunged his knife several times into its body; then, as suddenly jumping off behind, he seized it by the tail and with one cut severed the ham-string. These details made an impression upon me 'at the time which has never been effaced or weakened.

Years passed before another opportunity offered to extend my acquaintance with Indians, and then in a totally different sphere and under different circumstances, and with many different tribes. The lapse of time, however, gave opportunity for reflection, and I realized the fact that my former rude impressions, founded upon such authorities as Catlin, Cooper, and others, must be considerably modified; and I resolved that, should occasion ever offer, I would devote attention and time to the observation of Indian character as it is, and not as I had believed it to be from writers on the subject.

CHAPTER II.

March from Texas to El Paso. — The Lipans. — Their Personal Appearance. — Sait-jah and the Picture.

In the year 1849, I was prevailed upon by Dr. Thomas H. Webb, Secretary of the Massachusetts Historical Society, to forego my position on the *Boston Herald*, and accept an appointment on the United States Boundary Commission, then being re-organized under the Hon. John R. Bartlett. Mr. Bartlett selected some thirty of the Commission, and determined to proceed by way of the Northern Route, which, up to that period, had been traveled only three times, and was, consequently, but little known. The most valuable information relative to the route was received from Judge Ankrim — a brave, courteous and handsome gentleman. In accordance with the directions pricked out on Mr. Bartlett's traveling chart by Judge Ankrim, one portion of the Commission directed their way, leaving the great body, under Col. John McClellan, U. S. Topographical Engineers, to come on by what is known as the Southern Route, a well beaten and frequently used road. Many portions of the way selected by Mr. Bartlett had never before been gone over by white men. There was no trail to direct our course, nor did we possess any satisfactory knowledge of its ability to afford wood, water and grass. The maps, however, showed that it was crossed by certain streams at stated distances, and the venture was boldly undertaken.

On arriving within a short distance of the South Con-

cho river, we camped on a small stream named the Antelope creek, situated in the Lipan country. Early next
morning, as the party were about to resume the march,
an Indian was seen advancing at full speed. A halt was
ordered, and in a few minutes he was among us asking,
in Spanish, for the commander. I at once took him to
Mr. Bartlett, and, on approaching the Commissioner, our
red visitant commenced fumbling among his clothes,
from which he extracted a dirty piece of handkerchief,
which, being unrolled, disclosed another dirty rag, and
the unwrapping continued until five pieces of cotton
fragments had been unrolled, displaying a handsome
leopard skin pouch, in which were a number of recom-
mendations, signed by well-known Americans, and set-
ting forth that the bearer, Chipota, a Lipan chief, had, a
short time before, celebrated a treaty of peace with the
United States, and was entitled to the consideration and
kindness of all American travelers over those wastes.
During the interview, I attentively watched the Indian,
who gave slight indications of uneasiness as to the manner in which his overtures would be received; but these
were soon dissipated by the frank and amicable deportment of Mr. Bartlett, who invited his visitor to take a
seat in his carriage and proceed with him to the next
camp, which was about twelve miles further. Chipota
appeared to be about sixty years of age. He was short,
stout and sinewy, with an uncommonly high and expan-
sive forehead, and so singularly like the celebrated Lewis
Cass in appearance, that the fact was immediately remarked by all the party who had ever seen Mr. Cass or
his portrait.

The Commissioner traveled in a close carriage, drawn
by four fleet and powerful mules. His *compagnon de voy-
age* was invariably Dr. Webb, who could never be induced

to mount a horse. The inside of the carriage was well supplied with Colt's and Sharp's rifles, Colt's pistols, a double-barreled shot gun, lots of ammunition, a spy-glass, and a number of small but useful tools. Upon entering this traveling arsenal, old Chipota looked around him with ill-concealed astonishment, which was greatly heightened by Mr. Bartlett preparing the spy-glass, and permitting him to take a good look through it at a distant object. The Indian could hardly credit that the thing he saw so distinctly through the glass was the same object he beheld so dimly with his naked eye. Not until we arrived in camp, however, were his senses brought to the full stand-point of admiration by the rapid discharges and terrific effects of the fire from our repeating rifles and pistols. Looking around with un-dissembled amazement, he said in his own language, as if soliloquizing: "*Inday pindah lickoyee schlango pooha-cante.*" It was not until years had passed that I became aware of the meaning of these words, but I noted them at the time by asking him to repeat them, and took a memorandum of their sounds. Since then I have discovered that they mean—"These people of the white eyes are wonderful medicine men."

About two hours after camping, we were joined by four more Lipans, the leader being named Chiquito, a Spanish term, signifying "the little one." He was tall, thin, sinewy, and had the appearance of having been possessed of more than ordinary powers of endurance. The likeness of this chief to General Jackson was quite as remarkable and striking as that of Chipota to General Cass, and was a general subject of remark. The most prominent member of Chiquito's escort was a tall, strong, well-made and handsome young Lipan dandy, who re-joiced in the name of Sait-jah, disdaining to be known by any Spanish term. This fellow evidently believed himself of some consequence, and strutted about with a very decided aristocratic bearing. After a short time passed in displaying his colossal proportions, his splendid leopard skin saddle, quiver, leggins, etc., Chipota quietly beckoned to him and the others, and, I suppose, gave them a short account of the wonders he had beheld. His warnings were received with trust by all but Sait-jah, who, like most inexperienced and flattered young men, savage or civilized, preferred to rely on his own experiences. Our party being small, and offering many temptations, I kept a strict but unobserved watch over the Indians, and suspected the tenor of Chipota's discourse, from his gesticulations. In a few minutes Sait-jah came toward me in a swaggering manner, and said, in broken Spanish: "Our chief says you great medicine; he says your pistol fires six times without reloading; he says you bring the trees which are afar off close to the eye, so you can count the leaves; he says your guns reach a great way, and never miss; he says a great many other wonderful things, which I cannot believe. You have bewitched him." Drawing a six-shooter from my belt, I pointed out a tree about seventy-five yards distant, and commenced firing rapidly. Each shot struck the tree, and blazed off large fragments of the bark. Sait-jah was astonished at the power of the weapon, and made no attempt to conceal his surprise; but his admiration broke out into emphatic expression when he witnessed the precision and reach of our Sharp's rifles, and the rapidity with which they could be loaded and fired. His pride had evidently received a heavy fall, and his lofty bearing was toned down to the level of his white visitors.

In my possession was the miniature of a young lady, whose many graces of person, cultivated mind and amiable disposition, rendered her one of the most lovable of Boston's fairest daughters. Sait-jah happened to see this picture, and asked permission to take a good look at the pleasant features. The miniature was placed in his hand, and his eyes seemed to devour its expressive lineaments. Throughout the remainder of that day this Indian bored me with frequent requests for another look, and the next morning, so soon as the camp was astir, he offered me his bow, arrows and splendid leopard skin for the picture. These offers being refused, he then added his horse, and whatever other property he might have, for its possession; but, finding me deaf to his entreaties, he took one long, last look, vaulted on his horse, set off at full speed and rapidly disappeared in the distance.

The Lipans are a numerous and warlike tribe, roaming over a vast extent of country, and perpetually at war with the Comanches, Kaddos, and other tribes of Western Texas. Since acquiring the Apache language, I have discovered that they are a branch of that great tribe — speaking identically the same language, with the exception of a few terms and names of things existing in their region and not generally known to those branches which inhabit Arizona and New Mexico. The Mescalero Apaches, in their search for buffaloes, frequently meet the Lipans, and always on the best of terms. No conflicts are known to have ever occurred between them; but they act in concert against the Comanches, and all other tribes. All the remarks on the Apache race, which will be found in the succeeding pages of this work, apply with equal force to the Lipans, with the exception of their tribal organization, the Lipans having regular chiefs, whom they obey on all occasions, and whose acts are final; while the Apaches are pure democrats, each warrior being his own master, and submitting only to

2*

the temporary control of a chief elected for the occasion.

As no other Indians were encountered until after our arrival at Paso del Norte, the remainder of our journey with its many incidents, sufferings and dangers, will not be expatiated upon in this work, which is solely dedicated to descriptions of Indian life.

CHAPTER III.

In the latter part of January, 1850, Mr. Bartlett took
advantage of the march of Col. Craig, commanding the
military escort of the Boundary Commission, to order
Dr. Webb, Mr. Thurber and myself to the Copper Mines
of Santa Rita, as Col. Craig had determined to make
that place his head-quarters until the extended operations of the Commission should demand a more advanced
post. Dr. Webb, Secretary of the Commission, and Mr.
Thurber, Botanist, rode in Mr. Bartlett's carriage, which
he had loaned them for the trip, but I preferred to take
the saddle, being mounted on an uncommonly fine horse
I had bought from Capt. A. Buford, First United States
Dragoons. In order not to be distressed by the slow,
painful and tiresome marches of the infantry, Dr. Webb
invariably ordered Wells, the carriage driver, to hurry
forward to the next camping ground, and we generally
arrived three or four hours in advance of the troops, my
horse keeping up with the carriage, for I would not leave
my party in so dangerous an Indian country as the one
we were then penetrating. Sometimes, when the road
was rough and difficult for the carriage, I was accustomed to ride ahead in search of game, being always
armed to the teeth with two belt and two holster six-
shooters, a Sharp's carbine and a large bowie knife. On

the fourth day of our march, I advanced about three
miles ahead of the carriage, which was detained in making the passage through Cooke's cañon, a rough, rocky
and very dangerous defile, about forty miles east of the
Mimbres river, and having observed some antelope tracks,
looked around in hope of seeing the animals, when I
perceived myself surrounded by a band of about twenty-
five Indians, who advanced upon me from all sides, led
by a savage who rode several yards ahead of all others.
At that time I could have broken through the circle and
rejoined my party with but little risk, as my horse was
infinitely superior in strength and speed to their ponies,
but as I felt convinced that the carriage would heave in
sight within a short time, my resolution was immediately
taken to adopt another policy.   By this time their leader
was from twenty-five to thirty yards in advance of his
followers, and about the same distance from me, perceiving which I drew a heavy holster pistol with my right
hand and putting spurs to my horse, met him in a bound
or two, when I addressed him to the following effect, in
Spanish:

"Keep off or I will shoot you."

To this he replied: "Who are you, and whence do you
come?"

Observing that his warriors were closing upon me, I
said: "See here, Indian, you have plenty of warriors
against one man, but I have got you; your people may
kill me, but I will kill you, so tell them to hold back at
once."

Involuntarily the Apache waved his hand, and his warriors halted about forty yards off.   Not liking so short a
distance, I again urged the chief to let his warriors fall
back still further, at the same time giving a significant
shake of my pistol.   This, too, was done, and the Apaches

increased their distance to about one hundred and fifty yards. The chief, whom I afterwards found to be Cuchillo Negro, or the "Black Knife," then endeavored to gain my left side, but I foiled his attempt by keeping my horse's head in his direction wherever he moved. He then said, "Good-by," and started to rejoin his comrades, but I again brought him to a sense of his position, by telling him I would not permit it, and he must stay with me until my friends came up. This excited considerable surprise, for he evidently labored under the idea that I was alone, or nearly so. The following dialogue then took place:

Cuchillo Negro.—"What do you want in my country?"

American.—"I came here because my chief has sent me. He is coming soon with a large force, and will pass through this country, but does not intend to remain or do any harm to his Apache brethren. We come in peace, and will always act peaceably, unless you compel us to adopt other measures; if you do, the consequences will do you great harm."

Cuchillo Negro.—"I do not believe your words. You are alone. My people have been on the watch, and have seen no forces coming this way. If any such had been on the road, we would have known it. You are in my power. What more have you to say?"

American.—"Indian, you are foolish. Long security has made you careless. A company of soldiers is close behind me; but your young men have been asleep. The squaws have retained them in camp, when they should have been on the lookout. I am not in your power, but you, personally, are in mine. Your people can kill me, but not until I have put a ball through your body. Any signal you may make to them, or any forward movement on their part, will also be signal for your death. If you do not believe me, wait a few moments, and you will see my friends come round the point of yonder hill. They are many, and intend to remain several moons in your country. If you treat them well you will grow rich and get many presents, but if you treat them badly they will search you out among the rocks and hills of your country, will take possession of your watering places, will destroy your plantations and kill your warriors. Now choose."

Cuchillo Negro.—"For many years no white man has penetrated these regions, and we do not permit people to enter our country without knowing their purpose. If you had friends, as you say, you would not have left them and come on alone, for that is foolish. My young men have not been led away by the squaws, for there are none within two sun's march, and if you had a large party with you, they would have known it and given me notice. You have many guns, but I have many men, and you cannot escape if I give the signal."

American.—"Indian, I don't think you will give that signal so long as you and I are so close together. Wait a few moments, and see whether I tell the truth."

This proposition was finally agreed to by him, and we sat on our horses waiting the approach of the carriage. It is unnecessary to say what my feelings were during the next quarter of an hour, nor to explain the manœuvres each adopted to get or keep the advantage of his enemy. I feel incapable of doing justice to the occasion. At the expiration of the time mentioned, the carriage hove in sight, about a quarter of a mile off, rounding the point of the mountain, and it had been detained so much during the march through the rocky and terrible defile that the infantry had come up with it and presented a formidable array of glittering tubes immediately in its rear.

At this unexpected sight, Cuchillo Negro gazed for a moment like one in a dream, but quickly collecting himself, he advanced directly toward me, extending his right hand and saying, "*Jeunie, jeunie!*" which means friendly, amicable, good. I refused to take his hand lest he might suddenly jerk me off my horse and stab me while falling, but contented myself by saying, "*Estamos amigos*"—we are friends. He then turned quickly and rode off at full speed, attended by his warriors. They disappeared in another rocky cañon, about four hundred yards distant. It was subsequently my fate to meet this savage several other times, and I am satisfied that the remembrance of our interview on the occasion above narrated, did me no harm either with him or the balance of his tribe.

After leaving Doña Ana, our way led across the lower portion of the Jornada del Muerto until we arrived at what is known as the San Diego crossing of the Rio Grande, a mile or two below where Fort Thorne was subsequently built. As the Jornada del Muerto was the scene of another incident, its description is postponed for the present. The Rio Grande was crossed without much difficulty, and our camp formed near a large lagoon on the western bank of the river. This lagoon was infested by wild ducks and brant, and the Apaches took great numbers of them in the following manner.

In the early winter, when these birds commenced to arrive in great flocks, the Apaches took large numbers of gourds and set them adrift on the windward side of the lagoon, whence they were gradually propelled by the wind until they reached the opposite side, when they were recovered and again set adrift. At first, the ducks and geese exhibit dread and suspicion of these strange floating objects, but soon get used to them, and pay them no further attention. Having arrived at this stage, the Indians then fit these gourds upon their heads, having been furnished with holes for the eyes, nose and mouth, and, armed with a bag, they enter the water— not over five feet deep in any part—and exactly imitating the bobbing motion of the empty gourd upon the water, succeed in getting close enough to the birds, which are then caught by the feet, suddenly dragged under water, and stowed in the bag. The dexterity and naturalness with which this is done almost exceeds belief, yet it is a common thing among them.

About eighteen or twenty miles east of the Copper Mines of Santa Rita, is a hot spring, the waters of which exhibit a heat of 125 degrees Fahrenheit, and after having crossed the Mimbres, the whole party directed its course to this spring. After examining it thoroughly, and having the qualities of its water tested by Dr. Webb, we prosecuted our march; but my attention was soon after arrested by a number of antelopes feeding on the plain, not more than half a mile distant. Anxious to procure one, I left the party, and, galloping in the direction of the herd, arrived within five hundred yards of it, when I dismounted and tying my horse to a yucca bush, proceeded cautiously on foot, carbine in hand. Crawling from bush to bush, and hiding behind every stone which offered any shelter, I got within handsome range of a fine buck, and feeling sure that the animal could not escape me, I raised to fire, when, just as I was taking aim, I was astonished to see the animal raise erect upon its hind legs, and heard it cry out, in fair Spanish, " *No tiras, no tiras!*"—don't fire, don't fire! What I would have sworn was an antelope, proved to be a young Indian, the son of Ponce, a chief, who, having enveloped himself in an antelope's skin, with head, horns and all complete, had gradually crept up to the herd under his disguise, until his operations were brought to an untimely end by perceiving my aim directed at him. The Apaches frequently adopt this method of hunting, and imitate the actions of the antelopes so exactly as to completely mislead those animals with the belief that their deadliest enemy is one of their number.

We arrived at the Copper Mines, without further accident, one day in advance of our military escort, and had no sooner pitched our tent than we were visited by some eight or ten of the most villainous looking Apaches it is possible to conceive. Although the weather was exceedingly cold, with snow six inches deep on a level, and, in some places where it had drifted, as deep as three or four feet, the Indians were wholly nude, with the exception of a diminutive breech cloth. They bore no arms of any kind and pretended to be very friendly, having undoubtedly seen our train and escort crossing the plain from their various places of observation on the top of Ben Moore, which is eight thousand feet high. Our mules were hitched to the several wheels of the carriage and my horse in the rear, while one of our party kept constant and vigilant watch over the animals. When night fell Dr. Webb informed the Apaches, through me, that they must leave camp, which they did after receiving a few presents in the shape of tobacco, beads and some cotton cloth. A rousing fire was then made in front of the tent, and after a hearty supper our small party retired upon their arms, with one man on guard. It was afterwards discovered that among our visitors were the renowned warriors Delgadito, Ponce and Coletto Amarillo. These were their Mexican names—their Indian appellations I never learned.

About 11 o'clock, A. M., next day, Col. Craig appeared with his command, and formally took possession of the

Copper Mines, the great head-quarters of the redoubtable chief, Mangas Colorado, or the "Red Sleeves," beyond all comparison the most famous Apache warrior and statesman of the present century. The word statesman is used advisedly in his case, as will be made apparent to the reader in the course of his perusal. The term chief will also be found, hereafter, to have a very great modification, in so far as refers to the Apache race.

The Copper Mines of Santa Rita are located immediately at the foot of a huge and prominent mountain, named Ben Moore. These extensive mines had been abandoned for the space of eighty years, but were uncommonly rich and remunerative. They were formerly owned by a wealthy Mexican company, who sent the ore to Chihuahua, where a Government mint existed, and had the ore refined and struck into the copper coinage of the country. Although the distance was over three hundred miles, and every pound of ore had to be transported on pack mules, yet it proved a paying business, and mining was vigorously prosecuted for a space of some twenty years. Huge masses of ore, yielding from sixty to ninety per cent. of pure copper, are still visible all about the mine, and frequently considerable pieces of pure copper are met with by the visitor. The reason for its sudden and long abandonment was asked, and the following story related.

During the period that the Mexicans carried on operations at the mines, the Apaches appeared very friendly, receiving frequent presents, and visiting the houses of the miners without question. But every now and then the Mexicans lost a few mules, or had a man or two killed, and their suspicions were roused against the Apaches, who stoutly denied all knowledge of these acts and put on an air of offended pride. This state of affairs continued to grow worse and worse, until an Englishman, named Johnson, undertook to "settle matters," and to that end received *carte blanche* from his Mexican employers. Johnson ordered a *fiesta*, or feast, prepared, and invited all the Copper Mine Apaches to partake. The invitation was joyfully accepted, and between nine hundred and a thousand, including men, women and children, assembled to do justice to the hospitality of their entertainers. They were caused to sit grouped together as much as possible, while their host had prepared a six-pounder gun, loaded to the muzzle with slugs, musket balls, nails and pieces of glass, within one hundred yards of their main body. This cannon was concealed under a pile of pack saddles and other rubbish, but trained on the spot to be occupied by the Apaches. The time arrived; the feast was ready; the gun loaded and primed; Johnson stood ready with a lighted cigar to give the parting salute, and while all were eating as Apaches only can eat, the terrible storm of death was sped into their ranks, killing, wounding and maiming several hundred. This fearful volley was immediately followed up by a charge on the part of the Mexicans, who showed no pity to the wounded until nearly four hundred victims had been sacrificed at this feast of death. The survivors fled in dismay, and for several months the miners fancied they had forever got rid of the much hated Apaches. It was an ill-grounded hope, as the sequel proved.

The Copper Mines were entirely dependent upon Chihuahua for all supplies, and large *conductas*, or trains with guards, were employed in the business of bringing in such supplies, and taking away the ore. So regular had been the arrival and departure of these trains, that no efforts were made to retain provisions enough on hand in the event of a failure to arrive. Besides, no molestation of any kind had been experienced since Johnson's experiment. At length three or four days passed beyond the proper time for the *conducta's* arrival; provision was becoming exceedingly scarce; ammunition had been expended freely; no thought for the morrow had taken possession of their minds, and everything went on in the hap-hazard way of thoughtless Mexicans. No attempt was made to send a party in quest of the lost train, nor was any economy exercised. Two or three days more passed, and they were on the verge of starvation. The surrounding forests of heavy pines still furnished bear and turkeys, and other game in abundance, but their ammunition was becoming exceedingly scarce. In this dilemma some of the miners climbed Ben Moore, which gave a distinct view of the extensive plain reaching to and beyond the Mimbres river, but no sign of the *conducta* was visible. It was then ordered that a well-armed party should set out and discover its fate, but those who were to be left behind resolved to go also, as they would otherwise be forced to remain without means of defence or provisions. On a given day every man, woman and child residing in the Copper Mines took their departure; but they never reached their place of destination. The relentless Apaches had foreseen all these troubles, and taken measures accordingly. The party left, but their bones, with the exception of only four or five, lie bleaching upon the wide expanse between the Copper Mines of Santa Rita and the town of Chihuahua. Such is the narrative given me by an intelligent Mexican, whom I afterward met in Sonora. From that time for more than eighty years, the Apache had remained the unmolested master of this his great stronghold. This long interval of quiescence was rudely interrupted by the advent of the military escort to the Boundary Commission, which immediately commenced repairing the half-ruined presidio, and rendering some fifty small adobe buildings habitable for the members of the Commission. These proceedings were watched with great interest and unfeigned anxiety by the Apaches, who frequently asked whether we intended to remain at the Copper Mines, and as frequently received a reply in the negative. The real object of our stay was explained to them; but they could not conceive that people should take so much pains to build houses and render them comfortable only for a short residence, to be again abandoned at the very period when men could live in the open air without disquietude.

Shortly afterward, the whole Commission, numbering some two hundred and fifty well-armed men, arrived, making a total force of over three hundred men. This odds was more than the Apaches could face, with any prospect of success, and they relapsed into the better part of valor, under the advice of Mangas Colorado and his leading warriors. The gentle nomads pitched their main camp about two miles from the Copper Mines, and made frequent visits to observe our movements and to practice their skill in begging.

Although the Copper Mine, or Mimbres Apaches, have signalized themselves by many of the boldest and most daring exploits, they are not physically comparable to the Mescalero, Jicarilla and Chiricahui branches of the same tribe. But what they lack in personal strength they make up in wiliness and endurance. No amount of cold, hunger or thirst seems to have any appreciable effect upon an Apache. Whatever his sufferings, no complaint or murmur is ever heard to escape his lips, and he is always ready to engage in any enterprise which promises a commensurate reward. Ten Apaches will under-

take a venture which will stagger the courage and nerve
of a hundred Yumas, Pimos or Navajoes, although the
last mentioned tribe is an undoubted branch of the Apache
race, as will be shown in a subsequent chapter. The cunning of the Apache is only equaled by his skill and the
audacity with which he executes his projects, and every
success is chuckled over with undissembled gusto by the
whole tribe, the actors only assuming an unconcerned
air, as if wholly disconnected with the matter. Their
conversation is always carried on in low tones, and only
one person ever presumes to speak at a time. There is
no interruption to the speaker's remarks; but when he
ceases another takes the word, and either replies or in-
dorses the opinions of his predecessor. During a general
conversation on indifferent topics they separate into several small knots, and in each the above rules are strictly
observed.

I had selected the most lovely spot in the valley for
the site of my tent, which was some six hundred yards
distant from the rest, and shut out from sight by an intervening hillock. At this place the stream widened into a
handsome basin ten yards across, and with a little labor
I had built a sort of dam, which raised the water in the
basin to the depth of about three and a half feet, and
formed a delicious bathing pool, which was shaded by
a very large and spreading cottonwood tree. At this
place the Apaches frequently congregated in considerable numbers, maintaining a lively conversation, and
enabling me to make many observations I could not
otherwise have done. As I was the only member of the
Commission with whom they could converse, my tent
became their head-quarters during their visits, which were
almost daily for several consecutive months, until our
amicable relations were broken up by their irrepressible
rascality and treachery.

CHAPTER IV.

WERE I to diverge from the proposed plan of narrating
only what appertains directly to the elucidation of Indian
character, etc., this work might be continued through a
series of volumes; but the object of the writer is to con-
dense his remarks to such incidents as have relation only
to the various Indian tribes he encountered in the course
of nine years experience among them.

In May, the Commissioner resolved on a journey into
Sonora, to ascertain whether supplies of corn, flour, sheep,
and cattle, could be depended upon from that State for
the use of the Commission operating along its northern
frontier, and also for other objects immediately affecting
the welfare of the body under his orders, and the prosecution of the work committed to his charge. On the
afternoon of the third day we camped at a place where
several holes had been dug by previous travelers, and
being full of sweet water they offered us the first refreshment of the kind we had enjoyed for forty-eight hours.
The country for a long distance was a perfect plain, unbroken even by rocks or trees, with here and there a
shrub, but none over eighteen inches high. At this
place, on a subsequent occasion, an incident illustrative

of the Apache race occurred, and it is related here, although having no connection with our march, for the sake of condensation.

Several years after accompanying Mr. Bartlett, it became necessary for a small party of Americans, five all told, to visit Sonora for provisions, and knowing the road I served as guide. One evening we encamped at the place mentioned above, and again found water for our famishing party and their animals. It was a God-send, as we had been without water for nearly sixty hours. Indian signs in abundance had been observed during the day, and we were all alive to the importance of keeping the strictest watch; accordingly two were placed upon guard at a time. Richard Purdy and myself took the first watch, each one occupying a flank of the camp, certainly not a large one, but of the utmost importance. Knowing the nature of the savages, it was agreed that we should not walk our posts, but conceal ourselves as much as possible and keep a sharp lookout. Before nightfall, Purdy and myself took the exact bearings of each shrub within pistol range, and quietly assumed our positions flat down in the grass, each man being sheltered by a small bush. There was no moon, but a bright starlight enabled us to perceive objects at some distance. The evening passed quietly, and at eleven o'clock we called two more of our comrades, who assumed our places, after having pointed out to them our precautions. At two o'clock, A. M., we were again roused to resume guard, and each one took his position. Scarcely an hour had elapsed when it appeared to me that a certain small bush had changed position somewhat; but not liking to create a false alarm and be laughed at for my pains, I merely determined to watch it with earnest attention. My suspicions and precaution were amply rewarded by perceiving the bush to approach, very gradually indeed, but still unmistakably. I dared not call to Purdy, but got my rifle to bear, as nearly as possible, upon the root of the bush. When I thought my aim good, and felt tolerably sure of my sights, I pulled the trigger. The shot was followed by the yells of some fifteen Apaches, who had approached within thirty paces of our camp by covering their heads with grass and crawling upon their bellies. Our comrades jumped to their feet and commenced shooting at the Indians, who discharged one volley into our camp and left us masters of the field. We lost one horse, killed, and had another slightly wounded; but a search developed the Apache of the moving bush lying dead, with a hole through his head. Without waiting for dawn the animals were immediately got ready and the party again started on its trip, fearing that the Apaches might get ahead and waylay them in some dangerous pass or cañon.

Accompanying the Commissioner, in the course of time we arrived at Agua Prieta, from whence I was dispatched with Mr. Thurber and Mr. Stewart to discover the town of Fronteras, and ascertain whether it could be reached with wagons. Mounting our horses we pursued a straight line for the supposed site of the town, passing through some chapparel and over broken ridges, until we arrived upon an extensive and beautiful plain, over which we galloped with free rein. About half an hour before sundown, we discovered a few thin columns of smoke ascending to the right of our road, and nearly ahead, from the top of a slight eminence about three miles distant. A few minutes brought us to the spot, but we could perceive no inhabitants about the houses on the plain, but raising our eyes to the hill, we saw the entire population of some nine hundred souls, besides four hundred soldiers, huddled together in evident alarm. They had taken us for Apaches, and fled in dismay to the presidio and protection of the military; but when they discovered that we were Americans, nothing could exceed their wonder at our hardihood and folly, as they termed it, in penetrating the country with so small a party. This fact will give the reader some idea of the abject terror with which the poor Mexicans on the frontiers of Sonora, Chihuahua and Durango regard the Apache Indians.

To persons not aware of the causes, this timidity would appear as rank cowardice; but, however true such a charge would be of the masses, yet it must be acknowledged that there are notable exceptions. The Mexicans on the northern frontier are the very lowest and poorest of their countrymen. Living in hovels and sustaining themselves in some manner never yet determined or ascertained by any other people, almost wholly without arms or ammunition, and brought up from their earliest infancy to entertain the most abject dread and horror of the Apaches, they are forever after unable to divest themselves of the belief that an Apache warrior is not a man, but some terrible ogre against whom it is useless to contend, and who is only to be avoided by flight or appeased by unconditional submission.

At Fronteras I met with Gen. Carasco, Military Governor of Sonora, and an old enemy whom it had been my lot to confront during the Mexican war. The General received us with marked hospitality and kindness; offered us refreshments of which we stood greatly in need, and dispatched runners to show Mr. Bartlett the way into the town. During the evening's session, which lasted into the "wee sma' hours ayont the twal," the conversation turned upon the battle of Cerro Gordo, where the General commanded a brigade, and we discovered that he barely escaped falling into our hands. Discussing the character of the Apaches and the policy of the Mexican Government in their regard, the General made the following remarks:

"There is a small town named Janos, in Chihuahua, near the eastern boundary of Sonora, where the Apaches have for several years been received and provided with rations by the Government of that State, although the same Indians were at the time in open war with the Mexicans of Sonora. Not being able to comprehend the virtue of a policy which feeds Indians in one State that they might prey upon and destroy the citizens of another, I concluded that my duty was to destroy the enemy wherever I could find him. Acting upon this decision, I waited until the allotted time for the Apaches to visit Janos to obtain their regular quarterly rations, and, by forced marches at night, succeeded in reaching the place just as the carnival was at its height. We killed a hundred and thirty, and took about ninety prisoners, principally women and children. Col. Medina, commanding the State of Chihuahua, was so enraged at my action, that he made formal complaint to the Supreme Government, which, however, after some unnecessary delay, approved of my course."

I expressed much astonishment at such a condition of affairs, when Carasco added: "It is the old story; our territory is enormous, and our Government weak. It cannot extend its protecting arms throughout all portions of the country. Whole provinces are left for years to themselves, except in the matter of taxation, and things run to ruin. It is to this cause that frequent *pronunciamentos* are attributed. The richest man in either of the distant States is actual lord of the State, and can always set the Government at defiance, because it costs so much to reduce him to subordination. I will give you an instance in point. During the American war, Manuel Gandara loaned the sum of four hundred thousand dollars to the Supreme Government, receiving its acknowledgements for that amount, with interest at the rate of ten per cent. per annum. After the war, during the administration of Peña y Peña, an election for Governor took place in Sonora, in which Manuel Gandara and Manuel Monteverde were the competitors. These families were as deadly rivals as the houses of Romeo and Capulet; and when the voting was over, each candidate claimed the election. As usual, neither applied to the Supreme Government for arbitration, but each summoned its forces and engaged in civil war. Gandara was backed by his numerous friends, peons, and the Yaqui Indians, while Monteverde enlisted the interests of many prominent Sonorians, and the Opatah and Papago tribes. War raged for a long time, until Monteverde applied to the General Government for protection. Gen. Urea was sent with a force of three thousand regulars to suppress Gandara, and for a time succeeded. At this stage of the proceedings, Gandara called upon the Supreme Government to refund his loan of four hundred thousand dollars, threatening that if payment were not forthcoming, he would assign his claim to the British Government. This threat had its effect, and soon after Gandara was put in possession of an order, emanating from the Secretary of War, to the effect that Urea had been operating without proper warrant of authority, and that if Gandara could catch that officer, he was at liberty to suspend him by the neck. This thoroughly frightened Urea, who immediately returned to the capital."

" Now," added Carasco, "you can appreciate the delicate position in which I find myself. I am ordered to the military command of Sonora, but am supplied with neither men nor money. Every day I was pained by accounts of dreadful Apache raids, in which men were massacred; women and children carried off captives; horses and property destroyed, and extensive districts laid waste and abandoned. At length I resorted to forced contributions from the rich and impressed the poor, determined they should fight for their own interests. ¯ This makes me unpopular with all parties, and I expect, some day, to be assassinated for my zeal in their behalf." Prophetic words! In less than a year Carasco was taken off by poison; so, at least, it was reported.

Wending our way from Fronteras we reached Arispe, the former capital of Sonora, on the 31st of May, 1850. At the time of our visit the place contained about twelve hundred inhabitants; but no American can possibly conjecture the terror felt by the people, of all classes, whenever it was announced that the Apaches were near. The second day after our arrival five Apache prisoners—two warriors and three women—were brought into town under a strong guard of twenty-five soldiers, and lodged in the town jail to await their ultimate destination. Two days afterward the rain poured down in torrents; the night was exceedingly dark and stormy; reverberating peals of thunder shook the solid hills, and repeated flashes of the most vivid lightning inspired the beholder with awe. The Mexican guard over the prisoners retired within and lighted their cigaritos, or engaged in the hazards of monte. The doors were securely closed and all prepared to pass the watch away with as much relish as the circumstances would permit. A little after midnight certain peculiar noises were heard about the prison and were

repeated with an emphasis which compelled attention.
Instinctively the guard knew that these noises proceeded
from Apaches who were in quest of their incarcerated
friends, and the fact was quickly made apparent by the
prisoners, who commenced a chant in their native tongue
loud enough to be heard outside. Here was a dilemma.
The Indians were undoubtedly watching the door with
intense interest, and no one dared go forth in that im-
penetrable gloom to face the savage foe. The force of
the enemy was unknown. The citizens could not be relied upon for aid; no one would come to their assistance
if attacked; they only numbered eight men and a sergeant,
and they were panic-stricken. Perceiving this state of
affairs, the Apache prisoners boldly advanced and demanded to be let out, at the same time giving fearful
yells to apprise their friends of their designs, which were
seconded by repeated strokes of heavy stones against the
door. In their overpowering terror the guard mustered
its whole strength, opened the door slightly and permitted their savage charge to leave. It is needless to add
that they were never seen more. This is no figment of
the brain, but the real, undisguised fact, and is recorded
for the purpose of showing how completely the Apaches
have control of the Mexican race upon the frontier.

Another incident illustrative of this supremacy occurred
in the same town. A band of fifteen Apaches pursued a
pack train and overtook it within three hundred yards of
Arispe. The *arrieros* saved themselves by speedy flight,
but the train was plundered and the mules driven off.
Within an hour nearly two hundred armed men assembled
with the avowed purpose of pursuing the savages and recovering the plunder. I happened to be on the Plaza at
the time, and had just before observed the Indians making for the mountains lying east of the town. Which

way did they go? asked the Mexican leader. I pointed out the direction, and also called his attention to the volume of dust raised by the retreating savages. He thanked me, placed himself at the head of his column, cried out, "*Marchamos valientes*"—let us march, brave fellows—and took a course the very opposite of the one pointed out. I then and there made up my mind, that if a similar affair should ever happen where I was, and a Mexican should inquire the route of the Indians, I would indicate the opposite to the one actually taken.

On our return from Sonora we met a force of two hundred Mexican soldiers in the Guadalupe Pass, who informed us that a party of ten Americans had been waylaid by the Apaches near the town of Janos, in Chihuahua, and that one was killed and three others wounded, the panic-stricken survivors saving themselves by precipitate flight. I felt convinced that this villainy had been perpetrated by the Copper Mine Apaches, who had been so seemingly friendly with us, but could not substantiate the charge. Subsequent revelations satisfied me that my suspicions were well founded, for soon after our arrival at the Copper Mines Mr. Bartlett sounded Mangas Colorado on the subject, but he denied any knowledge whatever of the affair; yet two days afterward admitted that he knew about it, and said that it had been done by some bad young men over whom he had no control.

An Apache is trained from his earliest infancy to regard all other people as his natural enemies. He is taught that the chief excellence of man is to outwit his fellows. He is made to feel that the highest honors are bestowed upon him who is master of the greatest amount of rascality. The favors of the women are lavished upon the most adroit thief, because his dexterity enables him to furnish a more copious supply to their wants and caprices. As they never engage in any pursuit except that of war and the chase, all their worldly goods are the results of their skill and proficiency in these vocations. Polygamy being an institution among them, the man who can support or keep, or attract by his power to keep, the greatest number of women, is the man who is deemed entitled to the greatest amount of honor and respect. Gïanatah is a great brave, said one in my hearing—does he not keep seven squaws? and yet Gianatah was not, so far as personal bravery goes, the leading warrior of his band; but he was the most dexterous thief.

After our return to the Copper Mines, I was sitting in front of my tent one afternoon, writing a letter, when an Apache approached and for some reason regarded me attentively.

"What are you doing?" he at length inquired.

"Talking to my friends at home."

"But how can you talk to them so far off?"

"I will tell you. When the Apache desires to indicate speed he makes the figure of a bird; if he wishes to denote something beautiful or sweet, he delineates a flower; if he desires to express sloth, he makes the figure of a tortoise. These facts you know; but we do not use those symbols, and in their place we have agreed upon certain characters, which being put together make words and indicate ideas. For instance, you see we make such marks; well, I send this paper to my friends, and they know just what these marks mean, the same as you would know what a bird or a tortoise meant; because we have all agreed upon a distinct and special interpretation." These ideas were expressed to him in Spanish with great distinctness, and repeated until he seemed to comprehend their gist.

The savage pondered for a while, and then said: "I

do not believe you; those characters all seem alike; nobody can distinguish any difference among many of them; you are trying to fool me, and make me believe you are a great medicine man."

"Indian," I answered, "I will give you proof. You see yonder man? He is the sutler. I will give you a note to him, authorizing you to receive a piece of tobacco; he is at least four hundred yards away, and cannot know of this conversation. If he gives you the tobacco on the reception of my note, you must believe."

"Very good; my white-eyed brother speaks well. I will make the trial, and will see if he says truth."

The note was written and delivered to my copper-colored friend, who started off on a brisk trot until he reached the sutler, to whom he delivered his order. Having read it, the sutler handed him a piece of tobacco, which seemed greatly to excite his astonishment. My friend looked at the weed, then scratched his head and looked again, in undisguised wonderment, advancing toward my tent steadily. When within twenty yards, I noticed his eyes gleam with suppressed satisfaction, and hastily coming up, he said:

"Look here, white man, you try to make a fool of poor Apache. You and the other man made this thing up beforehand, to force me into the belief that you are a great medicine. Now, if you want me to believe you, just write another letter for another piece of tobacco, and if he gives it to me, then I will believe."

It is needless to add that the cunning ruse of the Apache to secure two pieces of tobacco, did not succeed.

Although my tent was so far removed from the rest of the Commission as to render me isolated from the protection of my comrades, I never experienced any alarm, as I possessed two very large and fine dogs, and was ac-

3*

companied by my servant, José, a faithful and brave Mexican boy, of some nineteen years of age. My armory consisted of four six-shooters, two rifles, a double-barreled shot gun, two bowie-knives, and plenty of ammunition for each weapon. I could discharge twenty-eight shots without reloading, and backed by José and my faithful dogs, which kept the strictest watch at night, I was satisfied that a moderate band of Indians could be kept at bay until assistance arrived. This fancied security was destroyed after a few weeks, by a circumstance which will be related in a future chapter; but it required very strong motives to induce my relinquishment of the most pleasant location at the Copper Mines.

CHAPTER V.

MANGAS COLORADO, or Red Sleeves, was, undoubtedly,
the most prominent and influential Apache who has
existed for a century. Gifted with a large and powerful
frame, corded with iron-like sinews and muscles, and
possessed of far more than an ordinary amount of brain
strength, he succeeded, at an early age, in winning a
reputation unequaled in his tribe. His daring exploits,
his wonderful resources, his diplomatic abilities, and his
wise teachings in council soon surrounded him with a
large and influential band, which gave him a sort of
prestige and sway among the various branches of his
race, and carried his influence from the Colorado river to
the Guadalupe mountains. Throughout Arizona and
New Mexico, Mangas Colorado was a power in the land.
Yet he could assume no authority not delegated to him
by his people. He never presumed to speak for them
as one having authority, but invariably said he would
use his influence to perform certain promises and engagements. Mangas, in one of his raids into Sonora, carried
off a handsome and intelligent Mexican girl, whom he
made his wife, to the exclusion of his Apache squaws.
This singular favoritism bred some trouble in the tribe

for a short time, but was suddenly ended by Mangas challenging any of the offended brothers or relatives of his discarded wives. Two accepted the wager, and both were killed in fair duel. By his Mexican wife Mangas had three really beautiful daughters, and through his diplomatic ability, he managed to wive one with the chief of the Navajoes; another with the leading man of the Mescalero Apaches, and the third with the war chief of the Coyoteros. By so doing, he acquired a very great influence in these tribes, and, whenever he desired, could obtain their assistance in his raids. His height was about six feet; his head was enormously large, with a broad, bold forehead, a large acquiline nose, a most capacious mouth, and broad, heavy chin. His eyes were rather small, but exceedingly brilliant and flashing when under any excitement—although his outside demeanor was as imperturbable as brass. This is the man we met at the Copper Mines; but as his name will be mentioned many times in the course of this narrative, in connection with his acts, no more need be added at present. His most immediate counselors and attachés were Delgadito, Ponce, Cuchillo Negro, Coletto Amarillo, El Chico, and Pedro Azul. These were all appellations bestowed by Mexicans, and not their Apache names, which I never learned.

The Indian force about the Copper Mines amounted, according to my calculations, to four hundred warriors, who were no match for the three hundred well armed and thoroughly organized Americans at the place. Four or five weeks elapsed in amicable intercourse with the Apaches; but from occasional expressions, I felt convinced that Mangas had sought aid for the purpose of expelling us at the earliest possible moment. Nothing, however, occurred to strengthen my suspicions, and I

had almost dismissed them entirely, when I was surprised one morning to see the camp full of strange savages, who proved to be Navajoes, and were on the best
terms with the Apaches. The new comers were fine
looking, physically, but carried in their faces that name-
less yet unmistakable impress of low cunning and
treachery, which I afterward found to be the leading
traits of their tribe. Although they are of the great
Apache race, speaking identically the same language
and observing the same general habits of life in all
respects, yet they are far inferior in point of courage,
prowess, skill and intelligence. Five Apache warriors
will undertake and accomplish an exploit which no
fifty Navajoes would venture to perform. A single
Apache will go off, unaided, and commit a daring robbery or murder which twenty Navajoes would shrink
from attempting.

Our new visitors were all mounted on small, but strong,
active and wiry looking horses, which they rode with
remarkable ease and grace. Feeling satisfied in my own
mind that they had come there at the request of Mangas
Colorado, I advised Col. Craig of my suspicions, and he,
in turn, imparted the idea to Mr. Bartlett. We learned
that four hundred Navajo warriors were encamped on
the Gila river, only thirty miles distant, and knew that
the Indian Commissariat could not support so great a
number for any length of time, and that no such assem-
blage would have been got together in that portion of
the country unless for some determined purpose. The
hunting grounds around the Copper Mines offered no
special inducement, as they must have crossed a hundred
and fifty miles of better hunting country to arrive where
they then were. There was no trading to rely upon, and
on special incentive other than to help Mangas in driv-

ing us out of the place, or assisting him to steal our animals.

Their visits were very regular for three or four days, when, probably finding us too strong and too much on our guard to attack, they disappeared for a while, to return some weeks after and help to carry off our horses and mules. During their stay, my tent and its neighborhood were crowded with these savages, who asked me a multitude of questions, but never answered one of mine. This reticence on their part taught me a lesson, and I soon learned to endure their presence with perfect equanimity and *nonchalance*, smoking and replying to their queries with a simple nod or wave of the hand. My six-shooters and knife were always upon my person during these interviews, and my boy José sat in the back part of the tent with a Sharp's carbine and double barreled gun, well loaded with buckshot, within easy reach. I never permitted a Navajo to get behind me, and, while treating them with courtesy, gave them to understand that I had no special feeling on the subject, but regarded their visits as a matter of course.

It was a noticeable fact that neither Mangas Colorado or any of his leading men ever mixed with the Navajoes while in our camp, and judging this conduct somewhat strained and unnatural, Mr. Wiems and myself determined to watch them. In pursuance of this object, we saddled our horses one evening after the Indians had retired, for they were never permitted in camp after sunset, and very quietly picked our way to their bivouac, about two miles distant at that time. Gaining a slight eminence that overlooked them, we applied our field glasses, and, by the light of their fires, distinctly saw Mangas and the principal men in close conference with the leading Navajoes. This fact was also reported to

Col. Craig, who took additional precautions, which had the effect of relieving us from the presence of the new comers. In after years, it was my lot to make a very extensive and sanguinary acquaintance with this tribe, and the opportunity was improved to the utmost. Thousands of them were subjected to my control, and quite a number of them remembered me from the time we met at the Copper Mines. In several conversations I accused them of coming to aid Mangas, and assisting him in getting rid of his unwelcome intruders; and on each occasion they frankly admitted that they had visited the Copper Mines with that intention. Mangas had sent messengers to tell them that a large body of Americans had come into his country; that they were very rich in horses, mules, cotton cloth, beads, knives, pistols, rifles and ammunition; that he was not strong enough to murder and plunder us himself, and therefore required their aid, in which case one half the plunder was to be theirs, in the event of success. Lured by these promises, and urged by their chief, who was the son-in-law of Mangas, four hundred of them had come down to help that renowned warrior. They met in council, and agreed to come in and spy out the land before commencing operations, little supposing that we would discern any difference between them and the Apaches proper. Should matters promise well, a sudden attack was to be made by their united forces; but if that was not practicable without great loss of life on their part, then the system of distressing us by stealing our animals and cutting off small parties, was to be adopted. All these statements I got from Manuelito and others, at Fort Sumner, thirteen years after our occupation of the Copper Mines in Arizona. The subject was frequently talked over, and remembered as vividly as if it were a thing of yesterday.

Mr. Bartlett, in order to retain the supposed friendship of Mangas, had a fine pair of blue pants, ornamented with a wide red stripe down the outside of the legs, made for that respectable individual. To this were added a good field officer's uniform and epaulettes, given by Col. Craig, a new white shirt, black cravat, and an excellent pair of new shoes, such as are furnished to our soldiers. It was my duty to invest Mangas in his new suit, but some difficulty was experienced in getting him to wear his shirt inside of his pants instead of outside. After a time he made his appearance in *grande tenue*, evidently in love with his own elegant person. During the whole day he strutted about the camp, the envied of all beholders, and as vain of his new dress as a peacock of his feathers. The next day Mangas failed to put in an appearance; but the day after he came, with his pantaloons wrapped around his waist; his shirt, dirty and partly torn, outside; his uniform coat buttoned to his chin; one epaulet on his breast, and the other fastened, bullion down, between the hind buttons of his coat. In this guise he fancied himself an object worthy of universal admiration; and as he walked along, he would turn his eyes over his shoulder to relish the brilliant flashes of his posterior ornament. In less than a week, coat, shirt, pants and epaulettes were sported by another Indian after his fashion. Mangas had gambled them away, and the wearer was the fortunate winner.

On the evening of the 27th of June, 1850, Mr. W. Bausman, Mr. J. E. Wiems and myself were standing in front of the sutler's store, when we perceived a light, resembling a camp fire, about two hundred yards distant, near the banks of the creek. We knew that Indians were prohibited from being there after sundown, and as none of the Commission dwelt in that direction, it was agreed to go and find out who were the campers about the fire. We approached cautiously, and found ourselves in a bivouac of Indians and Mexicans. Among them was a young and handsome girl, clothed in a tattered chemise, with a buckskin skirt, and another skin thrown over her shoulders. This girl, who was not an Indian, appeared to be the waitress of the party, for whom she was preparing supper. As our approach had not been observed, we quietly proceeded to the cook fire, which was about four yards from the party, and I asked the girl, in a low voice, who those people were. She seemed evidently alarmed, and refusing to answer, hurried away to wait upon her associates. We remained until she came back, when I told her that it was necessary for us to know who they were; to which she placed her finger on her lips, and betokened that she dared not tell. The question was, however, pressed, when she stated in a whisper that she was a captive, and that the Mexicans present had just bought her, and were going to convey her to New Mexico. As this thing was specially prohibited by the United States laws, we made our way immediately to Mr. Bartlett and laid the matter before that gentleman for his consideration. With great promptitude Mr. Bartlett communicated the facts, in writing, to Col. Craig, and asked that gallant officer for a force to rescue the girl from her unhappy condition. This request was granted as soon as possible, and Lieut. Green was ordered to take a file of men and bring the girl before the Commissioner. This was done without delay, and the captive placed for the night under the care of Mr. Bartlett, who assigned her a comfortable room, and placed a proper guard over her quarters.

In the meantime the Apaches had slipped away, but a guard was put over the Mexican traders for the night.

Next day they were summoned before the Commissioner
to account for their possession of the girl, and their intentions as to her future disposal. Next morning the
traders respectively gave their names as Peter Blacklaws
—a very appropriate nomenclature—Pedro Archeveque,
which, being translated, means Peter Archbishop—a very
inappropriate name—and Faustin Valdes. The testimony
extracted from these men was extremely conflicting, but
the tenor of it went to show that they were engaged, with
some fifty others, in unlawful barter and trade with the
Indians, selling them powder and arms, probably, in exchange for female Mexican captives of attractive persons,
horses, skins, etc. Mr. Bartlett felt fully authorized to
deprive them of the captive, but having no authority to
punish the scoundrels, they were released; they were immediately afterwards waited upon by several gentlemen
of the Commission, who gave them to understand that
any delay in getting out of that place would be attended
with imminent danger. In less than twenty minutes they
had left the Copper Mines, poorer but wiser men.

The young captive gave her name as Inez Gonzales,
the eldest child of Jesus Gonzales, of Santa Cruz, on the
frontier of Sonora. About nine months previous, she
had left Santa Cruz with her uncle, aunt, a female friend
and her friend's brother, for the purpose of being present at the *grande fiesta de Nuestra Senora de la Magdalena*, or, the grand feast of our Lady of Magdalena.
They were protected by a military escort of ten soldiers
and an ensign. The second day of their journey they
were ambushed by a large party of El Pinal Apaches,
who killed her uncle and eight soldiers, including their
officer, and carried off her and her two female friends,
with the boy. For seven months she had been in their
power, and made to perform all the hard labor of an

Apache squaw, receiving kicks and blows as her reward. One old woman of the tribe, who had a tongue which made even the warriors quail, however, took a passing fancy for Inez, and from that time protected her from insult or harm so long as she remained among them. Her companions in captivity were subsequently purchased by a band of New Mexican traders, who took them off in a northerly direction. She never saw or heard of them afterwards. A second party had seen and purchased her, with the view of taking her to Santa Fé, for speculative and villainous purposes, when she was rescued by the Commission, every member of which vied with each other to extend their protection and care over this poor and suffering girl. Although she remained among us until her restoration to her parents and home, the sequel of her adventures will be given now.

On the morning of the 27th of August, exactly two months from the date of her rescue, the Commission left the Copper Mines, to prosecute its duties in the field, and as it had become necessary to visit Sonora again, Mr. Bartlett determined upon giving himself the gratification of restoring the fair Inez to the arms of her mourning mother. After many days' wandering, during which our small party was frequently reduced to only five or six, by reason of sending off occasional detachments, and after having lost our way and been forced to the necessity of living upon purslain and water for several successive days, we finally arrived near the town of Santa Cruz, on the 22d of September, nearly a month subsequent to leaving the Copper Mines. On the morning of the 23d, just one year to a day from the date of her capture, two men were dispatched to inform the family of Inez of her safety, and to add that she would be with her relations in four or five hours. About three miles

from town we met a large and joyous party of Mexicans,
arrayed in their gaudiest holiday costumes, and headed
by the mother of our fair charge. They had come out to
welcome her return and release from captivity among the
Apaches, a thing never before known to have occurred.
Mr. Bartlett conceded to me the privilege of placing Inez
into the longing arms of her mother, who, after repeated
embraces, and amidst alternate tears, prayers, thanks-
givings and joyous cries, yielded her place to the strong
but inferior claims of other relatives and friends, all of
whom ardently and most affectionately embraced her by
turns. It was one of the most affecting scenes conceivable, and, in joyous procession, the whole party entered
the town, amidst the loudest acclamations of the entire
population. Inez immediately entered the church, where
the good priest was in attendance, and went through a
solemn ceremony and thanksgiving. These scenes and
all their attendant circumstances have ever been among
the most pleasant in my remembrance. They form a
delicious oasis amidst the unpleasant recollections of
"man's inhumanity to man." Her own father had been
deceased for some years, and the mother of Inez was
then married to a man named Ortis, a very excellent,
honest and reliable Mexican, who testified quite as much
joy at her release from a captivity far worse than death,
as if she had been his own child.

The future career of this young and attractive girl,
whose fate was so suddenly and providentially changed,
is worthy of record.

Some months after the Commission left, on its way toward California, Inez attracted and secured the admiration of a Captain Gomez in the Mexican Regular Army,
and, at that time, in command of the frontier town of
Tubac. The relaxed state of morals among the Mexi-

cans seemed to warrant the poor girl in becoming his mistress for a time, but he subsequently made amends by marrying her and legitimatizing the two fine boys she bore him. Many years passed before I again saw or heard of Inez, and it was not until the fall of 1862, that I learned, while in Tucson, that she was still alive, but quite unwell. Capt. Gomez had been dead some years, and she was again married to the Alcalde of Santa Cruz, and had borne him two children—a boy and a girl. Having casually learned that I was in Tucson, and an officer in the Union Army, she dispatched me a letter, begging that I would order some one of our physicians to visit and prescribe for her. Of course, the poor girl, in her ignorance, had asked what it was impossible to grant, and I sadly dismissed the subject from my mind.

In 1864, it was again my lot to be within fifty miles of Santa Cruz, when a bold Opatah Indian chief, named Tanori, who had been commissioned as Colonel by Maximilian, had the temerity to cross our frontier with nearly seven hundred men and fire upon the people of the American town of San Gabriel, located two miles north of the dividing line, and fourteen miles from Santa Cruz. The excuse for this outrage was, that he had pursued the Liberal General, Jesus Garcia Morales, across our lines, and that he had not transcended his duty in so doing. Complaint of this raid having been made to me by the town authorities of San Gabriel, I immediately took the saddle, with one hundred and forty troopers, and marched straight to that place. Upon my arrival, I obtained affidavits of all the facts, and, having received permission from the acknowledged authorities of Sonora, determined to pursue Tanori and punish that gentleman for his audacious conduct.

He had retired upon Santa Cruz, whither I followed

without delay; but, hearing of our approach, he hastened forward to Imurez with wonderful celerity, and,
although the Adjutant, Lieut. Coddington, was dispatched, at speed, to request a delay on his part so that
we could arrange matters, he excused himself by saying
that "his orders were imperative to reach Ures without
delay." As a proof with what rapidity the Mexican infantry can cover the ground when an enemy is in pursuit, it is a fact that Tanori, with over six hundred men,
mostly infantry, made the march from Santa Cruz to
Imurez, a distance of forty-three miles, in the space of
nine hours. He left Santa Cruz at five o'clock in the
morning, and I subsequently learned that he conversed
with the party from whom I received my information, in
the town of Imurez, at two o'clock in the afternoon of
the same day. About three hundred of his men were
there with him at the time mentioned.

My trip to Santa Cruz offered me the opportunity to
visit Inez, whom I found to be the respected wife of the
chief and most influential man in that little community.
She has an affectionate husband, who is by no means
cramped for this world's goods; is surrounded by a fine
and promising family of three boys and a girl, and is universally esteemed for her many excellent qualities. It
is needless to state that my reception was most cordial
and enthusiastic. This sequel of her history will undoubtedly be received with sincere pleasure by all who
were members of Mr. Bartlett's Commission, and by none
with more interest than Mr. Bartlett and Dr. Webb.

CHAPTER VI.

Rescue of Two Mexican Boys.—War Talk.—Exciting Scene.—Peaceful Termination.—Large Indian Forces.—An Apache killed by a Mexican.—Intense Excitement.—Fearless Conduct of Col. Craig.—The Apaches Pacified.—Another War Talk.—Amicable Result.—Necessity of Firmness and Precaution.

IT has already been stated that my tent was pitched several hundred yards from the rest of the Commission, and hidden from the view of my companions by an intervening hillock. This fact rendered me far more cautious than I otherwise would have been. Several days subsequent to the rescue of Inez, the afternoon being exceedingly hot and sultry, I was lying on my cot reading a work borrowed from Dr. Webb, while José was busy in front of the tent, washing some clothes in the pool. A very large number of Apaches were in our camp that day, but had not disturbed me, as was their usual custom. Suddenly, two boys, evidently Mexicans, darted into my tent, got under my cot, and concealed themselves between the side of the tent and the drooping blankets. This visitation, in such an abrupt and irregular manner, excited my surprise, and I asked who they were and what they wanted. "*Somos Mejicanos, caballero, y estamos cautivos con los Apaches, y nos hemos escondido aqui para escaparles. Por Dios no nos rinde otra vez entre ellos,*" which means in English—"We are Mexicans, sir, and we are captives among the Apaches, and we have hidden here to escape them. For God's sake, do not deliver us again among them."

I called to José, and asked: "Are there any Indians close by."

"No, sir," he replied, "but they are coming this way."

I instantly jumped from the cot, thrust two six-shooters in my belt, took two more in my hands, one in each, ordered José to sling the carbine over his shoulder and carry the double-barreled gun in his hands, and telling the boys to keep close to my side—one on the right and the other on the left—I sallied from the tent with the determination to take these captives to the Commissioner, for his disposal.

We had not proceeded twenty yards before a band of some thirty or forty surrounded us, and with menacing words and gestures, demanded the instant release of their captives; but, having made up my mind, I was determined to carry out my intention at all risks. I told José to place his back to mine, cock his gun and shoot the first Indian he saw bend his bow or give sign of active hostility; while, with a cocked pistol in each hand, we went circling round, so as to face all parts of the ring in succession, at the same time warning the savages to keep their distance. In this manner we accomplished about two hundred yards, when my situation was perceived by several gentlemen of the Commission, and, drawing their pistols, they advanced to my aid. The Indians relinguished their attempts and accompanied us peaceably to the Commissioner, to whom I surrendered the boys and detailed the affair. The boys were respectively named Savero Aredia and José Trinfan, the former aged thirteen, and a native of Bacuachi, in Sonora, and the latter aged about eleven, and a native of Fronteras, in the same State. The next day at night, Mr. Bartlett sent them to the camp of Gen. Garcia Conde, the Mexican Commissioner. They were accompanied by a strong guard, which delivered them safely to the General, who subsequently restored them to their respective families, much to their wonder and gratification.

Four or five days afterward, Mangas Colorado, Ponce, Delgadito, Cuchillo Negro, Coletto Amarillo, and some two hundred warriors, together with the fellow who claimed the boys, entered the Copper Mines, to have a "big talk." Mr. Bartlett was not at all displeased to see them, and determined to settle the matter at once. The mass of Indians formed themselves in a semicircle, two and three deep, facing the door of the room in which the talk was had, while the principal men and about a dozen of the Commission, well armed, occupied a large room in our adobe building. Pipes and tobacco were handed round and a "cloud blown" before the real business of the *seance* commenced. About a hundred and fifty of the Commission were near at hand with their arms ready. After a long and profound silence, the conversation was commenced by Mangas Colorado, on the part of the Apaches, and by myself, on the part of the Americans, every expression of the savages being taken down in writing, and then translated to Mr. Bartlett, who dictated a reply, if anything important occurred to him, or allowed the interpreter to respond, as the circumstances would permit. As the succeeding recital of the interview was originally written out in full by myself, and handed to Mr. Bartlett as the official record, and subsequently published by him without alteration, I deem myself justified in making use of it for this work.

Mangas Colorado spoke and said: "Why did you take our captives from us?"

Reply.—"Your captives came to us and demanded our protection."

4

Mangas Colorado.—"You came to our country. You were well received. Your lives, your property, your animals were safe. You passed by ones, by twos, by threes through our country. You went and came in peace. Your strayed animals were always brought home to you again. Our wives, our women and children came here and visited your houses. We were friends—we were brothers! Believing this, we came among you and brought our captives, relying on it that we were brothers and that you would feel as we feel. We concealed nothing. We came not secretly nor in the night. We came in open day, and before your faces, and showed our captives to you. We believed your assurances of friendship, and we trusted them. Why did you take our captives from us?"

Reply.—"What we have said to you is true. We do not tell lies. The greatness and dignity of our nation forbid our doing so mean a thing. What our brother has said is true and good also. We will now tell him why we took his captives away. Four years ago, we, too, were at war with Mexico. We know that the Apaches make a distinction between Chihuahua and Sonora. They are now at peace with Chihuahua, but at war with Sonora. We, in our war, did not make that distinction. The Mexicans, whether living in one or the other State, are all one nation, and we fought them as a nation. When the war was over, in which we conquered, we made peace with them. They are now our friends, and by the terms of the peace we are bound to protect them. We told you this when we first came here, and requested you to cease from hostility against Mexico. Time passed, and we grew very friendly; everything went well. You came in here with your captives. Who were those captives? Mexicans; the very people we told you we were bound to protect. We took them from you and sent them to Gen. Garcia Conde, who will set them at liberty in their own country. We mean to show you that we cannot lie. We promised protection to the Mexicans, and we gave it to them. We promise friendship and protection to you, and we will give them to you. If we had not done so to Mexico, you would not believe us with regard to yourselves. We cannot lie."

During the above conversation, which was carried on in a slow and dignified manner, Ponce was becoming very much excited, altogether too much so for an Indian, and being unable to restrain himself any longer, he arose, and, with many gesticulations, said:

Ponce.—"Yes, but you took our captives without beforehand cautioning us. We were ignorant of this promise to restore captives. They were made prisoners in lawful warfare. They belong to us. They are our property. Our people have also been made captives by Mexicans. If we had known of this thing, we would not have come here. We would not have placed that confidence in you."

Reply.—"Our brother speaks in anger, and without reflection. Boys and women lose their temper, but men reflect and argue; and he who has reason and justice on his side, wins. No doubt, you have suffered much by the Mexicans. This is a question in which it is impossible for us to tell who is wrong, or who is right. You and the Mexicans accuse each other of being the aggressors. Our duty is to fulfill our promise to both. This opportunity enables us to show to Mexico that we mean what we say, and when the time comes, we will be ready and prompt to prove the good faith of our promises to you."

Ponce.—"I am neither a boy nor a squaw. I am a

man and a brave. I speak with reflection. I know what I say. I speak of the wrongs we have suffered and those you now do us." Then, placing his hand on my shoulder, he said in a very excited manner—"You must not speak any more. Let some one else speak."

As this was rather more than I had bargained for, I immediately placed both hands on his shoulders, and, crushing him down on the floor, I said:

"I want you to understand that *I* am the very one to speak—the only one who can speak to you. Now, stay there. Do *you* sit down. You are a squaw and no brave. I will select a man to speak for the Apaches. Delgadito (beckoning to that warrior) do you come here and speak for your nation."

It is impossible to describe the smothered rage of Ponce, but he saw there was no chance, and never again uttered a word during the session.

Delgadito then arose and said: "Let my brother declare the mind of his people."

Reply.—"We wish to explain to our Apache brethren why we have done this thing, and what we can do for the late owner of those captives. We know that you have not acted secretly or in the dark. You came in open day, and brought your captives among us. We took them in open day, in obedience to orders from our great chief at Washington. The great chief of our nation said: 'You must take all the Mexican captives you meet among the Apaches and set them at liberty.' We cannot disobey this order, and for this reason we have taken away your captives."

Delgadito.--"We cannot doubt the words of our brave white brethren. The Americans are braves. *We know it*, and we believe a brave scorns to lie. But the owner of these captives is poor. He cannot lose his prisoners, who were obtained at the risk of his life, and purchased by the blood of his relatives. He justly demands his captives. We are his friends, and wish to see this demand complied with. It is just, and as justice we demand it."

Reply.—"We will tell our Apache brethren what can be done. The captives cannot be restored. The Commissioner cannot buy them. No American can buy them; but there is a Mexican in our employ who is anxious to buy and restore them to their homes. We have no objection that he should do so; and if he is not rich enough, some of us will lend him the means."

Delgadito.—"The owner does not wish to sell; he wants his captives."

Reply.—"Our brother has already been told that this cannot be. We do not speak with two tongues. Make up your minds."

A short consultation was then held among the leading Apaches, after which Delgadito said: "The owner wants twenty horses for them."

Reply.—"The Apache laughs at his white brother. He thinks him a squaw, and that he can play with him as with an arrow. Let the Apache say again."

Delgadito.—"The brave who owns these captives does not want to sell. He has had one of these boys six years. He grew up under him. His heart-strings are bound around him. He is as a son to his old age. He speaks our language, and he cannot sell him. Money cannot buy affection. His heart cannot be sold. He taught him to string the bow and wield the lance. He loves the boy and cannot sell him."

Reply.—"We are sorry that this thing should be. We feel for our Apache brother, and would like to lighten his heart. But it is not our fault. Our brother has fixed

his affection on the child of his enemy. It is very noble.
But our duty is stern. We cannot avoid it. It wounds
our hearts to hurt our friends; but if they were our own
children, and the duty of the law said: 'Part with them;
part with them,' we would. Let our Apache brother reflect, and name his price."

Delgadito.—"What will you give?"

To which Mr. Bartlett replied: "Come and I will show
you."

The whole conclave then broke up and adjourned to
the Commissary's stores, where goods, such as calicoes,
blankets and sheetings, to the value of two hundred and
fifty dollars were laid out for their acceptance. This was
more than Apache cupidity could stand; the bargain was
soon closed, and the affair passed away in peace. But it
was never forgotten, and I felt positive that the time
would come when they would endeavor to wreak their ill-
concealed vengeance. My expectations were justified by
the result, for they ultimately stole nearly two hundred
head of animals from the Commission.

At this period the band of Mangas Colorado, numbering some three hundred warriors, remained encamped
about four miles distant, while that of Delgadito, numbering nearly as many, occupied the valley of the Mimbres river, eighteen miles off. At the same time four
hundred Navajoes occupied the banks of the Gila, distant
twenty-eight miles. We were thus placed between three
large Indian forces, but took no notice of the fact, continuing our hunting excursions in twos and threes with
as much apparent indifference as ever, and adopting the
precaution of taking our six-shooters and plenty of ammunition, as well as our rifles.

On the 6th of July, a Mexican, named Jesus Lopez, in
the employ of the Commission, had a dispute with an

Apache, which terminated by the Mexican shooting his savage friend. Large numbers of Apaches, including Mangas Colorado and several prominent men, were in our camp at the time, but in a moment they mounted their active ponies and were fleeing in all directions. Col. Craig called upon me to follow him, and we rushed out and up the hills after the Apaches, telling them not to go, that we were friends, that the murderer was already a prisoner, and that full justice would be done them. After many persuasions, we induced them to calm their fears and come back. The prisoner was shown them with chains on his feet in care of the guard; while the wounded man was taken to the hospital and accorded every assistance. He lingered for a month and then died, surrounded by his friends, who had been witnesses to the care bestowed upon him. This affair brought on another talk, which took place a few days after his burial, which was performed by his own people in secret, having declined the offer of a coffin and sepulture at our hands.

A large body of Apaches had congregated to hear the talk, and they were evidently determined to have the best of it on this occasion. They had made up their minds to have the blood of the slayer, and had they succeeded would have attributed their triumph to fear on our part. Mr. Bartlett was quite as determined that American law only should have weight, and I was prepared for a lively scene. On that day the Commissary's and Sutler's stores were closed, and every man of us stood ready for active duty at a moment's warning. The smoking process over, the Apaches were addressed as follows, the same rules being observed as on the former occasion.

Commissioner.—" I feel sad, as well as all the Americans here, and sympathize with our Apache brothers for

the death of one of their braves. We are all friends.
The dead man was our friend, and we regret his loss. I
know that he committed no offence; that he even did not
provoke the attack upon him. But our Apache brethren
must remember that it was not by the hand of an American he died. It was by that of a Mexican, though employed by the Commissioner. For this reason it is my
duty to see justice done you, and the murderer punished. I am here in command of the party engaged in
tracing the dividing line between the United States—the
country of the Americans—and Mexico. I have fully
explained this to you before, and you now understand
it. Beyond this I have no powers. The great chief of
the Americans lives far, very far, toward the rising sun.
From him I received my orders, and those orders I must
obey. I cannot interfere in punishing any man, whether
an Indian, a Mexican, or an American. There is another
great chief who lives at Santa Fé. He is the Governor
of all New Mexico. This great chief administers the
laws of the Americans. He alone can inflict punishment
when a man has been found guilty. To this great chief
I will send the murderer of our Apache brother. He
will try him, and if found guilty, will have him punished
according to American laws. This is all I can do. Such
is the disposition I will make of this man. It is all I
have a right to do."

To my surprise, Ponce arose to reply; he said: "This
is all very good. The Apaches know that the Americans
are their friends. The Apaches believe what the Americans say is true. They know that the Americans do not
speak with two tongues. They know that you have never
told them a lie. They know that you will do what you
say. But the Apaches will not be satisfied to hear that
the murderer has been punished in Santa Fé. They

want him punished here, at the Copper Mines, where the band of the dead brave may see him put to death—where all the Apaches may see him put to death. (Here Ponce made the sign of suspending by the neck.) Then the Apaches will see and know that their American brothers do justice to them."

Commissioner.—"I will propose another plan to the Apaches. It is to keep the murderer in chains, as you now see him; to make him work, and give all he earns to the wife and family of your dead brave. This I will see paid in blankets, in cotton cloth, in corn, in money, or anything else the family may like. I will give them all that is now due to the man, and at the end of every month I will give them twenty dollars in goods or in money. When the cold season comes, these women and children will come in and receive their blankets and cloth to keep them warm, and corn to satisfy their hunger."

Ponce.—"You speak well. Your promises are good. But money will not satisfy an Apache for the blood of a brave! Thousands will not drown the grief of this poor woman for the loss of her son. Would money satisfy an American for the murder of his people? Would money pay you, Señor Commissioner, for the loss of your child? No; money will not bury your grief. It will not bury ours. The mother of the dead brave demands the life of his murderer. Nothing else will satisfy her. She wants no money. She wants no goods. She wants no corn. Would money satisfy me (striking his breast) for the death of my son? No! I would demand the blood of the murderer. *Then* I would be satisfied. Then I would be willing to die myself. I would not wish to live and feel the grief which the loss of my son would cause me."

Reply.—"Your words are good. You speak with the

4*

heart of feeling. I feel as you do. All the Americans feel as you do. Our hearts are sad at your loss. We mourn with this poor woman. We will do all we can to assist her and her family. I know that neither money nor goods will pay for her loss. I do not want the Apaches, my brothers, so to consider it. What I propose is for the good of this family. My wish is, to make them comfortable. I desire to give them the aid of which they are deprived by the loss of their protector. If the prisoner's life is taken, your desire for revenge is satisfied. Law and justice are satisfied; but this poor woman gets nothing. She and her family remain poor. They have no one to labor for them. Will it not be better to provide for their wants?"

A short interchange of opinions occurred at this period of the proceedings, and the mother of the murdered man was called on for her decision. Acting under the influence of the leading warriors, whose object is stated at the opening of this chapter, she vehemently demanded the blood of her son's slayer, and stated her determination to be satisfied with nothing else. In accordance with this decision Ponce resumed and said:

"If an Apache should take the life of an American, would you not make war on us and take many Apache lives?"

Reply.—"No; I would demand the arrest of the murderer, and would be satisfied to have him punished as the Apaches punish those who commit murder. Did not a band of Apaches attack a small party of Americans, very recently, on the Janos road? Did they not kill one of them and wound three others with their arrows? And did they not take from them all their property? You all know this to be true, and I know it to be true. I passed near the spot where it took place, three days afterward.

The Apaches did not even bury their victim. They left him lying by the wayside, food for the crows and the wolves. Why do not these Americans revenge themselves on you for this act? They are strong enough. They have many warriors, and in a few days can bring a thousand more here. But there would be no justice in that. The Americans believe this murder was committed by your bad men—by cowards. The Apaches have bad men among them; but you who are now among us are our friends, and we will not demand redress of you. Yet, as I told you before, you must endeavor to find the men who killed our brother, and punish them. Our animals feed in your valleys. Some of your bad men might steal them, as they have already done; but the Americans would not make war on you for this. We hold you responsible, and shall call on you to find them and bring them back, as you have done. While the Apaches continue to do this, the Americans will be their friends and their brothers. But if the Apaches take our property and do not restore it, they can no longer be the friends of the Americans. War will then follow; thousands of soldiers will take possession of your lands, your grazing valleys, and your watering places. They will destroy every Apache warrior they find, and take your women and children captives."

This rather menacing speech, with the firmness and determination evinced, brought our copper colored and belligerent visitors to a proper sense of the case, and after considerable "pow-wow" among themselves, the mother of the deceased agreed to leave the punishment of the murderer to the determination of our own laws, and to receive as equivalent for his loss all the money due the prisoner, and twenty dollars a month, the amount of his wages, while we remained at the Copper Mines.

During the foregoing talk I learned the important fact, that coolness and quiet determination will almost always overawe and subdue an Indian, provided the right is on your side. But however much he may yield, óne may make sure that he will seize the first favorable opportunity to "get even." Should such an opportunity never occur, it becomes his cherished object to wreak his vengeance on the next comer, entirely regardless of his antecedents. For this reason the utmost caution is always necessary; because, although one may feel wholly guiltless of act or intention against the savages, he is held strictly responsible by them for the acts and intentions of his predecessors.

CHAPTER VII.

Some time after the events above recorded, it became necessary for me to visit the town of Socorro, in New Mexico, for the purpose of assisting in the purchase of sheep. It was my most excellent fortune to possess a horse whose equal I have never seen. With high courage and almost fabulous powers of endurance; strong, swift and handsome, I had made him a special pet, and nobly did he answer my appeal when occasion demanded.

At that time Fort Craig had no existence, and the space between Doña Ana and Socorro—a distance of one hundred and twenty-five miles—is a large desert, well supplied with fine grama grass in some portions, but absolutely destitute of water or shade for ninety-six miles. This intervening strip of territory is known by the unattractive appellation of the *Jornada del Muerto*, or the Dead Man's Journey. Why it ever received this title I never distinctly learned, but suppose it was on account of the very numerous massacres committed on it by the Apache Indians. On the east the road is fringed for about sixty miles by the Sierra Blanca, a noted stronghold of that people; and from its heights they are enabled distinctly to perceive any party of travelers coming over the wide and unsheltered expanse of the *Jornada del Muerto*. As the plain affords no opportunity for ambush, they come sweeping upon the unsuspecting immigrant in more than usual numbers, and if successful in their attack, invariably destroy all of the party; for there is no possible chance of escape, and the Apaches never take any prisoners but women and young children, and they become captives for life.

At Socorro was a small American garrison, consisting of about half a company of the Second Dragoons, commanded by Lieut. Reuben Campbell, an officer whose acquaintance I had made during the Mexican war, and for whom I entertained a sincere regard.

I left Doña Ana about three o'clock A. M., and traveled leisurely until four in the afternoon, when I unsaddled my horse, staked him to a strong picket pin planted in a field of fine grass, and laid down under the lee side of a cactus to catch a modicum of shade. At twelve, midnight, I resumed my journey, and reached Socorro next day about eleven o'clock A. M., having traveled during the cool of the night at a much more rapid pace. During the trip I neither saw an Indian nor an Indian sign; and here let me add that the Apaches of the Jornada, or more properly the Mescalero Apaches, were at the time in a state of active hostility.

Most pleasantly did I pass two days with Lieut. Campbell, rehearsing scenes and incidents of the Mexican war, and each metaphorically "shouldering his crutch to show how fields were won." Having refreshed myself and rested my noble horse, I took leave of Campbell on the morning of the third day, at three o'clock, when we took the *doch and dorrish* with mutual wishes for each other's welfare.

My trip up had been unaccompanied by any event of interest, and I sincerely hoped that my journey down would be equally tame and spiritless; but this was not to be. I saved my noble beast all I could, frequently dismounting and leading him by the bridle, so as to retain his strength and speed in case of necessity. In this way we jogged on until about three o'clock in the afternoon, by which time we had accomplished about fifty miles, leaving some seventy-five yet to go. The sun was intensely oppressive, and glared like a shield of red-hot brass. A friendly bush, surrounded with fine grass, and standing about one hundred yards to the left of the hard and splendid natural road which runs through four-fifths of the Jornada, invited me to partake of its modest shade, and I turned my horse in that direction, but was surprised at noticing a column of dust to my left, in the direction of the Sierra Blanca, which had the appearance of being in violent motion, and coming my way. Instinctively I felt that it was caused by Apaches; and I took the precaution to tighten my horse's girths, see that the saddle was properly placed and re-cap my four six-shooters, two of which were in my belt, and two in my holsters. I also untied a Mexican *serape*, or blanket, which was lashed to the after part of my saddle, and doubling it, I passed it over my shoulders and tied it under my chin by a stout buckskin thong. By this time the character of the coming party was unmistakable, and they were evidently bent on cutting me off from the road. My gallant horse seemed to appreciate the condition of affairs almost as well as I, and bounded on like a bird. The pursuing party failed in their first attempt and entered the road about three hundred yards in my rear. Perceiving that my horse was infinitely superior in speed and power, I drew rein to save him all that I could, and allowed the Indians to come within fifty yards. There were some forty of them, and none with fire-arms, but mainly supplied with lances, only five or six of the num-

ber carrying bows and arrows. These last named pro-
jectiles commenced to whistle near me; but I paid no
heed, keeping steadily on my course, until one penetrated my blanket; but the effect was completely destroyed by the fluttering of its heavy double folds, which
were kept in a rattling motion by the speed at which we
were going. Perceiving that the force of the arrow had
been neutralized, I drew a heavy holster pistol, and
wheeling half round in my saddle, pointed it at the savages. This caused them to fall back in some alarm, and
I took advantage of that fact to redouble my speed for a
mile or so, gaining some six hundred yards on my pursuers, when I again drew rein to save my horse.

It required a long time for them to again recover shooting distance, but their yells and cries were perpetual.
In this manner, alternately checking and speeding my
horse, and presenting my pistol at the savages, we
scoured over many miles of that infernal Jornada. Several arrows were sticking in my blanket; one had grazed
my right arm, just bringing blood, and the other had
touched my left thigh. I then became convinced that
my horse was the main object of their pursuit. His
value and unequaled qualities were well known to the
Apaches, and they resolved to have him, if possible. Of
course, my life would have been sacrificed, if they could
only manage that little affair. I had bought the horse
of Capt. A. Buford, First United States Dragoons, who
assured me that his equal did not exist in the Territory.
He had been offered a hundred mustangs for the horse
by a Mescalero Apache, but refused, on the ground that
he could take care of one animal with ease; but if he
possessed a hundred, the Apaches would be likely to
steal them at any moment while grazing.

Near the foot of the Jornada, the road takes a bold

sweeping curve to the left, toward Doña Ana, being interrupted by a low but rugged series of small hills and deep ravines. About eight o'clock P. M., the moon being bright and not a cloud visible, I dashed round the first hill, and was surprised to note that the Apaches had apparently given up the chase, for I neither heard nor saw any more of them, although I was about four hundred yards ahead. Suddenly it flashed upon my mind that they might have some short cut-off, and had pursued it with the intention of heading me. For the first time I struck my rowels into the reeking flanks of my poor steed, and most gallantly did he respond to this last call. He fairly flew over the road. Hill after hill was passed with wonderful rapidity until nearly a quarter of an hour had elapsed, when I again heard my Apache friends, about eighty yards in my rear. No sooner did they perceive that their design had been penetrated and frustrated, than they recommenced their yells with additional vigor. But their horses were blown, as well as mine. They had come at their best pace the whole way, while mine had been saved from time to time. If I had come fifty miles at a slow gait in the early day, they had come fifteen at dead speed before they reached to where our race began.

In this manner we continued our career until I arrived within five miles of Doña Ana, about eleven o'clock P. M., when, feeling myself comparatively safe, I commenced emptying the cylinders of my heavy holster pistols among them. Their cries and yells were fearful at this time, but I did not cease firing until they had fallen back out of reach. The remainder of my journey was made without company, and I reached Doña Ana about twelve o'clock midnight, having made the distance of one hundred and twenty-five miles, on one horse, in the space of twenty-one hours, the last seventy miles being performed at a run.

So soon as I arrived, I threw off my serape, which had quite a number of arrows sticking in it, called my boy, José, and rubbed my horse down dry with good, soft straw. This operation required about two hours. I then washed him all over with strong whisky and water, and again rubbed him dry. This was followed by taking off his shoes, and giving him about two quarts of whisky and water as a draught. His whole body and limbs were then swathed in blankets, a mess of cut hay, sprinkled with water and mixed with a couple of pounds of raw steak, cut into small pieces, was given him to eat, and a deep bed of clean dry straw prepared for him to sink into. These duties kept me up until five o'clock A. M., when I refreshed my inner man with a wholesome whisky toddy, prepared by Buford, and sought repose, from which I did not awaken for all that day and the succeeding night. On the second day after the above adventure, I visited my horse and found him in as fine condition as any one could reasonably expect. He was neither foundered nor injured in any ostensible manner. On many a subsequent occasion he served me with equal zeal and capability, but never more under such exciting circumstances. Several efforts were afterwards made by the Apaches to get possession of that noble beast, but, I am proud and happy to add, invariably without success. At the Copper Mines he was saved to me by mere accident. On a certain occasion, remembering that he had lost a shoe, I sent José to bring him from the herd then grazing about a mile distant, under the care of a guard. The order was immediately obeyed, and in half an hour afterward the whole herd was carried off by the Apaches.

It may be entered up as an invariable rule, that the

visits of Apaches to American camps are always for sinister purposes. They have nothing to trade for; consequently, it is not barter that brings them. They beg, but in no wise comparably with other Indian tribes; and scarcely expect to receive when they ask. Their keen eyes omit nothing. One's arms and equipments, the number of your party, their cohesion and precaution, their course of march, their system of defence in case of attack, and the amount of plunder to be obtained with the least possible risk, are all noted and judged. Wherever their observations can be made from neighboring heights with a chance of successful ambush, the Apache never shows himself, nor gives any sign of his presence. Like the ground shark, one never knows he is there until one feels his bite. In nature and disposition, in habits, laws, manners and customs, in religion and ceremonies, in tribal and family organization, in language and signs, in war and in peace, he is totally different from all other Indians of the North American continent; and these facts will be set forth in future chapters, for the consideration of those who may peruse this work.

CHAPTER VIII.

THE main object of the author is to relate such incidents as will give his readers an insight into Indian character; but in each case the relation will be of facts occurring within his own personal experience. It is too much the habit to give details received from hearsay evidence, from which the writer draws his conclusions and offers them to his readers as the results of personal investigation and knowledge. This fault, for I so consider it, will be avoided in the present work, and nothing described which was not actually witnessed or experienced by the author, who leaves his readers to form their own conclusions.

After the shooting of the Apache at the Copper Mines by Jesus Lopez, matters resumed a pacific appearance for some weeks; but the calm was only on the surface. The Apache mind had been deeply exercised by the recovery of Inez and the two boys, and by our invasion and long retention of their favorite haunt. Gold mines had been struck a few miles from the post, and this fact threatened the existence of a permanent colony of Americans, which also served to aggravate the natural hatred and malevolence of the savages. This last mentioned fear proved well grounded, for at this day there are over three hundred Americans and others working those mines, and a considerable village has sprung up in their immediate vicinity.

Mangas Colorado, Ponce, Delgadito, Cuchillo Negro, Coletto Amarillo, and other prominent Apaches, have, since then, all been sent to their long account by the rifles of Californian soldiers and American citizens, but not without the loss of many innocent lives on our part, or the perpetration of atrocities on the part of the Apaches which make the blood curdle at the bare recital. These developments will form portions of succeeding chapters.

Toward the latter end of July, a number of mules for which Col. Craig was responsible, could not be found, although all the surrounding country, to the extent of thirty miles, was strictly searched. That gallant officer and accomplished gentleman invited me to his quarters, and asked my opinion on the subject. Without hesitation, I informed him that I thought the Apaches had stolen them, either for the hope of reward for bringing them back (as the Commissioner had invariably bestowed gifts on those of the tribe who brought in strayed animals, or those supposed to have strayed) or that they had made the initiative of a war campaign. After two or three hours of conversation, the Colonel fell into my idea, and determined to go and search for them himself. Taking thirty soldiers, he visited the Apache camp of Delgadito, on the Mimbres river. The Indians were much excited, and disclaimed any participation in the robbery, or any knowledge of the missing animals; but promised to hunt them up and restore them to that officer, if found. Eight days afterward they kept their

promise, in a truly Apache manner, by making another
descent upon the Colonel's herd of mules, and relieving
him of the necessity to guard twenty-five more of those
animals, and some fine horses. Having nothing but
infantry, Col. Craig felt himself unable to maintain an active campaign against these bold and well-mounted savages, and consequently invoked the aid of Capt. Buford's
company of dragoons, from Doña Ana. Soon after the
arrival of that officer, another batch of animals disappeared in the same mysterious manner, and a joint scout,
composed of the dragoons and mounted infantry, started
off to recover the lost animals, or punish the robbers, if
possible. This raid proved wholly ineffective, neither
animals being recovered, nor Indians punished; but during the absence of the force, intelligence was brought
that the Apaches had attacked the mining camp, about
three or four miles down the cañon, and were driving off
the cattle. About twenty of the Commission, headed by
Lieut. A. W. Whipple, mounted their horses and gave
immediate pursuit. The Indians were overhauled in a
thick forest, and one party, numbering about fifty warriors, stood to give us battle, while a detachment hurried
on with the cattle. The Indians concealed themselves
behind large pine trees, and retreated as fast as possible,
but still showing front. Our party dismounted, and,
being joined by Mr. Hay, the head miner, with four of
his associates, we left our horses in care of eight men,
and took to the trees, keeping up a lively fire from behind their friendly shelter.

Here, for the first time, all doubt as to the identity of
the robbers was set at rest, for they were headed by Delgadito, who kept at a safe distance and poured out torrents of the vilest abuse upon the Americans. This same
scoundrel had slept in my tent only two nights before,

when I gave him a good shirt and a serviceable pair of shoes.

The Government had furnished the Commission with several styles of newly-patented arms, and among these were some Wesson's rifles, which could throw their balls with fair accuracy a distance of four hundred yards—at that period a very remarkable distance. One of these rifles I had ordered to be fitted with new and fine sights, and at three hundred and fifty yards a good marksman could hit the size of his hat eight times out of ten.

Among our party was Wells, the Commissioner's carriage driver—an excellent, brave and cool man, and a crack shot. I pointed Delgadito out to Wells, and handing him my rifle, told him to approach as nearly as possible, take good aim and bring the rascal down. Wells glided from tree to tree with the utmost caution and rapidity, until he got within two hundred and sixty or seventy yards of Delgadito, who, at that moment, was slapping his buttocks and defying us with the most opprobrious language. While in the act of exhibiting his posteriors—a favorite taunt among the Apaches—he uncovered them to Wells, who took deliberate aim and fired. This mark of attention was received by Delgadito with an unearthly yell and a series of dances and capers that would put a *maitre de ballet* to the blush. The Apache leader was recalled to full consciousness of his exposed position by the whizzing of three or four balls in close proximity to his upper end, when he ceased his saltatory exercises and rushed frantically through a thick copse, followed by his band. We started back for our horses and having remounted, again pressed forward in pursuit. In fifteen minutes we had passed the woods and opened upon the plain, over which the Apaches were scouring for life. The pursuit lasted for thirty miles, and just at sundown we came once more upon the cattle, when the party in charge abandoned them and sought safety in flight with their beaten companions. Perceiving that further pursuit would be useless, we contented ourselves by bringing back Mr. Hay's herd. I afterward learned that the ball from Wells' rifle gouged a neat streak across that portion of Delgadito's person denominated in school parlance as the "seat of honor." His riding and general activity were spoiled for several weeks.

This celebrated Apache was subsequently killed by a Mexican, whom he was endeavoring to dupe and destroy. They were fording the Mimbres river on foot, and upon reaching the eastern bank, Delgadito caught hold of the projecting branch of a tree to assist himself, when the Mexican took advantage of his momentary neglect, and plunged his knife through the Indian's heart from behind. It is an actual fact that the dead savage was found, the next day, still clinging to the branch. This event took place two years after we had left the country. I never met with Delgadito after the affair in the woods; but had resolved to pistol him the very first time we got close enough to make my shot sure.

In every case the Copper Mine Apaches had been treated with the greatest kindness and hospitality by the whole Commission. They had received very many and valuable presents. For months they had the unrestricted freedom of our camp. All causes of dispute had been settled to their own satisfaction; nothing had occurred for weeks to disturb the existing harmony. Only two days before the affair above described, Delgadito and over a hundred warriors had been in the Copper Mines, and emphatically disavowed any participation in or knowledge of the wholesale robberies which had been committed on our people. Mr. Bartlett and Dr. Webb had

persisted in their theory, that "kind treatment, a rigid
adherance to what is right, and a prompt and invariable
fulfillment of all promises, would secure the friendship of
the Apaches;" but, although this kind of treatment had
been exactly carried out by Mr. Bartlett and his Commission, the Apaches took occasion to manifest their ap-
preciation and friendship by robbing over three hundred
head of our finest mules and horses, which had been
resting and growing fat and strong for future use. They
never served us again. There are cases where an individual Apache will conceive a personal regard for a particular man, and will do him almost any act of kindness
in his power, but this is far, very far, from being a general rule. From earliest infancy they are instructed to
regard every other race as natural enemies. Their suspicions and savage distrust are aroused and cultivated
before they ever come in contact with other people. An
Apache child of three years will run and yell with fear
and hate from a white man. Apache mothers hush their
children by naming an American. To rob or kill a Mexican, is considered a most honorable achievement; but to
commit successful outrage upon an American, entitles
the perpetrator to the highest consideration. Dexterity
in stealing is a virtue of no mean character. The most
adroit thief is precisely the man who is best capable of
maintaining his wives in plenty and bedecking them in
meretricious finery, of which they are inordinately fond.
The Apache woman who is saddled with the least work
and the most ornaments, is the envied of her sex. For
this reason, the young girls prefer to become the fifth,
sixth, or seventh wife of a noted robber, rather than the
single spouse of a less adroit thief. In the first case her
labors are divided by her associate wives, and are, therefore, measurably lessened, while her chances for obtain-

5

ing gew-gaws are quite as good or better. They unquestionably prefer polygamy, as it exists.

A really brave man does not rank as high as a really clever, thievish poltroon. His gallantry is admired, and in times of danger all flock around him for protection; but at other periods the young squaws give him the cold shoulder, and he is regarded as little better than a fool who will run into danger, but does not know how to steal, or enrich himself at the expense of others. "He is a very brave warrior," say they, "a man who will fight and shed his blood in our defense; but he is little better than an ass, because he is always poor and don't know how to steal and not be caught." I am not too sure that something of this characteristic does not obtain among people who profess to rank much higher than the Apaches in the scale of mankind. It might be as well, perhaps, to pull the mote out of our own eyes before we attempt to extract the beam from those of our savage brethren. Nevertheless, the Apache character is not lovely. In point of natural shrewdness, quick perception and keen animal instinct they are unequaled by any other people. They know what is just and proper, because in all their talks they urge justice and propriety, and profess to be guided by those virtues; but all their acts belie their words. Deceit is regarded among them with the same admiration we bestow upon one of the fine arts. To lull the suspicions of an enemy—and to them all other people are enemies—and then take advantage of his credence, is regarded as a splendid stroke of policy. To rob and not be robbed; to kill and not be killed; to take captive and not be captured, form the sum of an Apache's education and ambition, and he who can perform these acts with the greatest success is the greatest man in the tribe. To be a prominent Apache is to be a prominent scoundrel.

But the reader will have plenty of opportunities to judge for himself, as the succeeding pages will unfold incidents enough from which to form a criterion. They are far from cowardly, but they are exceedingly prudent. Twenty Apaches will not attack four well armed and determined men, if they keep constantly on their guard and prepared for action. In no case will they incur the risk of losing life, unless the plunder be most enticing and their numbers overpowering, and even then they will track a small party for days, waiting an opportunity to establish a secure ambush or effect a surprise. A celebrated warrior once told me: "You Americans are fools, for whenever you hear a gun fire you run straight to the spot; but we Apaches get away, and by and by steal round and discover the cause."

I have before stated that individual Apaches will sometimes conceive a regard for particular persons not of their tribe, and an incident illustrative of this fact occurred to Lieut. Diaz of the Mexican Commission. Mr. Diaz had been ordered to occupy a station on the top of a certain prominent height, and took with him a party of ten men. His camp was only about four miles from the camp of Gen. Garcia Conde; but getting out of provisions he left the mountain, accompanied by one man, for the purpose of ordering another supply. His course led him over a perfectly smooth plain for the distance of two miles. Not a tree, nor a bush, nor a rock was visible, but the grass was thick and about a foot high. Mr. Diaz and his man walked side by side, each with a six-shooter in his hand, for the Apaches were then hostile. About the middle of the plain Mr. Diaz felt his right wrist seized and his left arm pinioned, while his pistol was taken from his grasp, and he found himself in the power of Cuchillo Negro and a dozen other savages. His at-

tendant was also seized and a prisoner. Cuchillo Negro
looked at him for a moment, with a most gratified expression on his savage face, and then said:

"My friend, you see that you cannot escape us. But
I like you and will do you no harm. You must cease
from staying on that hill. I want it; it belongs to me.
You have intruded into my country; but you yourself I
like. I will keep these pistols; but send for the rest of
your men on the hill and take them away. For your sake
we will not kill them this time."

Poor Lieut. Diaz had not a word to reply except to
promise that the Indian's request would be granted in return for his generosity. It seems that Cuchillo Negro
had observed the movement of Mr. Diaz, and with his
band had buried himself under the grass, waiting the
auspicious moment when Mr. Diaz should pass him on
the road, when suddenly and noiselessly rising the savages grasped the unsuspecting Mexicans. I will here
add, that Mr. Diaz was the officer charged to blow up
the fortress of Chapultepec, should it fall into the hands
of the Americans; but when the time came his heart failed
him, and he was captured pistol in hand, as if about to
fire the magazine.

A few weeks after the incidents above described, the
Commission abandoned the Copper Mines, in order to
prosecute their labors to completion, and this abandonment was always regarded by the Apaches as the legitimate result of their active hostility. This fact came to
my knowledge twelve years subsequent to the period of
our removal, at which time it was again my province to
renew my acquaintance with Mangas Colorado, then the
only one living of the chiefs we had met at the Copper
Mines. Coletto Amarillo, Ponce and his son, were killed
in action by Californian soldiers, and it was the fate of
Mangas to die on the point of an American bayonet.

After a long travel through Sonora, visiting Santa Cruz, Bacuachi, Babispe, Tumacarcori, Imurez, Arispe, Ures, Hermosillo, Guaymas, and several other towns, Mr. Bartlett took passage by sea from Guaymas, leaving Dr. Webb, Mr. Thurber, Mr. Pratt and his son, myself and five others, making a party of ten, to reach California overland, and join him at San Diego. This was a very small party to travel through the Apache strongholds, especially at a time when those savages were at open war with us; but we were all splendidly armed, except Dr. Webb, who could never be persuaded to carry anything but a small five-inch five-shooter and a knife—and we were also tolerably experienced in the Apache style of warfare, and the nature of the country to be traversed. The magnificent Santa Rita, ten thousand feet high, with its majestic head wreathed in snow, Tubac, San Xavier del Bac and Tucson were successively reached and passed. The great desert of ninety miles without water—I speak of eighteen years ago, in 1850— between Tucson and the Gila river, was crossed safely, but not without much suffering; and we finally reached the Pimo villages, where we met Lieut. Whipple and party.

The Pimos have ever been most friendly to Americans, and I have yet to learn of a single instance in which they ever harmed a white man. These Indians are not nomads· Their villages have remained in the same localities for hundreds of years. As their country affords no game, and they are by no means a warlike tribe, they maintain themselves in comfort and abundance by tilling the ground, and limit their warlike propensities to punishing the raids made upon them by other tribes. These Pimos profess to have originally come from the far south. According to their tradition, their forefathers were driven from their native land many centuries ago, and sought an asylum by coming northward. They profess to have crossed through Sonora, and finally settled on the Gila, about twenty miles east of the eastern limit of the Great Gila Bend, where that river makes a detour to the north of nearly ninety miles, and, after sweeping round the base of a range of mountains, resumes its original course westward. Here they were visited by the Jesuit missionaries, who taught them how to till the ground, and supplied them with many valuable seeds, and also instructed them in the art of preparing and weaving cotton. A Pimo cotton blanket will last for years, and is really a very handsome and creditable affair. The men never cut their hair, but wear it in massive plaits and folds, which frequently descend to the calves of their legs. The front hair is cut even with the eyebrows. The women wear short hair, and are not permitted to have it more than eight or nine inches in length. They are a robust and well-formed race, and not at all revengeful, but exceedingly superstitious — far more so than any other tribe I ever met. They are hospitable, chatty, and exceedingly proud of the purity of their blood.

Living in the closest amity with them are the Maricopa Indians, who, like the Pimos, claim to be direct descendants from Moctezuma, but differ from them essentially in their language, laws, habits, manners and religious ceremonies. The Maricopa tradition, as given me by Juan José, a chief of some importance in former times, and subsequently confirmed by Juan Chivari, the present head chief of the tribe, is to the following effect.

About a hundred years ago the Yumas, Cocopahs and Maricopas composed one tribe, known as the Coco-Maricopa tribe. They occupied the country about the head of the Gulf of California, and for some distance up the

Colorado river. At that time a dispute occurred, and what is now known as the Cocopah tribe split off, and the secessionists were permitted to go in peace. This pacific policy soon afterward induced the party, now known as Maricopas, to secede also; but this defection incurred the severe displeasure and hostility of the remainder, who now form the Yuma tribe. Many sanguinary conflicts ensued, when the Yumas succeeded in obtaining the aid of the Cocopahs, and, together, they gradually forced the Maricopas up the Colorado, until the Gila was reached. Knowing that the country to the north was occupied by the Amojaves, a large and warlike tribe, the retreating Maricopas turned their steps eastward, and followed the windings of the Gila river, pursued by their relentless enemies, until they reached the Great Gila Bend. Their spies were sent across this desert and returned with the intelligence that they had met a tribe living in well constructed and comfortable houses, cultivating the land, well clothed, numerous, and apparently happy. A council was called and it was agreed to send an embassy to the Pimos, to negotiate a defensive and offensive alliance, and with the request that the Pimos would parcel out to them a suitable amount of land for their occupation. After much delay, and with true Indian circumspection, it was agreed that the Maricopas should inhabit certain lands of the Pimos; but it was made a *sine qua non* that the new-comers must forever renounce their warlike and hunting propensities, and dedicate themselves to tillage—for, said the Pimos, we have no hunting grounds; we do not wish to incur the vengeance of the Tontos, the Chimehuevis, the Apaches, and others, by making useless raids against them; they have nothing to lose, and we have, and you must confine yourselves solely to revenging any warlike

incursions made either upon us or upon yourselves.
You are free to worship after your own manner, and
govern yourselves according to your own laws; but you
must be ready at all times to furnish a proportionate
number of warriors to protect the general weal, and, in
the event of taking any booty, there shall be a fair divi-
sion made by a council of sagamores, composed of equal
numbers from each tribe, and their decision must be
final.

These equitable and generous terms were accepted by
the Maricopas, who immediately occupied a portion of
Pimo territory, and imitated them in the construction of
their dwellings and the cultivation of the land, being
supplied with seed by the Pimos. In this manner the
two tribes have continued together for one hundred
years; yet, as an instance of the pertinacity with which
an Indian will cling to his own particular tribe and customs, although many of them have intermarried, and
their villages are never more than two miles apart,
and in some cases not more than four hundred yards, to
this day they cannot converse with each other unless
through an interpreter. Their laws, religion, manners,
ceremonies and language, remain quite as distinct as on
the day they sought the Pimo alliance. Here we find
no difference of color or diversity of pursuit. There is
no clashing element, no cause for discordant controversy,
or contention. They are and have been the warmest of
friends for the period stated, have frequently intermarried, are bound together by one common sympathy and
one common cause, have the same enemies to contend
against and the same evils to deplore—the same blessings
to enjoy; yet they are no closer together now than they
were one hundred years ago. Ought not these indisputable facts to furnish us a lesson in Indian character?

Must we forever blind our eyes to such teachings of experience and fact, and indulge in the pleasing hypothesis that we can effect radical changes in their political and social economy? Enthusiasts will point to a few individual exceptions, who have, as it were, got rid of their Indian nature and elevated themselves to a higher sphere in the mental, social and political scales; but these exceptions are very few, and only serve to establish the rule that the leopard cannot change his spots, nor an Ethiopian his skin. The Cherokees, Choctaws and Chickasaws, are pointed out as triumphal examples of what the white man's instructions and precepts will do for the Indian races. But in what essential particulars have they demonstrated this wonderful improvement? It is true that many of them know how to read, write and compute; that they assume, to some extent, the vestments of the whites; that they have learned how to construct a better class of houses, and have improved their physical condition in other respects; but is this true of the majority? Have they not adopted, to the fullest extent, all the vices of the whites, while acquiring some of their minor virtues? If left to themselves, would they continue to advance and progress in wisdom and virtue, or would they retrograde into barbarism? Are not such changes and improvements as have taken place among them more attributable to the large admixture of white blood visible in these tribes, than to any other cause? How many of pure Indian blood are now to be found among them? Are not those people rapidly dwindling away, and will they not soon be among the things that were? Have their numbers increased, or have they become strong? Do they love us with any deeper affection, or do they show gratitude for their civilization?

But, says the christian philanthropist, it is our duty to

5*

continue even unto the end; to faint not by the way, nor become lukewarm. These people are God's children, as well as yourself. They are possessed of immortal souls, and if your lot has been cast, through the mercy of Providence, in a more elevated and useful condition of life, you should not contemn those who have been denied these benefits. The Almighty has created them for the express purpose of exercising your philanthropy, your brotherly love, and all your better and nobler qualities. Take the red man by the hand as you have done to his negro brother, and guide him gently, kindly toward a better state in this world and the hope of salvation hereafter.

I admit that these are very persuasive and forcible arguments; but, reverend sir, the red man absolutely refuses to come. He disdains to take my hand; he flouts my offered sympathy, and feels indignant at my presumption in proffering him my aid to improve his condition. He conceives himself not only my equal, but decidedly my superior. He desires only to be let alone. His forefathers lived well enough without our officious services, and he intends to do likewise. He is the man of the woods, the plains, the mountains, and looks upon us as the men of the towns and the cities. For no possible consideration would he change places or accept our domiciliary style of life, and without such domestication all our efforts are vain and idle. With calm and unruffled dignity he listens to all you say, and with unconcealed dislike he makes it a point to remember nothing he has heard, or, if remembering, to treasure it up as something to be avoided. Your counsels are considered as baits and traps, and your desire to domiciliate him as an effort to bring him under your control. You are and must ever remain, to him, an object of suspicion and distrust. You are understood to be his natural enemy, and all his faculties are awakened against your advances. Treasuring up his own vengeful purposes for months and years, he imputes to you the same, or kindred intention of doing him ultimate harm. No effort, no kindness on your part, can induce him to disabuse his mind of this idea, because he is not capable of such magnanimity, and regards it as the finest stroke of duplicity. Trained to treachery, he is ever on his guard against it in others. Even members of his own tribe are not trusted implicitly.

When you talk to him of a Creator, he replies that he admits that fact; and when you endeavor to explain the attributes of the Most High, he tells you of the necessity to propitiate the devil. Any attempt to make him comprehend the Trinity is laughed to scorn, and he hesitates not to tell you that you lie, simply because it is beyond his comprehension. He admires and envies our power to read, write and calculate, and would fain be master of those accomplishments; but ask him to send his children to school, in order that they might learn to do likewise, and straightway he regards you as one wishing to control and bewitch the beloved offspring. He is willing to obtain information by oral means, but scouts the idea of learning it by studious process, which he regards as a species of slavery, and detests the control exercised by the teacher over his free born, wild, and unfettered children. While he frankly admits that you are better clothed, better fed, and better conditioned in all respects than he is, he as frankly and persistently refuses all overtures and invitations to adopt your style of life. He is as dogmatically convinced of his superiority as you are of yours, and no effort of rhetoric or argument can bring him to a different opinion. Show him the wonders of magnetism, or a microscope, or explain to him the mechanism of a watch, or direct his admiring gaze through a telescope, and he will express unfeigned delight, but will, at the same time, regard you with additional distrust and suspicion. In fine, all your efforts are treated as the advances of an invidious enemy, and no expenditure of time or industry has ever been successful in this field of operation. How can we cultivate and improve human beings who resolutely refuse cultivation and improvement, and brand all our efforts as so many snares laid for their subjection? But it is useless to prolong a discussion of this subject; *experientia docet*, and experience has shown the futility of all attempts to cultivate, civilize and christianize the North American savage.

The deplorable condition of the Californian Indians, after years upon years of Jesuit teachings, and the foundation of numerous missions, surrounded with large and pacific Indian populations, only offers another proof that the savage tribes of this continent are not susceptible of permanent and radical improvement. Instead of being bettered, civilized and christianized, they have contracted all the worst features of the white race and retained all the more despicable characteristics of their own, while the native dignity, courage and primitive virtues of the Indian have been completely annihilated. In all the world there is no more despicable people than the indigenous tribes of California, which have been, for years, under the sway and tuition of the Jesuit fathers, who piously thought they were doing God good service. In all the attributes of manhood, in everything which dignifies uncivilized human nature, the untamed tribes are infinitely their superiors. Superstition, cowardice, filth, sloth, drunkenness, moral depravity, and the most revolting licentiousness have replaced the sterner and more simple qualities of the wild Indian tribes. In the desire to do them good, we have done them the most harm. In the hope of excising their savage defects, we have inoculated them with the most terrific vices. This is a sad picture, but it cannot be denied.

What was the result of bringing leading chiefs, like Black Hawk, Keokuk, Irritaba and Juan Chivari from their native wilds to behold and take lessons from the wealth, power, numbers and general superiority of our people? In each case those once renowned warriors lost their whole influence. They were regarded with suspicion and dislike by their own tribes. They were suspected of being bewitched. Their tales of the wondrous things they saw and heard were treated with scorn and unbelief, and, in some instances, such as in that of Irritaba and Juan Chivari, they barely escaped death at the hands of their former followers.

The North American savage gazes with ill-suppressed admiration upon our palatial buildings, our thronged streets, our splendid stores, our vast and complicated mechanical engineering, our big guns and great ships; but his teaching ends there. While wondering at these things, he pants for his own unbounded plains and dense forests. He is not animated to attempt any change in his own method of life. He has no idea of toiling throughout existence that his children's children, to the tenth or twentieth generation, may possess capabilities and advantages like those enjoyed by the white man. His ambition is not at all excited, and he philosophically concludes that each race has its appointed duties, and is engaged in its fulfillment. Indians who have been removed from their native scenes at an early age, and received the best education attainable in our seminaries of learning, have almost invariably returned to their wastes, and proved the most formidable enemies of those who congratulated themselves on having rescued them as "brands from the burning."

CHAPTER IX.

AMONG the most superstitious of all our Indian races, the Pimos take precedence. They entertain an unfaltering belief in witchcraft, sorcery, ghosts, the direct influence of the evil one, and the absolute necessity of propitiating the "gentleman in black." It is not, by any means, difficult to disturb their serenity and set them almost wild, by the exercise of the most simple processes known to us. I have often fancied to myself their unbounded wonderment and fear at a skillful exhibition of the magic lantern, or the more scientific feats of chemistry—such as converting fluids into solids, and *vice versa* —but so far none of these effects have been shown them.

After joining the party under Lieut. Whipple, that superior officer and thorough gentleman, invited me to accompany him one beautiful night to assist in observing an eclipse of the moon, which was to take place about ten o'clock. The opportunity to make observations was too valuable to be lost, and as Mr. Wheaton was ill, the invitation to fill his place was kindly tendered to the writer. The large telescope and other important instruments were carried by two men of Whipple's party, and we proceeded until the highest hillock in the neighborhood was surmounted. The Pimos and Maricopas soon learned that the white men were abroad with sundry curious looking weapons, and surrounded us by hundreds; but as we knew them to be thoroughly peaceful, and even generous, no notice was taken of their presence. The telescope was placed in position, and on being asked by a Pimo what it was, I carelessly replied that it was a terrific cannon, the shot of which would reach to the moon. Little did we think how quickly this answer would place us in imminent jeopardy. The round, full moon was sailing across the heavens in refulgent splendor. Not a cloud could be seen; the air was calm and tranquil; the night was pleasantly warm, and everything promised a satisfactory observation. By and by, the eclipse was about to commence. Mr. Whipple stationed himself at the telescope, and the rest of us stood ready to obey his directions. Every one was attentive, and wholly bent on making the occasion a success. At length the observation commenced. It was watched by the Indians, who kept their eyes alternately fixed on the moon and on Mr. Whipple; and as the disc of that luminary began to grow less and less, and darker and darker, the Chief, Culo Azul, said to me: "What are you doing?"

Not apprehending any difficulty, and relying on their well known and often tried amity, I replied: "We are shooting and killing the moon."

This was translated to the surrounding multitude, and immediately followed by the most dreadful yells I ever heard. A rush was made toward us, and weapons brandished with fearful and vengeful violence. Our party became alarmed, and prepared to sell our lives as dearly as possible; but the thought of our unsuspecting comrades in the camp compelled us to act with caution. The first object of the savages was evidently to destroy the weapon which they believed to be killing the moon; but its loss would have been irreparable, and their vengeance would not have stopped there.

"What are we to do without the moon?" inquired the Chief. "How are we to note time? How shall we know when to plant and when to reap? How can we pass all our nights in darkness, and be incapacitated from preventing Apache raids? What have we done to you, that you should do this thing to us?"

To these questions, asked with vehemence and rapidity, I replied, "Wait until I consult my superior," and immediately acquainted Mr. Whipple with all the facts. That officer had left the telescope in alarm; but immediately replaced himself with the greatest *sang-froid*, and, in an undertone, said:

"Tell them that, if they will keep quiet and promise not to make any hostile movement, we will restore the moon again, as full and as bright as ever."

His coolness, courage, and undisturbed self-possession excited my highest admiration, and I immediately translated his words to Culo Azul, who again made them known to his people. Under the direction of Mr. Whipple, I added:

"We can hit the moon, as you may see for yourselves," —at this time that luminary was obscured one-half by the earth's shadow—"and it is also in our power to restore it to health and strength; but if you harm us or injure our instruments, then the moon must remain dead, and can never be restored. We have only the kindliest feelings toward the Pimos and Maricopas, and we only wished to destroy the moon in order to prevent its light from guiding the Apaches and Yumas to your villages.

But as our brethren have signified their dislike to the proceeding, we will restore the moon to its original splendor. If in a little while it does not reappear, our Pimo and Maricopa friends may take their vengeance and destroy our instruments. But they must remember that we alone are the medicine men; our brethren in the camp are as innocent as you, and should not be disturbed or held accountable in any event."

This promise restored some degree of tranquility, and they gave us their word not to injure or interfere with our unsuspecting comrades.

It has often occurred to me what a dreadful fate would have been ours if a sudden storm had arisen at that period, and prevented the moon from being seen again immediately after the eclipse. But the heavens were specially bright and cloudless, and not the slightest incident occurred to dash our courage. In the course of time the observation reached its fullest extent, and the anxiety of our Indian friends became intense. Yells and moanings rent the still night air, maledictions and curses were lavished upon us, weapons were drawn, and every indication given of speedy dismissal from this vale of tears; but the grand old chief, who seemed to have absolute control of his people, stood between us and harm, and quietly awaited the issue. By and by the moon began to exhibit her brilliant shield once more. Its silver disc grew larger and larger. Gradually, but surely, it sailed from behind the earth's shadow and assumed its pristine proportions, until she was again unveiled in full majesty. To describe the joy, the amazement and the homage of the savages is quite impossible. We were lifted up on their arms, patted on our backs, embraced, and dignified to their utmost extent. All this time Mr. Whipple had been quietly taking his observations and writing them in his book. At no period did he appear ruffled or concerned. His equanimity won respect, and his influence with the Pimos became all powerful. In a subsequent chapter will be found detailed another and no less curious incident among those Indians.

The Pimos and Maricopas both pretend to trace their descent from Moctezuma, whoever that renowned gentleman may be, but they have entirely different ideas about the matter. The Pimos believe Moctezuma to have been a god, who resided on earth for a time, and became the founder of their race, but was treacherously and basely murdered. Before yielding up the ghost, he threatened his slayers with future punishment, foretold the scattering of the various tribes he had created and organized, and promised to come again and assume control of their affairs when all his children should be reunited under his rule.

The Pimos invariably resort to the ceremony of cremation when any of their tribe dies. The body is placed upon a funeral pyre and rapidly consumed. No effort is made to collect the ashes of the dead, but all his friends and relatives take a portion, and, mixing them with the dissolved gum of the mesquit tree (which is a species of the acacia, and yields a concrete juice similar to gum arabic), they daub their faces with the odious compound, and permit it to remain until it is worn away.

The chastity of their women is proverbial, but this is probably more the result of the fear of detection than from any natural virtue. Among themselves loose women are tolerated, but the Pimo girl who may be caught in carnal intercourse with any other than a Pimo man, runs nine chances out of ten to be stoned to death. If a white man be a trader among them, and has been there for a long time, and has acquired something of their language, he is more or less considered entitled to the privileges of the tribe; but, even then, disclosure of concubinage is attended with imminent danger to the guilty female. The women of this tribe are particularly fine looking, possessing elegant forms, nicely shaped and well tapered limbs, brilliant and perfect white teeth, small hands, and the easy carriage of the unfettered Indian girl who never saw a pair of corsets, nor inclosed her form in the net-work of crinoline. The men are rugged and tolerably well made, but in nowise remarkable for size nor physical strength. Their powers of endurance are about on a par with most other Indian races, but bear no comparison with those of the Apaches. They are almost all bow-legged, with long trunks and arms, deep chested, narrow shouldered and big headed. Their noses are flatter, wider and more fleshy than those of other tribes, while their feet, in both sexes, are unusually large and splayed. Prior to receiving muskets and ammunition from the American Government—a favor granted them through the wise intercession of Gen. James H. Carleton—their weapons consisted of a bow and arrow, and a lance or knife. Their arrows differ from those of all the Apache tribes in having only two feathers instead of three, and in being much longer, with the single exception of the Coyoteros, who use very long arrows of reed, finished out with some hard wood, and an iron or flint head, but invariably with three feathers at the opposite end.

The Maricopas invariably bury their dead, and mock the ceremony of cremation. They, like the Pimos, and most other Indian tribes, believe in the existence of two gods, who divide the universe between them. One of the divinities is the author of all good, the other the father of all evil. The good god is deemed a quiet and inactive spirit, who takes no decisive part in the affairs of mankind, but relies more upon their desire to escape the evils brought upon them by the bad spirit than upon any direct efforts of his own. He contents himself with the knowledge that after mankind has been sufficiently tormented by his great adversary, they will seek him as a source of refuge. On the other hand, they invest the evil spirit with powers of unequaled and inconceivable activity. He is everywhere at once, and takes the lead in all schemes and pursuits, with the view of converting them to his ultimate use. The first duty of the Indian, exposed as he is to the influences of these two spirits, is to propitiate the most active of the two, and the one which will control his every day avocations. His next object is to approach the good spirit and ask his pardon for having made terms with his one great enemy. This method is something in the style of Louis XI's prayers, but is really in use among these Indians. Their women are not noted for chastity, but are very cautious against detection, which is severely punished, although not to the extent that obtains among the Pimos. They are quite as good looking as their neighbors, and the men generally are credited with a superior reputation as warriors. Their dress, arms, accoutrements, and general style of person are so nearly similar as not to arrest the attention of travelers; but their religion, language, laws and customs are wholly different. The Maricopas seem to have more general recklessness and cordiality of manner than the Pimos, who are constrained and stiff in their intercourse with strangers. The Pimo believes in a future state, in which material modifications will exist; but the Maricopa thinks that the existence of man, after death, closely resembles his earthly career—that his wants and requirements will be very similar to those he experienced in this world.

Acting on this belief he will sacrifice at the grave of a warrior all the property of which he died possessed, together with all in possession of his various relatives. The decease of a warrior therefore becomes a *bona fide* cause for mourning; for each of his immediate relations is stripped of any goods they may own, in order that his spirit may assume a proper place and distinction among his predecessors in the other world. This solemnity of course impoverishes all his relations, and its exaction creates sincere grief. How completely is this custom at variance with ours. How clearly does it exhibit the difference between savage and enlightened views on a point of no common importance. This custom, so strictly enforced among the Maricopas, does not exist among the Pimos; but in the case of an intermarriage between the two tribes the deceased is invariably sepultured in rigid accordance with the views of his or her tribe. Self-interest is, after all, as strong a motive among Indians as among whites, and for this reason intermarriages between the two tribes are so rare, even after one hundred years of undivided co-existence on the same lands, and prosecution of the same general objects.

A more marked dissimilarity is observable in their superstitions regarding warfare. The American officer can take a body of Pimos and follow up the trail of a hostile force until he has run his game to earth, when a fight takes place, in which he can depend upon the pluck and courage of his followers; but should the contest result in the death of a single enemy, or in that of a Pimo, he must bid adieu to any further effort for the time being, for the Pimos will immediately about face and return to their villages, to undergo the process of purification from blood. No threats, no inducements can make them alter or modify this course. It is a part of their religion, and they will observe its dictates. One, or twenty, or a hundred of the enemy may be killed during the engagement, but if blood be spilled the Pimos will return to their villages for the purpose above stated. Not so with the Maricopas, although they are prone to abandon the war path after the enemy has been met and overcome; but if led by energetic white men they will continue and obey them to the end. The reader cannot fail to have remarked some singularly diverse traits of character in these two tribes; and this difference is the more extraordinary in view of the fact that they have been domiciled together for so many years, and been acting under one common bond of sympathy and interest. It only affords another convincing proof, if any such were required, of the unchangeable and unimpressible character of the North American savage.

The country inhabited by the Pimos and Maricopas is a dead flat with clayey soil, which is extremely tenacious when wet, and sparsely covered with mesquit trees. It is a fine wheat land, and the Indians raise very abundant crops of wheat, melons, pumpkins and corn; but their supplies are almost wholly limited to these articles. As before recited, they manufacture a very superior quality of cotton blanket, which will turn rain, and is warm, comfortable and lasting. Dr. David Wooster of San Francisco, who resided among them for some time, and compiled a vocabulary of their language, is, perhaps, better informed with regard to these tribes than any other white man. He was indefatigable in his researches, and received the confidence and affection of these Indians for his many benevolent acts, and his self-sacrificing attention to their sick, without the hope or prospect of pay or reward. The remembrance of his many kind deeds is cherished among them, and they charged me, on my last visit, to make known that fact to their benefactor.

We left the Pimo villages with much misgiving, as we had learned that the Yumas, on the Colorado river, had declared war with the Americans, and our party at that time was only ten strong, seven Americans and three Mexicans, among whom was the step-father of Inez, who had consented to act as guide and arriero for our party. Just as we were about to depart an incident occurred explanatory of Indian character, and for that reason worthy of a place in this work.

Gen. Garcia Conde had been to the Colorado river with his command, and returned to the Pimo villages, bringing with him a noted Yuma chief, named Antonio. This brave had signalized himself in the frequent contests between the Yumas and Maricopas, and had earned the undying vengeance of the latter tribe. Gen. Conde, however, persuaded him to act as guide for his party, promising to protect him from all harm, and to have him safely returned to his country and people. On arriving at the Maricopa village, which was the first to the westward, it was soon bruited abroad that Antonio was with the Mexicans and under their protection. Hundreds of Maricopas and Pimos visited Gen. Conde's camp to get a sight of their famed enemy, but no overt demonstrations were made, as Gen. Conde warned them that he would protect Antonio at all hazards, and they had no disposition to provoke his power to enforce his promise. The next morning Antonio was found dead, his body pierced in many places. Gen. Conde was much grieved, but as the deed had already been consummated, and there was no clue whatever of the murderers, he contented himself with giving decent christian sepulture to the remains, and then immediately prosecuted his journey.

Two days afterward we passed down the road, going

westward, and it was my lot to be something like a mile
or two in the rear of my comrades, but being better
mounted than they, this fact gave me no concern, especially as I knew that we were among peaceful and in-
offensive tribes. Just south of the last village inhabited
by the Maricopas, a low, flat-topped hill is met, with its
northern base close to the highway along which I had to
pass. On arriving near this hill, I observed a very large
crowd of Indians on its summit and sides, who appeared
to be performing a series of most unusual antics, accompanied with occasional discordant and ear-splitting
yells. At first I feared that my comrades had committed some act that had aroused their vengeance, but cooler
consideration convinced me that they were not the men
to do foolish acts. I rode forward at a round gallop,
with the intention of passing the hill and its occupants
as quickly as possible without appearing to be in flight,
but I was not destined to escape so easily. Four or five
stalwart warriors placed themselves in the road and beckoned me to hold up, and, believing discretion to be the
better part of valor, on this occasion at least, I obeyed
their summons. One took my horse, while another assisted me, most courteously, to dismount, and then
taking my hand, led me up the ascent, accompanied by
his associates. It beggars all my descriptive powers to
depict the scene which met my astonished gaze when I
reached the summit and was introduced inside the inner
ring. From four to five thousand Indians were present.
The squaws were formed in three complete circles nearest the center, leaving a space of two hundred yards
diameter. Around these were great numbers of warriors,
of greater or less fame, and boys from ten to fifteen years
of age. In the center of the open space a human head,
and the forearms with hands attached, were placed upon

the ground —the head standing on the stump of the neck, which was supported by a stick driven into the ground and thrust up through the throat, and the arms and hands crossed, one over the other, immediately in front of the face. I recognized the head to be that of Antonio, the murdered Yuma chief, and concluded that the present gathering was held for the purpose of a grand jubilee over his death. My conjecture was correct, but before I had time to reflect, I was seized by the hands of two powerful Indians, who joined others, until a small ring of sixty or seventy were got together, and was hurried round and round, in a regular dance, about the horrid spectacle for the space of several minutes. Showing signs of fatigue from the violent rotary motion, I was rescued by a friendly Pimo, who said: "Do you like this thing?"

"Certainly," I replied, "it is your way of rejoicing over the death of your enemies, and as the Pimos and Maricopas are our friends, I do not see why I should not rejoice with you."

This response delighted him greatly, and he immediately translated it to the multitude, who greeted me with terrific yells of approbation. Availing myself of the good feeling engendered, I desired my robust friend, whose every limb quivered with excitement, to state to the multitude that my party had gone on a long time before; that the country over which I had to pass was frequently the scene of Apache horrors; and that I had sufficiently expressed my sympathy with the occasion to be allowed to depart in peace. This speech was received with another chorus of yells, and I was gently conducted down the steep, at the base of which I found my horse in safe keeping. My conductors were warmly thanked, and I set off at full gallop to join my comrades, delighted

6

at having so easily escaped the well meant but revolting hospitality of the savages.

Twelve miles further on we entered the Gila Bend desert. At this point the Gila river trends to the north and describes a curve of one hundred and twenty miles around the northern base of a long range of mountains, resuming its original course westward about fifty miles from the point of departure. This space of fifty miles is entirely without water, and is the highway for the Coyoteros and some of the Sierra Blanca Apaches making raids upon Sonora. The probabilities were very much in favor of meeting one or more war parties of those tribes, and we kept a strict lookout during the transit, but failed to see any, although we may have been observed by them.

On the afternoon of the third day after leaving the Pimos, we came upon the scene of the Oatman massacre, and as the coyotes had dug up the remains of the murdered party, they were carefully and safely re-interred by us. Here was another caution to beware the treachery and malice of the Apaches. The lesson was well heeded by our little band; but we felt ourselves able to whip five times our number in fair fight, and the strictest vigilance was observed in passing any place which could shelter an ambush. Next day we camped on the Gila, under a splendid grove of high and clear cotton-wood trees. There was no underbrush for hundreds of yards in every direction, and our rifles could easily reach the surrounding expanse, in case of attack, while the friendly trees would afford us good shelter. Every one was busy —some collecting dry wood for the guard fire, others in cooking, others again in securing the animals and providing their food—when I suddenly perceived an Indian running toward us with both arms raised above his head.

I was about to draw a bead upon the fellow, but seeing that he was alone and unarmed, I refrained, and beckoned him to come forward, which he did with decided good will. He spoke Spanish well enough for all practical purposes, and informed us that he was a Maricopa and had been captured by the Yumas, together with a woman of his tribe, some months before, but had managed to effect his escape a few days before meeting our party, and as he and his companion were starving, they came to ask our assistance, having struck our trail at the entrance to the camp ground. He then uttered a peculiar cry, and was immediately joined by the woman, who had concealed herself to await the issue of his visit. The poor woman presented a thin, worn and suffering appearance, which did not require the use of language to explain. Our first care was to supply these poor creatures with food and a spare blanket each; for, as we had left the higher and colder regions, and were entering upon the warmest known on the globe, and as our means for transportation were becoming beautifully less, we could afford to be generous in this respect, especially as the probabilities were greatly in favor of abandoning or cacheing the major part of our effects, among which were a number of costly instruments, which could neither be eaten nor drunk. No further questions were pressed upon our guests until their hunger had been appeased, when, sitting at the camp fire, the man gave us the following narration, corroborated in all points by his companion.

Some five months previous, a large war party of the Yumas had come up the Gila with the intention of cutting off small detachments of Maricopas and Pimos, who annually visit the Gila Bend desert to collect the fruit of the petajaya, a gigantic species of cactus. This fruit is dried in the sun and closely resembles our figs in point

of size, taste and shape, but the external husk or covering is not edible. They also macerate it in water after
being dried, when the saccharine qualities causes the
liquid to ferment, and after such fermentation it becomes
highly intoxicating. It is upon this liquor that the Maricopas and Pimos get drunk once a year, the revelry continuing for a week or two at a time; but it is also a universal custom with them to take regular turns, so that
only one-third of the party is supposed to indulge at
one time, the remainder being required to take care of
their stimulated comrades, and protect them from injur-
ing each other or being injured by other tribes. The
Yumas are well acquainted with the custom, and the
party referred to had gone up the Gila to profit by the
circumstance. In that raid they succeeded in killing a
few Maricopas and taking prisoners the man and woman
who were then our guests and informants. Of course
any species of labor and hardship that could be imposed
they were compelled to undergo, until the arrival of a
band of twenty-one Americans with a great many sheep
which they were driving to California. The military,
consisting of a Sergeant and ten men, had been driven
off by the Yumas just before the advent of these visitors,
who were wholly ignorant of the fact, and quite unprepared to expect the hostility which terminated with their
massacre. They were received by the Yumas with every
profession of friendship, the Indians bringing in large
quantities of slim, straight and dried cotton-wood
branches to build fires with, and rendering them other
kindly services, so that all apprehension was completely
lulled. While the evening meal was in preparation, the
Yumas interspersed themselves thickly among the Americans, who had some four fires going, built by the
Yumas, who had placed the long, smooth cotton-wood

branches across each other, in every direction, and the fire as nearly to the center as possible. So soon as those sticks had burned through so as to leave an effective club at each end, a single sharp cry gave the signal, upon which each Yuma present, probably a hundred, seized his burning brand, and commenced the work of death, dealing blows to the nearest American, while another large party rushed fully armed upon the scene, and quickly dispatched their unprepared and unsuspecting visitors. The Americans fought with desperation, discharging their six-shooters and using their knives with bloody effect, but were soon overcome by resistless numbers, and slain to a man. It was during this contest, which engaged the whole attention of the Yumas, that our two guests managed to effect their escape. They had traveled for four days without food, hiding themselves from morning till night, and prosecuting their way only after dark. Seeing a small party of Americans, whom they knew were always friendly to their tribe, and incited by the double motives of obtaining food and warning us of our danger, they had sought our camp.

Our danger was indeed imminent. Our party consisted only of seven Americans and three Mexicans, and our ammunition had been reduced to forty rounds for each weapon. A party of well armed men, more than three times our number, had been massacred only a few days before by a hostile tribe of Indians, through the heart of whose country we would be compelled to make our way, if we continued. The enemy had driven off the miserably small garrison, and were flushed with the success of their last great robbery and murder. The Colorado river was impassable without a launch, and that was in possession of the Indians. We were in a "regular fix," and a council of war was immediately held.   I am free to acknowledge that I was afraid to go forward, and used every argument to show the foolhardiness of such an attempt, but all my objections were met by the imperturbable Dr. Webb, who contented himself with saying—"Our provisions are nearly exhausted, our ammunition is nearly expended, we are ordered to go on, and it is our duty.   We may be killed, but it is better to die fighting, since we have been warned and are on our guard, than to die of starvation on these terrible deserts.   In any case, it is only a choice of deaths, but it is certain destruction to turn back, while we may manage to escape or pass the Yumas in safety."   It was finally agreed to adopt his views—keep a sharp lookout, fight if need be, to the bitter end, and die like men in the proper discharge of a recognized duty.   This determination was duly imparted to our Maricopa friends, who could not restrain expressions of amazement, and gave us some additional valuable information about the existence of the launches in which to cross the Colorado, the nature and habits of the Yumas, their treacherous manner of approach, and the best means for us to adopt. Those kindly people were then supplied with provisions enough to last them to their villages, and took leave of us with unfeigned regret, expecting never to see one of our number again.   My next meeting with them will be found in a succeeding chapter.

Early next morning we resumed our journey down the Gila, and prosecuted it for several days until we reached the Colorado near its junction with the Gila.   At that period the whole country was a wilderness, and the place now occupied by large houses and well filled stores, with an American population of six or seven hundred souls, was waste and desolate.   The approach to the river was hidden by a dense mass of young willow trees, through which we had to pass in order to reach water, of which ourselves and animals were greatly in need. The thermometer stood at 118 degrees Fahrenheit, in the shade, and we had marched twenty-four miles that day without water. On emerging from the willows to the banks of the broad, red, swift and turbid stream which met our gaze, we discovered, on the opposite side, within easy rifle reach, a large number of Yuma men, women and children, a fact which assured us that our approach had not been known by that tribe. They instantly fled in all directions, thereby proving their fear and suspicions, which would not have been entertained if the two people had been at peace with each other. Having watered our suffering animals, we prosecuted our way down the Colorado, and encamped upon an open sand beach, with three hundred yards of clear ground in the rear and the river in front. No weapon in possession of the Yumas could reach anything like that distance, while our rifles commanded the whole area. Our animals were drawn up in line on the river side with a careful guard, and were fed with an abundance of young willow tops, which they eat greedily. Our fires were well supplied and kept blazing brightly, so as to shed light on the surrounding shore and disclose the approach of any enemy. In this manner we passed an anxious night.

The next day, soon after dawn, an Indian presented himself unarmed, and with reiterated assurances of the most cordial friendship for the Americans. He subsequently proved to be Caballo en Pelo, or the " Naked Horse," the head chief of the Yumas. Our reception was not calculated to excite his hopes, every one extending his left hand, and keeping a revolver in his right, and it was not long before Caballo en Pelo found that he had committed himself to the tender mercies of men who entertained the deepest suspicion of his professed amity. To test his sincerity, Dr. Webb asked what had become of the soldiers, to which he replied that they had voluntarily withdrawn three months before. This we knew to be a lie, as Gen. Conde had informed us of their presence with a couple of good launches to assist the crossing of immigrants, and we had met the General only twenty days previous, when this information was received from him, who had come directly from the Colorado in eleven days. The report of our Maricopa visitors also disproved the statement of Caballo en Pelo, and we immediately consulted together as to our future course, which was afterward carried into effect, as the reader will discover, and to it I attribute our escape from the treacherous Yumas.

We subsequently learned that the persons massacred by the Yumas just before our arrival, were John Gallantin and his band. This man had the reputation of being one of the worst scoundrels who ever existed even in that demoralized and villainous region. It is reported of him, that the Governor of Chihuahua, having offered a premium of thirty dollars for every Apache scalp, Gallantin got together a band of cut-throats and went into the business. But all his activity and cupidity failed to find the Apaches, and scalps became very scarce. Determined to make money out of the Governor's terms, he commenced killing Papago, Opatah and Yaqui Indians, whose scalps he sold in considerable numbers at thirty dollars each, declaring that they had been taken from the heads of Apaches. But the ease with which Gallantin and his band supplied themselves, without producing any sensible diminution of Apache raids, excited suspicion, and he was actually caught taking the scalps from the heads of several Mexicans murdered by his people in cold blood. Finding that he had been discovered in his unspeakable villainies, he fled to New Mexico, where, by stealing and by purchase, he collected about two thousand five hundred head of sheep, with which he was passing into California, when he encountered his well-merited fate at the hands of the Yumas. Not a soul of his band escaped death.

At the period about which I am writing, Arizona and New Mexico were cursed by the presence of two or three hundred of the most infamous scoundrels it is possible to conceive. Innocent and unoffending men were shot down or bowie-knived merely for the pleasure of witnessing their death agonies. Men walked the streets and public squares with double-barreled shot guns, and hunted each other as sportsmen hunt for game. In the graveyard of Tucson there were forty-seven graves of white men in 1860, ten years after the events above recited, and of that number only two had died natural deaths, all the rest being murdered in broils and barroom quarrels. Since Carleton's occupation of those Territories with his California Column, a great change for the better has taken place, and this melioration promises to gain ground.

6*

CHAPTER X.

THE foregoing digression is excusable, on the ground
that it exposes, to some extent, the character of the
American people who first made the intimate acquaintance of the Indian tribes occupying the country on the
direct route of migration between the Atlantic and Pacific States, and, in a measure, accounts for their hostile
advances. The Pimos and Maricopas must, however, be
excepted from this category, as they never, on any occasion, no matter how much goaded, exhibited any vengeful or adverse spirit toward Americans. In like manner, these remarks cannot apply to the Apaches, who
never, at any time, ceased their active hostility and
treacherous attacks.

Soon after Caballo en Pelo, or the "Naked Horse,"
entered our camp, he made a signal to his associates,
and we soon had an accession of fourteen more, embracing several of the principal men in the Yuma tribe.
They were all unarmed, and each one expressed his desire to maintain friendly relations with our people. Dr.
Webb, with his usual blunt honesty of character, and
total neglect of policy, abruptly asked them — "If
you mean as you profess, why did you drive away the

small body of soldiers left here to assist the Americans in crossing the river and supplying their needs, and, why did you massacre the American party with sheep, who came here on their road to California?" These unexpected queries discomfited the savages, and threw us "all aback," as may readily be supposed. Caballo en Pelo, Pasqual, and several other leading men, undertook to deny these charges *in toto*, but we were too well informed, and their denials only tended to put us more than ever on the *qui vive*.

A few words interchanged between the members of our party decided our course of action. In any case we were fully committed, and nothing but perilous measures could decide the result of our desperate surroundings. It was determined to hold all the Yumas present as captives, subject to instant death upon the exhibition of any hostility on the part of that tribe. We felt that our lives were at the mercy of those savages, but also resolved that we should not be sacrificed without a corresponding amount of satisfaction. Their principal men were in our camp unarmed; we had the disposal of their lives in our power, and knew that they could not escape in the event of any hostile act against our small party. These deliberations were fully unfolded to the chiefs, who were informed that no more of their tribe would be admitted into our camp without jeopardizing the safety of those already there. They were also told, that having come of their own free will, they would be expected to remain during our pleasure, and, in the meantime, be fed from our very limited resources. They were furthermore informed that the launch which they had taken from the soldiers would be needed for our conveyance across the Colorado, and as we knew it to be in their possession, it must be forthcoming when required. The

first act of Caballo en Pelo was to signalize his people
not to approach our camp, which was located on a sand-
spit, with three hundred yards clear rifle range on all
sides not covered by the river.   He then went on to dis-
claim any inimical design, quoting the fact that he and
his chief men had sought us unarmed, when they might
have overwhelmed our paltry force with hundreds of
warriors.   He also stated that they had no hostile feelings toward white men coming from the east, but would
oppose all from the west, as they had learned that a
force from that quarter was being prepared for a campaign against them.   They were not at war with Americans generally, but solely with those whom they expected from California with warlike intentions.   Caballo
en Pelo then asked if he and his companions were to
consider themselves prisoners.   To this home question
Dr. Webb, who was in charge of our party, directed me
to answer—yes, they were; and would be held as such,
until the launches they had taken from the soldiers were
produced for our passage across the Colorado, and they
had given satisfactory evidence of their peaceful intentions.   This abrupt announcement was not pleasing to
our savage guests, who exhibited alarm, mingled with
half-uttered threats of vengeance; but the old motto,
"in for a penny, in for a pound," was the only one we
could adopt under the circumstances, and our resolution
was as unalterable as the laws of the Medes and Per-
sians.

Dr. Webb furthermore informed the Yumas that they
must order their warriors, who were gathering thickly on
our side the river, not to approach within three hundred
yards, adding, "we suspect your motives, and intend to
have the first blood, if any is to be shed.   Your chief
men are in our power.   Your people can kill us, as they

are so much more numerous, but we will kill you first, if they do not obey our orders which shall be promulgated through you."

This was undoubtedly the "tightest fix" our visitors ever got in. They were by no means prepared for such a decided stand, and were quite at a loss for expedient. Seeing resolution in each man's eye, and knowing that it was our determination to put them to death the moment any decidedly hostile step should be taken by their people, they concluded to make the best of a bad bargain, and escape by strategy from the trap they had prepared to spring upon us, but in which they had caught themselves.

Caballo en Pelo made a few signs to the surrounding and anxious multitude, which then quietly retreated out of sight among the dense willows which grew with remarkable luxuriance about three hundred yards from the river. We then dug two holes, about twenty feet apart, parallel to each other, and each about five feet long by one and a half wide and two deep. In these holes we made blazing fires which rose about two or three feet above the surface of the ground, and between these fires we ordered the Yumas to lie down, side by side, while a sentinel with a cocked six-shooter paraded along the line of their heads, and another along the line of their feet. A flank escape was impossible, as it was prevented by a bright and hot fire on each side. Our few remaining animals were drawn up in line on the river side of the camp, with a guard outside of them and within twenty feet of the whole party. We slept but little that night, and at early dawn we were once more afoot, and in discussion with the Yumas, who stoutly denied any hostile motive, and professed indignation at their treatment. We gave them a good breakfast, as we had given them a plentiful supper the evening previous, and then reiterated our demand for the launches, while they as stubbornly denied any knowledge of their existence.

That day we moved down the river about eleven miles and selected a good camp ground early in the afternoon. Again we were surrounded by hundreds of Indians, but the personal fears of our hostages kept them at bay, and they did not approach nearer than three hundred yards. The night passed as the previous one had done, and we perceived it was the intention of the Yumas to wear us out, and then seize their opportunity; but this scheme was frustrated by the nerve and decision of Dr. Webb, who next morning informed Caballo en Pelo and his chief followers, that "we were well aware of the existence of the launches by oral as well as written intelligence; that they were absolutely necessary to cross the Colorado; that we knew the Yumas had driven away the small garrison of American soldiers and had the launches in their possession; that we had met the escaped Maricopas, who told us all about the massacre of Gallantin and his party, and the appropriation of the launches by the Yumas; and, finally, that if those launches were not forthcoming by twelve o'clock the next day, we should at once proceed to extremities and kill him and all the Yumas in our camp."

It may well be supposed that this sort of talk aroused the liveliest alarm among our prisoners, who commenced an excited conversation in their own tongue, which culminated in a request from Caballo en Pelo that one of his young men be permitted to leave our camp and make inquiry if the launches really were in existence, and if so, to bring it down river to our camp. This was agreed to, and a young lad, about eighteen years of age, the son of Pasqual, selected for the business. He was allowed to depart with the positive assurance that we would keep our words in regard to his father and the other head men of the Yuma tribe in our camp.

That night we observed more than the usual precautions, for one-half our number were on guard at all times. Next morning no Indians were to be seen, but at ten o'clock A. M., a large launch, capable of holding half our party with their baggage, was seen approaching under the conduct of two Yumas. It was moored in front of our camp, and immediate preparations were made for crossing. Five of us, taking half the Yuma prisoners, immediately embarked with rifles in hand, ready for use, and as we could easily sweep both sides the river, our party was really as strong as ever. Our mules and horses were made to swim across under the lead and direction of two Yumas, who were kept within range of our rifles, and in this manner we succeeded in gaining the western bank of the Colorado, after three most exciting days of detention amidst overwhelming numbers of hostile savages; but our troubles were not yet ended. We had still to undergo another ordeal, even more perilous, because we had no hostages as securities for our safety from attack.

Having gained the western bank of the Colorado in peace, the Yumas demanded to be released from captivity, but our safety would not permit such a course, and Dr. Webb informed them that they must remain in camp that night and would be set free next day. The utmost precaution was again observed throughout the night, and at three o'clock next morning we were once more *en route* toward California, accompanied by the leading Yumas, who were kept closely guarded. That day we penetrated twenty-eight miles into the great Colorado desert, halting about four o'clock P. M., in a place where

neither water nor wood existed, and completely surrounded by hills and banks of white sand. With much
toil several of our number ascended one or two of the
highest hillocks, but as far as the eye could reach nothing was to be seen but one unbroken expanse of sand—
white, dazzling under the rays of a burning sun, unre-
lieved by a single bush or shrub—broken and fretted
with countless hillocks, and utterly void of animal life.
This part of the Colorado desert is much more frightful
than the great Sahara of Africa. The absolute stillness
and repose is something awful; it is death in life; it is
the most impressive lesson of man's feebleness, and the
most startling reproof against his vanity. In our case
these sensations were not mitigated by the knowledge of
being surrounded by a fierce, warlike and numerous Indian tribe, thirsting for our blood, and eager to revenge
the indignity they had suffered by the captivity of their
head chiefs, and the failure of their treacherous schemes.

As before stated, we halted and made preparations as
if to encamp. Dr. Webb then directed Mr. Thurber to
ascend the highest sand hill in the neighborhood, examine all around with his field glass and report if the Indians were upon our trail. In about half an hour Mr.
Thurber returned, and assured us that from two to three
hundred Yumas were within five miles of our position,
and heading toward our camp. There was no time to
lose. Caballo en Pelo with his fellow captives were immediately informed that they must take the back track
and return to the river, that our road was toward the
west, that we had no more provisions to give them, and
that it was indispensable for us to part company then
and there. To these requirements the wily chief demur-
red, and stated his desire to go on with us to California.
He was overruled by the strong persuasive force of draw-

ing our pistols, and giving him the sole alternative of obeying or dying. They chose the former, and decamped with haste. So soon as they disappeared round the base of a friendly sand hill, we immediately repacked our wagon, and drove on with all possible speed, hoping to escape in the fast coming darkness.

Eleven years afterward, Pasqual himself told me that they met about three hundred of their warriors half an hour after being expelled from our camp, and the whole band came in pursuit of us, but as the Indian never risks life when he thinks the same end can be accomplished by strategy, and as time is of no moment to them, it was agreed to fall foul of us just before daylight the next morning, and by a rapid and combined assault massacre our little party with comparative ease and impunity. Acting on that policy, they approached our abandoned camp with extreme caution, and commenced a survey from surrounding hillocks. They were not surprised to see no fire, as they knew there was no wood in that part of the desert, and they remained quiescent until nearly morning, when their scouts gave them the unwelcome information that we were gone.

Our flight was continued all night and part of the next day, until overtaken by one of those dreadful sandstorms which prevail on the Colorado desert. The day was intensely hot, and the most oppressive silence seemed to reign absolute. Suddenly a dark, dense and singular looking cloud arose in the west and moved toward us with incredible velocity. Great masses of heavy sand were lifted as if they were so many feathers and carried high into the air with extreme violence. The places formerly occupied by huge hillocks containing many thousand tons of sand, were swept clean as if by magic in a few moments, and the vast banks removed to other lo-

calities in the twinkling of an eye. Our mules fell flat
upon their bellies and thrust their noses close to the
ground, our horses followed their example—none of us
could stand against the force and might of the storm—
and we, too, laid down flat, hauling a tent over us. In
a few moments the tent was so deeply covered with sand
as to retain its position, and every now and then we were
compelled to remove the swiftly gathering mass, to avoid
being absolutely buried alive. Amidst the distress, the
horrible sensations, and the suffocating feelings occa-
sioned by this sirocco, we entertained the grateful sense
of protection from our savage pursuers, who were quite
as incapable of facing that terrific storm as we were.
For forty-eight hours we had not tasted food, and were
more than a day without water in the hottest climate
known to man, and our distress heightened by the intense craving for water invariably attendant on those
scorching blasts of the desert. These sensations were
not alleviated by the fact of knowing that we had yet a
journey of forty miles before we could find water.

About three o'clock P. M., the storm passed off, and we
instantly resumed our way without cooking food, for eating could only add to our already terrible thirst. All
that night our weary feet trod that infernal desert until
the glowing morning sun shone upon us like a plate of
molten brass, but we had arrived at a fine camp ground,
thickly supplied with shady mesquit trees and abounding with excellent grass for our worn-out animals, which
had dwindled down to less than one-half the number we
boasted before crossing the Colorado. About an hour
after camping, the step-father of Inez, who served us as
guide, reported that he saw an alamo tree a short distance off, and he believed that there must be water in its
neighborhood. Several of us proceeded to the spot and

in a short time discovered a small pool containing about twenty gallons of water deposited in a hollow by a former copious rain, and sheltered from the sun by friendly brush. The joyful news was soon made known to the rest of our comrades, and our raging thirst slaked, after which the remainder of the water was equally divided among our famishing stock. As Carisso creek was then within a day's march, no thought was taken for the morrow, and after a most refreshing night's rest, we re-commenced our journey at early dawn, reaching Carisso creek about five o'clock on the afternoon of the same day. At this place we felt ourselves wholly safe from the Yumas. There was abundance of pasture, and water and wood, and we would have remained for a day or two to obtain much needed rest, but our provisions had entirely given out, and we had still one hundred miles of travel before us without an ounce of food, unless such as might possibly be procured in the way of game.

With sad hearts and weakened frames we pushed forward until we reached Vallecito, where we found an American garrison consisting of a company of infantry and three officers. By these warm-hearted and gallant gentlemen we were received with the greatest courtesy and kindliness, and entertained by them with a warmth of hospitality which has found an abiding place among my most grateful recollections. Some time had elapsed since supplies were received from San Diego, and they were themselves on "short commons," and unable to furnish us with the provisions needed to complete our journey; but gave us freely to the extent of their power. It would have been gross ingratitude to remain there, living upon the very diminished stores of our kind entertainers, and we again pushed forward the next day. Our course lay over the Volcan mountain, and upon its mag-

nificent height we found a rancho owned and inhabited
by a big-hearted gentleman, who ministered to our wants
and furnished us with two fresh mules. Next day we
resumed our march, and soon after passing the old battle
ground of San Pascual met Col. Heintzleman, in command of three hundred troops, on his way to chastise
the Yuma Indians for their many murders and robberies.
The officers were surprised to meet us coming from the
river, and asked many questions, which we were delighted to answer, giving valuable information.

Col. Heintzleman's force was subsequently increased
to five hundred men, and after two years' active warfare
he succeeded in reducing the Yumas, who have never
since presumed to contend against our power. Since
then Fort Yuma has become a noted frontier fortification,
surrounded by many hundreds of American citizens, who
live, for the most part, on the eastern bank of the river,
and carry on a lucrative trade with the interior of Arizona and the Yumas, Cocopahs, Cushans, Amojaves and
other tribes. The waters of the Colorado are now plowed
by half a dozen steamers, and my old enemies, the Yumas,
do the "chores" and menial offices for the whites. The
next day after meeting Col. Heintzleman we reached San
Diego, devoutly thankful to Providence for our many
and almost miraculous escapes from the tomahawks and
scalping knives of the Indian tribes through which we
had passed for the distance of two thousand eight hundred miles.

CHAPTER XI.

A WEEK after our safe arrival in San Diego, worn-out and suffering from nearly two years' wandering upon the uninhabited deserts of Texas, Arizona, northern Sonora, and a portion of New Mexico, I received a warm, cordial and brotherly letter from the Hon. Jere Clemens, Senator from Alabama, who had been my Lieutenant-Colonel during a portion of the Mexican war, after the death of Col. Ransom, and the capture of Chapultepec, which letter informed me that although the appropriation for the Boundary Commission had passed Congress, yet John B. Weller, Senator from California, had managed to have inserted in it a proviso which would have the effect of rendering that appropriation unavailable, and that the probabilities were we would be disbanded in the deserts, without money, or the means of return to our friends and home at the East. He also advised me to leave the Commission, as we had arrived within the precincts of civilization, and pursue some other avocation. The advice and arguments of my former superior, whose kindness and remembrance had followed me throughout our toilsome and dangerous career, convinced my mind of their value, and I resigned my place in the Commission. Three weeks afterward it returned toward the East, while I remained in San Diego.

About a month after the Commission had departed, carrying with it my warmest and most kindly esteem toward its gallant and noble-hearted members, a small party of ten men was formed for the purpose of entering and exploring a portion of Arizona, with a view to locate and exploit some of its valuable gold and silver mines, and I was engaged as the interpreter and guide of the party, on a salary of five hundred dollars per month.

On an appointed day we started, and after a tedious march, reached the Colorado, which was then the theater of an active war against the Yuma Indians. Col. Heintzleman had arrived with his troops and had begun a vigorous campaign. We were immediately crossed by the guard in charge of the launch, and cautioned about the Yumas, who were then supposed to be in force on the Gila, about thirty miles from its junction with the Colorado. In consequence of this warning, we determined to proceed by night instead of day until we had passed the field occupied by the savages. The rumbling of our two wagons, and the watchful stillness of our party, impressed the savages with the belief that we were an armed body stealing a march upon them, and we passed unmolested in the dark, arriving at Antelope Peak in our march from Fort Yuma. Here we considered ourselves comparatively safe from the Yumas, although exposed to visits from the Tonto Apaches, who inhabit the northern side of the Gila from Antelope Peak to the Pimo villages. Our party was well armed, each person having two revolvers, a good rifle and a large knife, and we felt ourselves equal to four or five times our number of Indians in an open fight, but were also aware that the utmost precaution was necessary at all times.

Just below and about what is known as Grinnell's Station the road is covered from four to five inches deep with a fine and almost impalpable dust, containing an abundance of alkali. The lightest tread sends it in clouds far over head, and a body of men riding together in close column are so thoroughly enveloped as to prevent the recognizing of each other at the distance of only three feet. In some places the road passes through the middle of an extensive plain, apparently incapable of affording covert to a hare. We had arrived at one of these wide openings, and were inclosed in a cloud of dust so dense as completely to bar the vision of all except the two who occupied the advance. One or two others attempted to ride on one side of the road, but the terrible thorns of the cactus and the pointed leaves of the Spanish bayonet which soon covered their horses legs with blood, and lamed the poor animals, induced them to resume the dusty road. No one expected an attack in so open, exposed and unsheltered a place, yet it was the very one selected for such a purpose. The wily savages knew that we would be upon our guard in passing a defile, a thick wood, or a rocky cañon; and also judged that we might be careless while crossing an open plain. They were well acquainted with the dusty character of the road, and relying on it to conceal their presence, had secreted themselves close to its southern edge, awaiting our approach.

At a certain spot, where a dozen or two yucca trees elevated their sharp-pointed leaves about four feet above ground, and while we were shrouded in a cloud of dust, a sharp, rattling volley was poured into us from a distance of less than twenty yards. It has always been a matter of astonishment to me that none of our party were either killed or wounded; but we lost two mules and three horses by that fire. The dense dust prevented

the Apaches from taking aim, and they fired a little too
low. It was no time for hesitation, and the order was
at once given to dismount and fight on foot. We could
distinguish little or nothing; shot after shot was expended in the direction of the savages; now and then a
dark body would be seen and made a target of as soon
as seen. Each man threw himself flat upon the ground;
but scarcely any could tell where his companions were.
It was pre-eminently a fight in which each man was on
"his own hook."

While we laid prostrate the dust settled somewhat,
and we were about to obtain a good sight of the enemy,
when John Wollaston cried out—"Up boys, they are
making a rush." Each man rose at the word, and a
hand to hand contest ensued which beggars all description. It was at this juncture that our revolvers did the
work, as was afterward shown. Again the dust rose in
blinding clouds, hurried up by the tramping feet of con-
tending men. We stood as much chance to be shot by
each other as by the savages. The quick rattling of pistols was heard on all sides, but the actors in this work
of death were invisible. The last charge of my second
pistol had been exhausted; my large knife lost in the
thick dust on the road, and the only weapon left me was
a small double-edged, but sharp and keen, dagger, with
a black whalebone hilt, and about four inches long on
the blade. I was just reloading a six-shooter, when a
robust and athletic Apache, much heavier than myself,
stood before me, not more than three feet off. He was
naked with the single exception of a breach cloth, and
his person was oiled from head to foot. I was clothed
in a green hunting frock, edged with black, a pair of
green pants, trimmed with black welts, and a green,
broad-brimmed felt hat. The instant we met, he ad-

vanced upon me with a long and keen knife, with which
he made a plunge at my breast. This attack was met by
stopping his right wrist with my left hand, and at the
same moment I lunged my small dagger full at his abdomen. He caught my right wrist in his left hand, and
for a couple of seconds—a long time under such circumstances—we stood regarding each other, my left hand
holding his right above my head, and his left retaining
my right on a level with his body. Feeling that he was
greased, and that I had no certain hold, I tripped him
with a sudden and violent pass of the right foot, which
brought him to the ground, but in falling he seized and
carried me down with him. In a moment the desperate
savage gained the ascendant, and planted himself firmly
on my person, with his right knee on my left arm, con-
fining it closely, and his left arm pinioning my right to
the ground, while his right arm was free. I was completely at his mercy. His personal strength and weight
were greater than mine. His triumph and delight glared
from his glittering black eyes, and he resolved to lose
nothing of his savage enjoyment. Holding me down
with the grasp of a giant, against which all my struggles
were wholly vain, he raised aloft his long, sharp knife,
and said—"Pindah lickoyee das-ay-go, dee-dah tatsan,"
which means, "the white-eyed man, you will be soon
dead." I thought as he did, and in that frightful moment made a hasty commendation of my soul to the Benevolent, but I am afraid that it was mingled with some
scheme to get out of my predicament, if possible.

To express the sensations I underwent at that moment
is not within the province of language. My erratic and
useless life passed in review before me in less than an instant of time. I lived more in that minute or two of our
deadly struggle than I had ever done in years, and, as I

7

was wholly powerless, I gave myself up for lost—another victim to Apache ferocity. His bloodshot eyes gleamed upon me with intense delight, and he seemed to delay the death-stroke for the purpose of gladdening his heart upon my fears and inexpressible torture. All this transpired in less than half a minute, but to me it seemed hours. Suddenly he raised his right arm for the final stroke. I saw the descending blow of the deadly weapon, and knew the force with which it was driven.

The love of life is a strong feeling at any time; but to be killed like a pig, by an Apache, seemed pre-eminently dreadful and contumelious. Down came the murderous knife, aimed full at my throat, for his position on my body made that the most prominent part of attack. Instantly I twisted my head and neck one side to avoid the blow and prolong life as much as possible. The keen blade passed in dangerous proximity to my throat, and buried itself deeply in the soft soil, penetrating my black silk cravat, while his right thumb came within reach of my mouth, and was as quickly seized between my teeth. His struggles to free himself were fearful, but my life depended on holding fast. Finding his efforts vain, he released his grasp of my right arm and seized his knife with his left hand, but the change, effected under extreme pain, reversed the whole state of affairs. Before my antagonist could extricate his deeply-buried weapon with his left hand, and while his right was held fast between my teeth, I circled his body and plunged my sharp and faithful dagger twice between his ribs, just under his left arm, at the same time making another convulsive effort to throw off his weight. In this I succeeded, and in a few moments had the satisfaction of seeing my enemy gasping his last under my repeated thrusts. Language would fail to convey anything like my sensations during that deadly contest, and I will not attempt the task.

About the same time the battle terminated with the defeat of our assailants, who lost ten killed and several wounded, how many we never knew. On our side, we lost one man—James Kendick—and had three wounded, viz: John Wollaston, John H. Marble and Theodore Heuston. Heuston and Marble died of their wounds soon after reaching Tucson, although they received the kindest nursing and attention from that noble Castilian gentleman, Juan Fernandez, and his amiable family. This sad result broke up the party, and I returned to San Diego shortly afterward with a party of immigrants coming to California.

The above was one of the few occasions wherein the Apaches have boldly attacked travelers from whom they could expect no great booty and lose many lives in a conflict. They were probably incited to the surprise by some more than usually daring spirit, who planned the affair and trusted for success in its distinctive and unexpected nature. We were precisely in a portion of the country which afforded no ostensible covert, and consequently made us less cautious. They knew the character of the road, and the blinding nature and volume of the dust. They depended upon the first fire to slay a number of our party, and produce a panic among the survivors. They counted upon a surprise and an easy victory, and expected to inherit our horses, mules, arms and provisions. They had conceived well, and acted gallantly, but were frustrated, although the results were of the saddest nature to our small company, as they completely upset our original intentions by the death of Theodore Heuston, who was the capitalist and founder of the expedition.

This event initiated me into another phase of Apache character I had never before seen. It proved that they are capable of bold and dangerous undertakings under very adverse circumstances, or when the chances are nearly evenly balanced; but this seldom occurs, as they almost invariably have opportunities to examine, at their leisure, all persons or parties who enter the regions inhabited by them, and form their plans so as to take every advantage with the least possible chance of losing a man.

After my return to San Diego, I determined to forsake my wild, almost nomadic life, and return to civilized existence. I was tired and disgusted with the incessant watchfulness, the unceasing warfare, and unrequited privations I had suffered. Life had been a round of contentions for two years. I had passed through an unbroken series of tribulations and dangers during that period. Hunger, thirst, severe cold and excessive heat, with much personal peril, had been my invariable concomitants, and I panted for a more quiet life. San Francisco held forth the only inducement on this coast, and thither I wended my way, on the steamer Sea Bird, then commanded by Capt. Healey, with Gorman as mate.

As this narrative is wholly devoted to incidents and adventures among Indian tribes, the author will be excused from giving a recital of his life until he was again compelled, in obedience to orders, to renew acquaintance with nomadic races. It is sufficient to say, that twelve years elapsed before such intimacy was effected, faithful details of which will be given in the succeeding chapters.

During the period of quiescence from exciting life which succeeded two years' eventful wanderings across the North American continent, abundant opportunities existed for reconsidering and drawing just inferences from the past. The conclusions arrived at then appeared well founded, if judged from the light of the experiences through which I had passed; but a subsequent career, under unusually favorable circumstances, gave me to comprehend how much my early judgment had erred. I had seen but the outside—had witnessed but the husk; the interior—the kernel of the nut—still remained untasted and unknown. I had flattered myself with having achieved a fair knowledge of Indian character. I believe my personal observations had been sufficient to instruct me on that subject. Former travels through South America, from Buenos Ayres to Valparaiso—when I was a sort of captive among the Pategonian Indians for seven months—seemed to justify me in thinking I had made a correct analysis of Indian traits. But I was much in error. Sufficient credit had not been given to their mental powers, their ability to calculate chances, to estimate and foresee the plans of others, to take precautions, to manœuvre with skill, to insure concert of action by a recognized code of signals, to convey information to succeeding parties of the route, numbers and designs of those who preceded, and to bring together formidable bodies from distant points without the aid of messengers. Much, very much, was yet to be learned.

A boy of twenty years is very apt to credit himself with having acquired a very satisfactory idea of human nature, and no amount of instruction and advice from his elders will induce him to change his views until a fuller experience makes him realize the fact that when he thought himself master of the situation, he was in reality only entering upon its rudimental knowledge. Of all people, Americans seem less inclined to receive and profit by the advice of others founded upon a larger and more matured experience. They want to know for themselves, and place the most abiding faith in their own judgment and readiness of resource. They seem to regard a warning as a sort of reflection upon their personal courage or skill, and frequently treat friendly counsel with somewhat of petulance. A most lamentable instance of this nature occurred to myself. After my second term of military service in Arizona, I was returning home via Fort Yuma, when I received an introduction to a Paymaster, with the rank of Major, in the Regular service. Dr. Tappan, Assistant Surgeon of Volunteers, was present at the time, and asked me to favor him with some instructions in reference to the marches, camping grounds, distances, and dangers to be met on their projected route up the Gila river to the place formerly known as Fort Breckinridge. It was clearly my duty, as well as my pleasure, to put him in possession of all the knowledge I had gleaned in reference to these points, and I closed my information by tracing a map of the route, and volunteering advice to the following effect.

You must never, said I, permit your zeal to outrun your discretion. Remember that a well appointed and careful party may travel through Arizona from one year's end to the other, without ever seeing an Apache, or any trace of his existence, and from this cause travelers frequently become careless and fall an easy prey to their sleepless watchfulness. Indeed, it is not difficult to point out many who have no faith in their apparent ubiquity, but believe that they must be sought in their strongholds. There are others again who will not be convinced that the eyes of these Indians are always upon them, because they see nothing to indicate that fact; but the truth is, every move you make, every step you advance, every camp you visit, is seen and noted by them, with the strictest scrutiny. If they perceive that you are careful, prepared for any contingency, and always on your guard, they will hesitate about making any attack with ten times your force, especially if your party does not offer sufficient inducement in the matter of plunder. But if they observe the least neglect, or want of precaution on your part, you will be assaulted at the very moment, in the very place, and under circumstances when least expected, with every probability of success in their favor. I further remarked, your party, I understand, will be a small one, of not more than ten or twelve persons, including an escort of nine men of the Regular Infantry. None of these men have probably ever been in an Indian country, and, if they have, no experience elsewhere will avail them among the Apaches, whose mode of warfare is so entirely at variance with those of all other tribes. The Regular soldiers, in order to preserve the polish and fine appearance of their guns, are in the habit of carrying them in covers and unloaded. This should be avoided. The men should be made to carry their muskets loaded, capped, and ready for action at a second's warning. They must be restrained from straggling, and moved in such order as will guarantee the greatest amount of security to every individual. Special care should be observed soon after entering a camping ground, when the men generally lay aside their weapons and separate into detachments to bring wood and water. I cannot too strongly impress you with the necessity for a rigid observance of this caution in all cases where the party is small, and no sufficient armed body left in camp, or provided as guards for the protection of those engaged in other necessary duties.

Dr. Tappan thanked me cordially for the information

imparted, and especially for the advice given in relation
to the Apaches, but the Major rather coolly intimated
that he was quite capable of managing his own affairs,
and had seen enough of Indian life to put him in possession of all necessary information. I touched my cap and
withdrew somewhat mortified. Soon afterward intelligence was received that the Major, Dr. Tappan and three
others had been killed at the Cotton-wood Springs, by
the Apaches. It seems that soon after entering upon
the camp ground, the party broke into small unarmed
squads, which went in search of wood and to bring water, when their ever-watchful and tigerish foes seized
the opportunity to dash in and massacre all they could.
In this miserable manner the lives of two valuable officers and three brave men were sacrificed for the want of
a little caution which could have been easily exercised.

Let it be borne in mind at all times that the Apaches
have scarcely ever been known to make a fighting attack
at night. Under cover of the darkness they will steal
into camp and conceal themselves from detection with
wondrous skill, in the hope of effecting a robbery; but
that is the extent of their night operations, unless they
become emboldened by the most reckless and foolhardy
carelessness. Their onslaughts are almost invariably
made by day, and at such times and places as tend to
impart the greatest sense of security. When they mean
mischief no marks are to be seen—no traces, no tracks,
no "signs" discoverable. The unsuspecting traveler,
lulled into a fatal belief that none of them are near, relaxes his caution, and is caught as surely as the spider
meshes the confiding fly. I have seen men, who, being
in company with large and well armed parties, had never
seen an Apache after a year of wandering in their country, actually doubted the existence of those savages

except amidst their strongholds, until a recklessness begotten of unbelief, induced them to relax their watchfulness and incur special risks. In some cases, they have succeeded and got off scot free, but in ninety out of a hundred they have either fallen victims to misplaced confidence, or escaped almost by miracle. Let no one flatter himself with the idea that, from the moment he has passed the Pimo villages, he is at any time unobserved by the Apaches. Being a non-productive race, subsisting wholly on plunder and game, and incapable of providing a commissariat which will maintain any considerable body for even a week or two, they are scattered in small but active parties throughout the whole of Arizona, a large part of New Mexico, and all the northern portions of Chihuahua and Sonora, and in some parts of Durango. The territory over which they roam, and in which they appear to be ubiquitous, is more than three times larger than California; and California possesses more area than all the New England States, together with New York and New Jersey. This is to say, that the country over which the Apache race holds the mastership—which is literally the fact—is nearly as extensive as all the States which border on the Atlantic and the Gulf of Mexico put together. No great expenditure of arithmetic is necessary to prove that, to domineer over a region so vast, to guard all its passes, to keep watchmen on all the principal heights overlooking the plains usually traveled, to keep up a regular system of videttes over its expanse, to strike a half dozen places two and three hundred miles apart at the same time, to organize parties for scouring the wide valleys and attending the movements of travelers, and to be a terror and a scourge throughout its whole area, must employ the utmost resources, activity and energy of a

7*

numerous people, exceedingly vigilant and rapid in their movements.

Casual observers have, unintentionally, done serious evil by underrating their real strength, to an extent almost inconceivable among those who are better informed. I have been in company with a body of fifteen hundred at the very time that intelligence was received that a half dozen other parties, numbering from twenty to three hundred each, were actively engaged in committing depredations at other points embraced in a radius of five hundred miles, and yet I have seen the number of Apaches estimated as low as fifteen hundred and two thousand. Nearly eight years of personal experiences have satisfied me that the Apache race, collectively, will number fully twenty-five thousand souls. In this estimate the Navajoes and Lipans are not included, but those are who inhabit portions of northwestern Mexico. Of this number five thousand are capable of taking the field and bearing an active part in their system of warfare. A boy of fourteen is quite as formidable an antagonist as a man of forty. From behind his rocky rampart or wooded covert he speeds a rifle ball as straight to the heart of his foe, while his chances for escape, in the event of failure, are greater than those of his more aged and heavier associate. Many of the women delight to participate in predatory excursions, urging on the men, and actually taking part in conflicts. They ride like centaurs and handle their rifles with deadly skill. I cannot conceive why the bullet sped by a woman should not be quite as much an object of danger as the one shot from the weapon of a man. In the estimate made, no account is taken of the fighting women, who are numerous, well trained, and desperate, often exhibiting more real courage than the men.

If any one indulges the idea that the Apaches are weak and few; that they can be reduced to submission by the establishment of scattered forts in the regions occupied by them; that they can be tamed, and rendered peaceable under any circumstances; that they are to be bound and holden by treaty stipulations; that they are susceptible of any law except the *lex talionis*, or are to be constrained by any rule but that of the *argumentum ad hominum*, they are wonderfully in error. The succeeding chapters of this unpretending volume of personal experience—acquired after nearly eight years of extraordinary facilities to learn the truth—will probably have the effect to disprove these sophistries in a convincing manner. And here, *I assert*, that I was in every way predisposed to offer every kindly act toward that race. Admiring their unyielding resistance; their acknowledged prowess; their undisputed skill and dexterity; their undoubted intelligence and native force of character; acquainted with their language, traditions, tribal and family organizations, and enjoying their confidence to a degree never before accorded to any but an Apache, I strenuously used every effort in consonance with my orders and plain duties, to better their condition, and instill such information as would best conduce to their future peace and happiness. These facts will appear in the course of my narrative, together with the lamentable failure of all conciliatory schemes, which were notably aided and seconded by the commanding General and his subalterns.

CHAPTER XII.

TEN years had passed away before I renewed acquaintance with "Lo." It had been my fervent desire and solemn resolve never more to revisit the scenes of so much suffering and personal risk. No pecuniary offer would have proved a sufficient inducement to forego that resolve. But the dreadful war of rebellion burst with fury over our heads. My country needed the help of all her loyal sons, and I quietly placed myself in their ranks as Captain of a company of the Second Cavalry, California Volunteers. General James H. Carleton was ordered to advance into Arizona and New Mexico, with a column of nearly three thousand Californian soldiers, consisting of artillery, infantry and cavalry. He did me the honor to select my company from my regiment and make it a part of his force. Although flattered by the compliment, as mine was the only company of the Second Cavalry attached to his column, I felt by no means delighted with the prospect of again traveling those arid, extensive, and most inhospitable deserts, mountain gorges, and scorching plains, over which the Apache held almost undisturbed rule. In military life obedience to order is the first requisite of a soldier, and of course I submitted without murmur to this unexpected and disagreeable mandate.

It is foreign to the text of this work to enter into details of experiences not indicative of Indian character, and I will, therefore, pass over the many occurrences of military life during the trying winter of 1861 and 1862, when nearly the whole State was overflowed, and over sixty millions of dollars worth of property destroyed by the floods. It is not necessary to recite the gigantic labors performed by the column from California, in making roads; digging and restoring wells in desert places; constructing bridges; establishing depots; escorting trains, and sending forward advanced bodies of observation; for certain intelligence had been received that the enemy were advancing upon the frontiers of this State, and were not far from Fort Yuma. All these details have no connection with this volume, and will therefore be ignored.

I was ordered in the advance by Gen. Carleton, with instruction to occupy the pass at Antelope Peak until his arrival. On reaching that place I found that the Gila river had made great inroads upon the *mesa* or tableland between it and the hill, until only a passage of something like a hundred yards intervened. Of this pass I took possession, drawing up my two wagons and picket line in such a manner as to intercept all travel, while a lookout was maintained during the day from the top of the peak, and a well ordered patrol scoured the country for a space of ten miles to the eastward at all times of day and night. During our occupancy of this pass a band of Yumas, about thirty in number, all warriors, came up from the Colorado river to collect stones, and make *metates* for their wives. The *metate* is a slightly hollowed hard stone, upon which soaked maize is laid,

and then reduced to paste by the vigorous friction of another oblong and partially rounded stone, in the hands
of squaws "who love their lords." The paste so formed
is then patted between the hands until it assumes a flat,
thin and round appearance, when it is laid on a hot pan
and baked into a *tortilla*. As no stones of a suitable
character are found in the neighborhood of the Colorado
river, nearer than Antelope Peak, the Yumas yearly visit
that place to obtain them, as the *metate* is an indispensable culinary utensil.

Three days after we had occupied the pass we were
visited by the Yumas, who immediately set to work selecting stones and hewing them into the required shape
in their rude manner. But it was soon discovered that
several blankets, and a revolver, for which I was responsible, had disappeared, and I determined to get rid
of my Yumas friends soon—by stratagem if possible, by
force if need be. The deadly feud between the Yumas
and the Maricopas and Pimos has already been stated,
and the knowledge of this feud served me in the case.
The sentinel on the hill was instructed to give the alarm
to indicate the advance of a body from the east, and to
answer, when questioned, that they were Indians. As that
side of the compass was occupied only by the Maricopas
and Pimos, such an arrangement would probably have
the effect of alarming the Yumas and ridding us of their
presence. In obedience to order the signal was duly
made and the programme carried out. The Yumas were
greatly alarmed, and inquired whether I would protect
them from the Maricopas. My answer was, that I had
nothing at all to do with their quarrels; that the Maricopas were as much our friends as the Yumas; that I
possessed no power to take sides, but was entirely sub-
servient to the orders of my chief, and that, if they

would procure such an order, I would obey it to the
letter, but under any other circumstances refused to take
action in the premises. This was enough. Hastily bund-
ling up their *metates* they decamped with the utmost celerity and left us undisturbed during the remainder of
our stay at Antelope Peak.

Sometime afterward we reached the first Maricopa village, where I was ordered to establish my camp and
keep up communications between the column and California. Lieut.-Col. Theodore Coult, of the infantry, was
in command at the central village, twelve miles beyond
my post, and successive orders of his reduced my force
to the Orderly Sergeant, E. B. Loring, (subequently Captain of Co. A, Second Cavalry, Cal. Vols.) one man with
a broken arm, and myself. My chief bugler and Quar-
termaster-Sergeant, George Shearer, had been dispatched
across the Gila Bend, sixty-five miles, with the mails, and
orders to bring forward the return mails from California.
Our camp was located on an extensive, clear plain, covered with short, green alkaline grass, wholly unfit for
our animals, of which we had twenty-seven, including
horses and mules. There was also about fifty thousand
dollars worth of Government property to be guarded,
and for which I was responsible. By digging a foot
or two, water was obtainable in abundance, but it was
so deeply impregnated with alkali as to be almost un-
drinkable. However, there was nothing else for it,
and we were compelled to use it or die of thirst. The
camp ground was nearly two miles west from the nearest Maricopa village, and had frequently been invaded
by the Apaches. As our animals were sickened by the
grass about us, it became indispensable to graze them in
a more favorable locality which existed about three miles
further westward, and exactly where the Apaches were

frequently visitors. Fortunately, we escaped their at-
tentions at that time. Our far-reaching carbines swept
the whole expanse around us, and we had formed a sort
of redoubt of earth, as a defense in case of attack, within
which our ammunition, spare arms, provisions and personal effects were ensconced. One kept guard while
the other slept. Our animals were placed in a line which
could be swept by our fire, and the wagons so arranged
as to furnish additional defense. In this unpleasant and
inglorious manner several days passed, until the arrival
of Col. E. A. Rigg, who was quite astonished at the facts
brought to his knowledge and immediately imparted
them to the commanding General, by whom I was ordered once more in the advance, and the major part of
of my company reunited under my control.

The grazing ground to which we resorted during our
stay near the Maricopa villages had been the scene of a
desperate conflict between that tribe and the Pimos, on
one side, and the Yumas, Chimehuevis, and Amojaves,
on the other. Victory rested with the Maricopas and
Pimos, who slew over four hundred of the allied tribes,
and so humiliated them that no effort has ever been
made on their part to renew hostilities. This battle occurred four years before our advent, and the ground was
strewed with the skulls and bones of slaughtered warriors. Every day large numbers of the Maricopas visited
my camp and were received with kindness, which they
never failed to appreciate. On one occasion the head
chief, Juan Chivari, and his Lieutenant, Palacio, paid
me a visit, and almost immediately recognized me as the
man who, ten years before, they had dubbed with the
title of "Captain Killmoon," by reason of the part I
took when Lieut. Whipple was observing an eclipse of
the moon. I acknowledged the soft impeachment and

was received with every demonstration of regard and kindness. Messengers were dispatched to inform the Maricopa man and woman we had succored more than twelve years before; and, although they resided some ten miles distant, in another village, in less than four hours they were hugging and embracing me as if I were their warmest friend. This recognition and gratitude for the slight services rendered touched me nearly, especially when the priceless information they imparted at the time was probably the means of saving our lives. Every little gift within my possession was freely and gratefully conferred upon these two deserving beings, savages though they were, who had married and were passing their peaceable lives together.

One afternoon Palacio said to me: "You killed the moon once, and brought it to life again. That was good. You are a great medicine. You were then among us. You are here once more. I have told my young people of the affair; but they will not believe, although hundreds were witnesses. When can you kill the moon again, and prove the fact?"

An almanac happened to be within reach, and I referred to it for the next lunar eclipse. To my great surprise, it stated that a full eclipse of that luminary would take place two nights from that date. Preserving the greatest composure, I told Palacio that if he would bring his people to my camp two nights from that time, and wait till a certain hour, I would again kill the moon, and again restore her to life. This piece of news was extensively spread throughout all the villages; and next day my camp was thronged, from morning till night, with Maricopas and Pimos anxious to know if Palacio had reported correctly. They were answered in the affirmative, and sent away with very mixed sensations.

Before the time for slaughter arrived, I visited the grazing ground and selected seven finely polished skulls of Yumas, which I kept concealed in a sack. A quantity of powder was then mixed and made into a paste, and so arranged as to compose fuses. A few iron filings were mixed with several of these fuses, and a number of carbine caps arranged in such a manner as to flash and snap when required. The skulls were placed in a circle, the center of which I was to occupy. In each one was a burning candle, the light from which shone through the eye sockets. In front of every skull was a small fuse, and from each fuse led a train of dry powder to the center of the ring. Back of the fuses were placed considerable charges of dry powder, which would explode so soon as the fuses burned to their locations, and which explosion would immediately extinguish the candles, leaving all in darkness. The skulls were also attached to each other by a fine but strong thread, and the thread to a small twine, which, when drawn in, would bring the whole affair in a pile, and allow of their secretion. All my designs were confided to Loring, the Orderly Sergeant, and our plans laid.

Long before the appointed time, (about ten o'clock P. M.) the camp was crowded by excited Pimos and Maricopas. Probably three thousand were present. It was necessary to distract their attention from my movements, and I directed Sergeant Shearer to draw them off by some device from my immediate neighborhood. In this he succeeded admirably. No one was present to observe what I did. The skulls were properly arranged; the fuses, powder and caps laid, and candles lighted; and I took my place in the center, armed with a sabre, my head and right shoulder bare, and my gaze fixed on the moon, which was about to be obscured. The signal was given, and Shearer led the excited crowds toward my position. With great ceremony I drew a circle round the lighted skulls, and forbade the already frightened audience from passing that bound on pain of death. I sat in the center of the circle, with my head between my hands, waiting for time to pass until the eclipse should be complete, or nearly so. The silence and anxiety of that immense crowd of savages was something fearful. I was undertaking a dangerous experiment. If it failed, the consequences might be fatal; if it succeeded, my influence among them would be almost unbounded. Circumstanced as I was, the thing was worth trying. As an officer of my country, I felt the necessity of obtaining a moral as well as physical ascendancy of these populous tribes, which occupied the highway of immigration between the East and the West. I was almost alone among them, and they had begun to despise the paucity of my force. It had become necessary to re-assert our superiority, and the adventitious circumstances before related favored my attempt. Crouched down, with a naked sabre in my hand, gleaming with the lights thrown through the sightless sockets of the encircling skulls, I impatiently waited the time to apply the match to my train. It came at last. The train was touched; the brilliant flame flashed with the speed of lightning and ignited the fuses, which fizzed and sputtered, and sent forth streams of bright sparks, lighting up the scene with somewhat of radiance, when suddenly the whole affair terminated in darkness. The change from intense light was so great that no one observed Shearer draw in and secrete the skulls, and when vision was restored the whole paraphernalia had passed away. In the meantime, the moon began to reappear; its disc became rapidly more observable and brilliant, until she again " O'er the dark her sil-

ver mantle threw" in all its splendor. The effect upon
the surrounding Indians I can not pretend to describe;
but the *sobriquet* of "Captain Killmoon" was unani-
mously adopted as a very proper appellation. About
one o'clock A. M. the savages retired, and left us to the
enjoyment of a hearty laugh and undisturbed repose.

Two days afterward I had occasion to visit the head-
quarters of Col. Coult, and received his hospitality.
That officer informed me that since our arrival the Indians had increased their prices for ground provisions,
poultry, etc., five and six hundred per cent. Chickens,
which had been a drug at a bit a piece, were then worth
seventy-five cents. I told the Colonel that I could obtain all I required at twenty-five cents each, and he commissioned me to purchase a dozen or more on his account.
This statement of mine had been made off-hand, and
without any deliberation. I had bought only three or
four chickens, and had no right to determine the market; but as the promise was given, it was my duty to fulfill it, even at expense to myself. Here, again, strategy
came into play. "Captain Bob Shorty" was once more
at his old tricks.

I was the fortunate possessor of a powerful magnet
and a fine pocket compass, and with these instruments I
resolved to test the acumen of my savage friends. A
strong burning glass aided me greatly, as it did on
subsequent occasions, to obtain their implicit trust and
confidence. Armed with these peaceable weapons, I informed the Maricopas that chickens would find a ready
market in my camp, and in a few hours several dozen
were proffered. Determined upon paying only a fair
price, I coolly commenced rolling a cigarito, at the same
time giving one to a Maricopa, who went to the camp
fire and got a light, with which he returned and prof-

fered me the civility of igniting my cigarito from his. This did not suit my purpose, and taking my burning glass, I said—"Do you think that a 'Great Medicine' like me would light his cigar from common fire? No; I will draw it from heaven," and, suiting the action to the words, I drew a focus in that glaring sun, which soon gave me the needed fire. This simple achievement filled them with unbounded astonishment, and prepared them for the reception of other miracles. Turning to a warrior who appeared a person of some consequence, I ordered him to produce his chickens, whereupon half a dozen of fair quality were offered for sale. I took them one by one in my hand, appeared to go through a most careful examination, and then suddenly turning to the man, inquired what he meant by trying to deceive me. The poor fellow was exceedingly mortified, and asked in what particular. The reply was, you have offered to sell me sick chickens, unfit for food, and are therefore attempting an imposition. He stoutly denied the charge, insisting that the chickens were sound and well. We will soon test that, I answered, and then deposited my fine pocket compass on the ground, holding the magnet concealed in the hollow of my left hand. The needle soon ceased oscillating and settled down to its proper pointings, when the Indian was requested to turn the compass round, which he did, and, to his great wonder, the needle again resumed its normal situation. After several essays of this kind, he became convinced that the north pole would invariably point northward, no matter what changes were made in the position of the case. So soon as the required impression had been effected, they were told to lay their chickens, one after the other, either on the east or west side of the compass, and informed that if the birds were good and healthy no change would be observed in the instrument; but if not, the north pole

would point directly at the object and detect the imposition. These injunctions were implicitly followed, and
keeping the magnet in my left hand, with the index finger of the right, I approached the instrument, muttering
several cabalistic words, and described a half circle close
to and about the case. Of course, no movement followed, and the chicken was accepted at the price asked.
In this manner two or three were bought; but then came
my turn. Changing the magnet into the hollow of my
right hand, I again approached the compass, at the south
pole, and instantly it commenced to circle round in obedience to well known causes, and under full control of
the magnet, until the north pole pointed exactly toward
the doomed chicken. There! I exclaimed, in a tone of
simulated indignation, did I not tell you that some of
your chickens were sick and bad? Do you expect to
cheat a "Great Medicine?" If you are not more honest
for the future, you may possibly be visited by a malady,
which will kill off all your fowls.

By this time a large and anxious crowd had assembled
to witness this new and extraordinary test, and any attempt to describe their wonderment would be fruitless.
Realizing the impression made, I then continued in the
following strain: I do not believe that you meant to be
bad, but rather give you credit for ignorance, and I only
claim that all the sick chickens shall be forfeited to me,
for I can cure them, and make them ultimately useful.
This proposition was eagerly accepted, *nem. con.*, and in
this manner I secured six dozen of excellent birds at the
rate of two bits each, while only twelve miles distant my
brother officers were paying six bits each for inferior
birds. The Indians, knowing us to be in their power
for supplies of this kind, had raised the prices five hundred per cent., and I had turned the scales against them
by a very simple process.

CHAPTER XIII.

IN consequence of the report made by Lieut.-Col. E. A. Rigg, Gen. Carleton again ordered me in the advance, with Capt. Thomas Roberts, Co. E, First California Infantry. Arriving at the San Pedro river, it became necessary to learn whether Dragoon Springs, some twenty-eight miles further on, could supply both companies, at a time, with water, or whether we would be obliged to break into detachments. Capt. Roberts took the advance with his infantry and three wagons, having also selected seven of my best mounted men to serve as scouts and couriers. I remained behind with fifteen of my cavalry and ten of Roberts' company, including the detachment left as a garrison at the river, where a tolerable adobe building, erected by the Overland Mail Stage Company, afforded decent shelter, and a defensible position.

The night after Roberts left was one of the most stormy I ever witnessed. The rain descended in floods. Earth and sky appeared thunder riven; blazing lightnings leaped from the inky clouds, and absorbed the Cimmerian darkness with their blinding flashes. The San

Pedro roared and foamed, the animals quailed and bent before the storm, and all nature seemed convulsed. I was in charge of sixteen wagons with their mules and precious freight, and my chief attention was elicited to secure their safety. Experience had taught me that the Apaches would select exactly such a time to make a bold attempt, and I doubled my sentries. Throwing myself on the earthen floor, in front of a decent fire, without removing my side arms or any portion of my clothing, I endeavored to obtain some repose. About two o'clock A. M., I was aroused by the Sergeant of the guard, who informed me that strange lights were visible coming down the hills on the west, north and south sides. A hasty survey showed me four lights, as of large burning brands, on three different sides of the compass, and apparently approaching the station. I felt convinced from this open demonstration, that no attack was meditated, for, in that case, the greatest secrecy and caution would have been observed by the Apaches. Nevertheless, the garrison was summoned and disposed to the best advantage. All fires were extinguished, and all lights shrouded from observation. In the course of a few minutes seven or eight more lights made their appearance, and seemed to be carried by persons walking at a rapid pace. Some of them approached within, what I considered, two hundred yards of the station, and at one time I felt greatly inclined to try the effect of a chance shot from my rifle, but gave up the idea from the conviction that no Apache would carry a torch within that distance, and maintain an erect position, while my fire might expose the persons of my men and draw a more effective return. After an hour and a half of anxious watch, the lights gradually united and faded away toward the east.

It was not until more than a year had elapsed that I

learned the meaning of this occurrence. A celebrated leading man of the Mescalero Apaches, named Gian-nah-tah, or "Always Ready," gave the desired information, which precisely tallied with succeeding events. He said that, as the Apaches are a dispersed and perpetually wandering race, it is impossible for one detachment to know where others might be at any time; but that when a great body of them was needed for any joint undertaking they made smoke signals of a certain character by day, and signals of fire by night. That, on the occasion of which I write, the nature of the country prohibited fire signals from being seen except from very short distances, and runners were hurried through the district, bearing torches, which would indicate that the aid of all within sight was required. In fine, it was the "speed, Malise, speed," of the Apache. This explanation will account for what followed.

Between three and four o'clock A. M., just after the lights had disappeared, the sound of horses advancing at a fast gallop was heard approaching the station. The sentinel challenged, and was immediately answered with the round Saxon response, "Friends." It proved to be two of my own company, who had been sent back by Capt. Roberts with the information that there was abundance of water at Dragoon Springs, and instruction to join him with the train without delay. The poor fellows had ridden twenty-eight miles through that terrible storm, and in the heart of a country swarming with hostile and ever vigilant savages. Two days subsequently they had a splendid opportunity to test their gallantry, and most nobly did they respond to the appeal. In obedience to order, we set forward before daylight to join Captain Roberts, and reached Dragoon Springs, without incident, at three o'clock P. M. A long and fatiguing march

8

of forty miles had to be made before reaching Apache
Pass, where the next water was to be had, and as we
were in doubt as to the quantity, it was again agreed
that I should remain at Dragoon Springs until next
morning, while Capt. Roberts was to push ahead with
his infantry and seven of my company, leaving the train
under my charge.   At half-past five o'clock P. M. he set
out, and the strictest vigilance was maintained in camp
the whole night.   By daylight next morning we were
again in the saddle, and the train duly straightened out
for the long and dreary march.   Had we not been en-
cumbered with wagons my cavalry could have made the
distance easily in seven hours; but we were compelled
to keep pace with those indispensable transports of food,
ammunition, clothing and medicine.   A little before dark
we arrived at Ewell's Station, fifteen miles west of the
pass, and I determined to park the train, as the mules
had almost given out, and were quite unable to accomplish the remainder of the march without some rest.
Just as I had come to this conclusion we perceived several riders coming toward us with all speed, and they
soon proved to be the detachment of my company which
had been detailed to act with Capt. Roberts.   Two of
them were mounted behind two others, and all had evidently ridden hard.   Sergeant Mitchell approached, and
saluting, said: "Capt. Roberts has been attacked in
Apache Pass by a very large body of Indians.   We
fought them for six hours, and finally compelled them
to run.   Capt. Roberts then directed us to come back
through the pass, and report to you with orders to park
the train and take every precaution for its safety.   He
will join you to-night.   On leaving the pass we were
pursued by over fifty well armed and mounted Apaches,
and we lost three horses, killed under us, and that one—

pointing to a splendid gray—is mortally wounded. Sergeant Maynard, now present, has his right arm fractured at the elbow, with a rifle ball, and John Teal we believe to be killed, as we saw him cut off by a band of fifteen or twenty savages, while we were unable to render him any assistance."

The wagons were ordered to be parked; every man was supplied with ammunition and posted to the best advantage; proper attention was paid to my wounded sergeant, and the camp arranged in such a manner as to insure a warm reception to a large body of savages. We remained on the *qui vive* until one o'clock A. M., when to my extreme surprise and sincere gratification we were joined by John Teal, who was supposed to have been killed. He brought with him his saddle, blanket, sabre and pistols, having lost his horse and spurs. His narrative is so full of interest, and so well illustrates a phase in Apache character, that it is worth recording.

"Soon after we left the pass," said he, " we opened upon a sort of hollow plain or vale, about a mile wide, across which we dashed with speed. I was about two hundred yards in the rear, and presently a body of about fifteen Indians got between me and my companions. I turned my horse's head southward and coursed along the plain, lengthwise, in the hope of outrunning them, but my horse had been too sorely tested, and could not get away. They came up and commenced firing, one ball passing through the body of my horse, just forward of his hind quarters. It was then about dark, and I immediately dismounted, determined to fight it out to the bitter end. My horse fell, and as I approached him, he began to lick my hands. I then swore to kill at least one Apache. Lying down behind the body of my dying animal, I opened fire upon them with my carbine, which being a breech-loader, enabled me to keep up a lively fusillade. This repeated fire seemed to confuse the savages, and instead of advancing with a rush, they commenced to circle round me, firing occasional shots in my direction. They knew that I also had a six-shooter and a sabre, and seemed unwilling to try close quarters. In this way the fight continued for over an hour, when I got a good chance at a prominent Indian and slipped a carbine ball into his breast. He must have been a man of some note, because soon after that they seemed to get away from me, and I could hear their voices growing fainter in the distance. I thought this a good time to make tracks, and divesting myself of my spurs, I took the saddle, bridle and blanket from my dead horse and started for camp. I have walked eight miles since then."

It is needless to add how gratified I was to receive this brave and loyal soldier again, and find him free from wound or scar. We subsequently ascertained that the man he shot was no less an individual than the celebrated Mangas Colorado, but, I regret to add, the rascal survived his wound to cause us more trouble.

About an hour after Teal had come in, I was joined by Capt. Roberts with thirty men, and then got a full description of the fight. I omitted to mention that two twelve-pounder mountain howitzers were with our little force, and to these guns the victory is probably attributable. It seems that about one hundred and thirty or forty miners had located themselves at the Pino Alto gold mines, or the same mines mentioned in a former portion of this work as the scene where Mr. Hay and his family were attacked and their cattle stolen by the Apaches, and also where Delgadito got badly scored by Wells. This was the great stronghold of Mangas and his band, and finding himself unable to dislodge the unwelcome intruders without help, he had dispatched messengers to Cheis, the principal warrior of the Chiricahui Apaches, to assist him in expelling the miners. Cheis was too much occupied by the advancing column of American troops to give heed to this call, and failed to attend. Such want of faith was inexplicable to Mangas, who knew nothing of our approach, and at the head of two hundred warriors he visited Cheis, to inquire the reason for his apparent defection from the Apache cause. In reply Cheis took Mangas to the top of the Chiricahui and showed him the dust made by our advance guard, and told him that it was his first duty to defend himself, and that if Mangas would join in the affair, they could whip the "white eyes," and make themselves masters of the spoil. This arrangement was immediately agreed to by Mangas, and their united forces, amounting to nearly seven hundred warriors, so disposed as to take Roberts by surprise and insure his defeat. But "the best laid plans of men and mice, aft gang aglee," and these finely fixed schemes were doomed to be terribly overthrown.

Roberts, entirely unsuspecting any attack, entered the pass with the ordinary precautions. He had penetrated two-thirds of the way, when from both sides of that battlemented gorge a fearful rain of fire and lead was poured upon his troops, within a range of from thirty to eighty yards. On either hand the rocks afforded natural and almost unassailable defenses. Every tree concealed an armed warrior, and each warrior boasted his rifle, six-shooter and knife. A better armed host could scarcely be imagined. From behind every species of shelter came the angry and hissing missiles, and not a soul to be seen. Quickly, vigorously, and bravely did his men respond, but to what effect? They were expending ammunition to no purpose; their foes were invisible; there was no way to escalade those impregnable natural fortresses; the howitzers were useless, and the men doubtful how to attack the foe. In such strait, Roberts determined to fall back, reform and renew the contest. The orders were given and obeyed with perfect discipline. Reaching the entrance to the pass the troops were reorganized, skirmishers were thrown out over the hills so as to command the road; the howitzers were loaded, and belched forth their shells whenever found necessary. In this manner the troops again marched forward. Water was indispensable for the continuance of life. Unless they could reach the springs they must perish. A march of forty miles under an Arizonian sun, and over wide alkaline plains, with their blinding dust and thirst-provoking effects, had already been effected, and it would be impossible to march back again without serious loss of life, and untold suffering, without taking into account the seeming disgrace of being defeated by seven times their force of Apaches. What would it avail those brave men to know that the Indians were as well armed as they; that they possessed all the advantages; that they outnumbered them seven to one, when the outside and carping world would be so ready to taunt them with defeat, and adduce so many specious reasons why they should have annihilated the savages?

Forward, steadily forward, under a continuous and galling fire, did those gallant companies advance until they reached the old station house in the pass, about six hundred yards from the springs. The house was built of stone, and afforded ample shelter; but still they had no water, and eighteen hours, with a march of forty miles, including six hours of sharp fighting, had been passed without a drop. Men and officers were faint, worn-out with fatigue, want of sleep, and intense privation and excitement; still Roberts urged them on, and led the way. His person was always the most exposed; his voice ever cheering and encouraging. Immediately commanding the springs are two hills, both high and difficult of ascent. One is to the east, and the other overlooks them from the south. On these heights the Apaches had built rude but efficient breastworks by piling rocks one upon the other so as to form crenelle holes between the interstices. From these fortifications they kept up a rapid and scathing fire, which could not be returned with effect by musketry from three to four hundred feet below. The howitzers were got into position, but one of them was so badly managed that the gunners were brought immediately under the fire from the hills without being able to make even a decent response. In a few moments it was overturned by some unaccountable piece of stupidity, and the artillerists driven off by the sharp fire of the savages. At that juncture, Sergeant Mitchell with his six associates of my company, made a rush to bring off the howitzer and place it in a better position. Upon reaching the guns, they determined not to turn it down hill, but up, so as to keep their fronts to the fire. While performing this gallant act, they were assailed with a storm of balls, but escaped untouched; after having righted the gun, brought it away, and placed it in a position best calculated to perform effective service. So soon as this feat had been happily accomplished, the exact range was obtained and shell after shell hurled upon the hills, bursting just when they should. The Apaches, wholly unused to such formidable engines, precipitately abandoned their rock works and fled in all directions. It was nearly night. To remain under those death-dealing heights during the night,

when camp-fires would afford the enemy the best kind
of advantage, was not true policy, and Capt. Roberts
ordered each man to take a drink from the precious and
hardly-earned springs, and fill his canteen, after which
the troops retired within the shelter afforded by the
stone station house, the proper guards and pickets being
posted.

In this fight Roberts had two men killed and three
wounded, and I afterwards learned from a prominent
Apache who was present in the engagement, that sixty-
three warriors were killed outright by the shells, while
only three perished from musketry fire. He added—
"We would have done well enough if you had not fired
wagons at us." The howitzers being on wheels, were
deemed a species of wagon by the Apaches, wholly inexperienced in that sort of warfare.

Capt. Roberts suffered his men to recruit their wasted
energies with supper, and then taking one-half his company, the remainder being left under command of Lieut.
Thompson, marched back to Ewell's Station, fifteen
miles, to assure the safety of the train under my command, and escort it through the pass. As before stated,
he reached my camp a little after two o'clock A.M., where
the men rested until five, when the march toward the
pass was resumed. Several alarms were given before
his arrival, and we heard the Apaches careering around
us; but they made no attack, and kept out of sight. At
five o'clock A. M., the train was straightened out with
half my effective cavalry force three hundred yards in
the advance, and the other half about as far in the rear,
while the wagons were flanked on either side by the infantry. In this order we entered that most formidable
of gorges, when the bugles blew a halt. A considerable
body of the infantry were then thrown out on either side

as skirmishers, with a small reserve as the rallying point, while the cavalry were ordered to guard the train, and make occasional dashes into the side cañons. "Up hill and down dale" went the skirmishers, plunging into dark and forbidding defiles, and climbing steep, rocky and difficult acclivities, while the cavalry made frequent sorties from the main body to the distance of several hundred yards. Being without a subaltern, Gen. Carleton had assigned Lieut. Muller, of the First Cavalry California Volunteers, to service with my command. This officer soon after gave sufficient proof of his gallantry and zeal, for which I now gratefully return thanks.

In this manner we progressed through that great stronghold of the Apaches and dangerous defile, until we joined the detachment under Lieut. Thompson, at the stone station house, where we quartered for the remainder of that day. Let it be borne in mind that Capt. Roberts' company of Californian Infantry had marched forty miles without food or water, had fought for six hours with desperation against six times their numbers of splendidly armed Apaches, ensconced behind their own natural ramparts, and with every possible advantage in their favor; had driven that force before them, occupied their defiles, taken their strongholds, and, after only one draught of water and a hasty meal, had made another march of thirty miles, almost absolutely without rest. I doubt much if any record exists to show where infantry have made a march of seventy miles, fought one terrible battle of six hours' duration, and achieved a decided victory under such circumstances.

The shrill fife, the rattling drum and the mellow bugles sounded the reveille before dawn of the next day. The camp-fires were soon throwing up their lively jets of flame and smoke, while the grateful odors of frying

8*

bacon and browning flap-jacks saluted the appreciative nostrils of the hungry troops. But we had no water, and without water we could have no coffee, that most coveted of all rations. There was reason to believe that the Apaches intended to put our metal to another trial. They had again occupied the heights above the springs, and also the water sources, which were thickly sheltered by trees and willow underbrush. Roberts again made preparations to dislodge the savages, and ordered his howitzers into the most favorable positions. Just then I saluted him, and said, " Captain, you have done your share of this fight; I now respectfully ask for my chance. If you will throw your shells on the heights above the springs, I will charge the latter with my men, and clean out the Apaches in a very few moments. I certainly think this concession due me."

Roberts reflected a few moments, and replied—" I am truly sorry that your wish cannot be granted. Yours is the only cavalry I have, and their safety is indispensable to ours. We are going to the San Simon river, where I am ordered to establish a depot and await the arrival of other troops with supplies. You are to take back this train for those supplies, and you will have enough to do in your proper turn. I cannot, under the circumstances, grant your request."

To this I replied: " Your objections appear cogent; but I cannot perceive why all these things cannot be accomplished, and still permit my men, who are burning with anxiety, to charge those springs and disperse that wretched horde of savages. They are already cowed, and will immediately flee before a vigorous assault."

Capt. Roberts replied: " You have had my answer, Captain, and it should be enough. I do not intend to jeopard my own men, but will shell the heights and springs, and effect a bloodless victory, in so far as we are concerned."

After this rebuff I could make no further personal appeal, but instructed Lieut. Muller to beseech Capt. Roberts, and, if possible, induce him to change his mind. Muller argued for half an hour, until Roberts told him either to obey or be placed under arrest. This ended the colloquy. The howitzers then opened fire—the shells burst splendidly; large numbers of Apaches were observed to decamp from the heights in the most hurried manner; the springs also underwent a similar cleaning, and in less than twenty minutes the troops were permitted to advance and fill their canteens, while my cavalry, without waiting further orders, made a rush after the retreating savages until the rapid rise and terribly broken nature of the ground checked their career. The hillsides were covered with fleeing Apaches, who seemed imbued with supernatural powers of locomotion. Upwards they sped with the celerity of Alpine goats, until they disappeared behind the crests of tall mountains and rugged hills. In peace and quiet we partook of the precious fountain. Our horses and mules, which had not tasted water for forty-eight hours, and were nearly famished from so dusty a road and so long a journey under the hottest of suns, drank as if they would never be satisfied. An hour later we moved through the pass, entered upon the wide plain which separates it from the San Simon river, and reached our camp on that creek, without further trouble, about four o'clock P. M.

CHAPTER XIV.

BUT short breathing space was afforded me at the San
Simon. On the morning of the third day after our arrival, and the trying tests to which we had been subjected, I received orders from Capt. Roberts to escort
the train of twenty-six wagons back to the San Pedro,
in order to furnish the required transportation for the
provision, ammunition, clothing and other supplies of
the column. For this duty I was assigned fourteen of
my troopers, and seven men of Roberts' company. The
intervening country had been well examined through
fine field glasses, and on two occasions a thorough re-
connissance had been made by the cavalry, which showed
that a very excellent passage existed to the north of the
Chiricahui range, over nearly a level plain, and that the
distance would be only some seven miles longer. This
route, with the approbation of Capt. Roberts, was at
once selected for our return, and for the following reasons: The safety of our train was of the very first importance, as upon it depended the success of the unprece-
dented march the "Column from California" was then
attempting. In the next place, if the Apaches had given

us such a strong and determined fight when we mustered one hundred and twenty-nine men and two mountain howitzers, what great chance would I have of safely conducting a train of twenty-six wagons with only twenty-one men, and without artillery, through such a terrific stronghold? In the third place, nature provided a passage nearly as short, much less laborious for men and animals, well supplied with water, wood and grass, and by its open character, affording the very best field for the operations of cavalry, and the widest range for our splendid breech-loading weapons of long reach. It was not a question whether we should again fight the Indians, but whether we could forward the main object of the expedition. Indeed, strict orders had been given to refrain from Indian broils as much as possible, to suffer some wrong rather than divert our time and attention from the great purpose contemplated, which was to liberate Arizona from Confederate rule and effect a junction with Gen. Canby as soon as possible. Had we been exclusively on an Indian campaign, other means would have been adopted.

Having taken a final survey, I started in the evening just after sundown, to prevent the Apaches from seeing the dust raised by the column, and directed our course over the open plain, north of the Chiricahui range, and between it and the mountains from which it is divided some four miles by an open and elevated piece of clear land, without trees or rocks, and thickly covered with the finest grama grass. We traveled all night with the cavalry covering the front and rear, and the seven infantrymen sleeping in the empty wagons, with their weapons loaded and ready at a moment's warning. Every little while the cavalry were required to patrol the length of the column, to ward off any sudden and unforeseen attack. The infantry were allowed to sleep, in order that they might be fresh to keep guard throughout the day. In this manner we progressed until five A. M., next day, when I ordered a halt, had the wagons handsomely corralled nearly in a circle, with the animals and men all inside, except the guard, and the camp properly prepared against surprise. We were then exactly north of the Chiricahui mountains, and south of another range, each being about two miles distant. I could distinctly see large numbers of Apaches riding furiously up and down the steeps of those heights, and sometimes advancing on the plain, as if to attack. But experience had taught them that our carbines and Minnie rifles were deadly at nearly a mile of distance, and they did not approach within their reach. Our horses were tied to the picket rope which extended across the open end of the corral, and covered by a sufficient guard. Finding that the Apaches did not care to make an onslaught, the cavalry and teamsters, all of whom were well armed, retired to rest, after partaking of a hearty meal. Next evening, at dark, we again hitched up and pursued our journey as before. I was in the advance with Sergeant Loring, when our horses suddenly jumped one side and our ears were greeted by the spiteful warning of a rattlesnake, coiled up directly in our path. To avoid this malignant reptile the train diverged about twenty yards from the road, and after a little while entered it again. This sort of thing occurred many times during the night, until we again struck the regular highway nearly due west of Apache Pass. Our next halt was made six miles from Ewell's Station, and we had come seventy miles in two nights. That day we saw no Indians, although the same precautions were adopted as if we were surrounded by large numbers. Our next march was to the Ojo de los Hermanos, or the "Brothers' Springs," so as to avoid stopping to water at Dragoon Springs, which were two miles up a deep and dangerous cañon, where the enemy would possess every possible advantage, and where the animals would have to be led to water a mile or more from the wagons, with the delightful prospect of not finding anything like a sufficiency.

In due course of time, we regained the San Pedro river, where Gen. Carleton had arrived with a considerable body of troops. I turned over my train, and was ordered to advance once more with head-quarters. Apache Pass was again entered and traversed; but it seemed as if no Indian had ever awakened its echoes with his war-whoop—as if it had ever been the abode of peace and silence. I rode beside Dr. McNulty for a while, and described to him the terrible conflict which had taken place there only eight days previous. That true soldier and soldiers' friend frequently exclaimed— "By George, I wish I had been here!" "What splendid natural breastworks are these, old fellow!"—a peculiar expression of his—"I am glad you came out of it all right!" Next day we emerged from the pass without molestation, or seeing an Indian sign; but, instead of directing our course toward the San Simon, diverged by another route toward the Cienega, a flat, marshy place, at the foot of the next easterly range of mountains, of which Stein's Peak is the most prominent. The San Simon creek, as it is called, sinks about a mile south of the station bearing that name, and undoubtedly furnishes the supply of water which is to be had at the Cienega, located on the same plain, and about eight miles south of the spot where the creek disappears.

We had progressed about two miles beyond the pass, when we suddenly came upon the bodies of thirteen persons, pierced in many places with bullet and arrow holes, and some with the arrows still sticking, driven deeply into their frames. After some examination, the verdict was that they were the bodies of white men killed by the Apaches but a short time before. This conclusion proved correct, as was afterward ascertained beyond all doubt, and as their destruction was compassed by a trick peculiarly illustrative of Apache character, I will relate it *in extenso*.

My readers will bear in mind the place described as Santa Rita del Cobre, where the Boundary Commission remained for several months, where Inez Gonzales and the two Mexican boys were rescued from captivity, where Delgadito made his attack upon Mr. Hay, and where he got handsomely seamed by Wells. The gold mines worked by Mr. Hay at that period, twelve years prior, had proved to be very rich, and attracted many bold adventurers, among whom were a number of celebrated Indian fighters, who had passed years upon our frontiers, and were universally dreaded by all the wild Indian tribes of Arizona and New Mexico. In a short time the mining population at that point amounted to something like two hundred, of whom one hundred and fifty were well armed, fearless and experienced men. The presence of such a party was far from pleasing to Mangas Colorado and his band, as they claimed exclusive proprietorship to that whole region, which was their main fastness. They also regarded the miners as the legitimate successors of the Boundary Commission, with whom they had parted in deadly enmity after a short season of simulated friendship. Mangas made many skillful efforts to dislodge the miners, and divert their attention from the Copper Mines, but without effect. He privately visited some of the more prominent among them, and professing the most disinterested friendship, offered to show them where gold was far more abundant and could be obtained with less labor, accompanying his promises with something like the following style of inducement:

"You good man. You stay here long time and never hurt Apache. You want the 'yellow iron;' I know where plenty is. Suppose you go with me, I show you; but tell no one else. Mangas your friend, he want to do you good. You like 'yellow iron'—good! Me no want 'yellow iron.' Him no good for me—can no eat, can no drink, can no keepee out cold. Come, I show you."

For a while each person so approached kept this offer to himself, but after a time they began to compare notes, and found that Mangas had made like promises to each, under the ban of secrecy and the pretense of exclusive personal friendship. Those who at first believed the old rascal, at once comprehended that it was a trap set to separate and sacrifice the bolder and leading men by gaining their confidence and killing them in detail, while their fates would remain unknown to those left behind. The next time, after this *éclaircissement*, that Mangas visited that camp, he was tied to a tree and administered a dose of "strap oil," well applied by lusty arms. His vengeance was more keenly aroused by this deserved treatment, and from that time forth every sort of annoyance was put into operation against the miners. They were shot at from the cover of trees and rocks, their cattle and horses were driven off, their supply trains robbed and destroyed, and themselves reduced to want. But Mangas desired their utter extirpation. He wanted their blood; he was anxious for their annihilation, and feeling himself unable to cope with them single handed, he dispatched emissaries to Cheis, the most famed warrior of the Chiricahui tribe, to come and help him oust the Americans.

Just at that time news was received by Cheis that the Americans were advancing from the west, and were about to overrun his country. "Charity begins at home," was the motto of that prominent Apache, and, instead of going to the relief of Mangas, notified him of the newly threatened invasion, and asked his assistance, promising to help Mangas, in his turn. The proffer was accepted, and Mangas joined Cheis at the Apache Pass with two hundred warriors, which accounts for the large force against which Roberts had to contend in that formidable gorge.

While these united forces were occupying Apache Pass, waiting our arrival, they descried a small band of Americans approaching from the east, across the wide plain intervening between that place and the Cienega, and determined to cut it off. Those wily Indians soon recognized in the new-comers a small, but well armed, party of the hardy and experienced miners from the Santa Rita del Cobre, and knew that such men were always on their guard and prepared to defend their lives with the greatest courage and determination. They also knew that they would be specially on the *qui vive* after having entered the pass, and that any attack upon them would probably result in the loss of several of their warriors. How to compass their ends and obviate this last possibility, became the chief objects of their attention. Two miles east of the pass, right in the clear and unobstructed plain, there is a gully, formed by the washing of heavy rains through a porous and yielding soil. This gully is from six to eight feet deep, a quarter of a mile long, three or four yards wide, and cannot be seen from horseback until the rider is within fifty yards of the spot. With consummate cunning a large body of the Apaches ensconced themselves in this gully, knowing that the travelers would be somewhat off their guard in an open plain, apparently without place of concealment, and awaited the approach of their victims. The scheme proved eminently successful. Wholly unapprehensive of a danger they could not see and had no reason to suspect, the hardy miners rode forward with their rifles resting in the slings across their saddle bows, their pistols in scabbards, and their whole attention absorbed in the pass they were about to enter. When they had arrived within forty yards of the gully or ditch, a terrific and simultaneous fire was opened upon them by the concealed Indians, which killed one-half their number outright, and sent the remainder wounded and panic stricken to seek safety in flight. They were immediately pursued and massacred to a man. Theirs were the bodies discovered by us soon after emerging from Apache Pass, and although we grieved over their death, as brave men grieve for each other, the circumstance taught us another and most instructive lesson in Apache character, and the wondrously shrewd calculations made by those people when determined to effect a desired object.

I subsequently learned that the victims had with them a considerable sum in gold dust, nearly fifty thousand dollars' worth, all of which fell into the hands of their slayers, who had become well acquainted with its value. Their bodies were as decently interred as circumstances would permit, after which we moved forward toward the Cienega, in mournful and somewhat vindictive mood.

Mangas Colorado returned with his diminished band to the Pino Alto country after his disastrous defeat in Apache Pass, but he returned with a carbine ball in his chest, fired by John Teal, whose gallant conduct has already been described. It was owing to this chance shot that the Apaches abandoned their attack upon Teal, in order to give succor to so prominent a man as Mangas. He was carefully conveyed to Janos, in Chihuahua, where he received the enforced attendance and aid of a Mexican physician, who happened to be in that place at the time. It was a case of the practice of surgery under unique circumstances. If the patient survived, well and good; he would return to his native wilds to again renew his fearful devastations; but if he died, the doctor and all the inhabitants were assured they should visit the spirit land with him. The ball was extracted, Mangas recovered, and the people were saved; but his was a short lease of life, for he was soon afterward captured by Capt. E. D. Shirland, of the First California Volunteer Cavalry, and killed while attempting to effect his escape from the guard house. In this manner perished Mangas Colorado, the greatest and most talented Apache Indian of the nineteenth century. In truth, he was a wonderful man. His sagacious counsels partook more of the character of wide and enlarged statesmanship than those of any other Indian of modern times. His subtle and comprehensive intellect enrolled and united the three principal tribes of Arizona and New Mexico in one common cause. He found means to collect and keep together, for weeks at a time, large bodies of savages, such as none of his predecessors could assemble and feed. He quieted and allayed all jealousies and disagreements between different branches of the great Apache family, and taught them to comprehend the value of unity and collective strength. Although never remarkable for personal prowess and courage, he knew how to evoke those qualities in others, and appropriate the credit to himself. Crafty and skilled in human nature, he laid plans and devised schemes remarkable for their shrewdness of conception and success in execution. In council he was the last to speak, in action he was the last to come on the field, and the first to leave if defeated; yet he had the reputation among all his people of being the wisest and bravest. That he was the wisest has never been denied; that he was the bravest has never been proved. But, take him for all in all, he exercised an influence never equaled by any savage of our time, when we take into consideration the fact that the Apaches acknowledge *no* chiefs, and obey no orders from any source. They constitute a pure democracy, in which every man is the equal of every other. Each is sovereign in his own right as a warrior, and disclaims all allegiance. But this subject will be treated at length in another portion of this work.

The life of Mangas Colorado, if it could be ascertained, would be a tissue of the most extensive and afflicting revelations, the most atrocious cruelties, the most vindictive revenges, and widespread injuries ever perpetrated by an American Indian. We read with sensations of horror the dreadful massacre at Schenectady, the bloody deeds at Wyoming, the cruelties of Proctor's savage allies, and others of like character; but they sink into absolute insignificance beside the acts of Mangas Colorado, running through a series of fifty years, for Mangas was fully seventy when sent to his last account. The northern portions of Chihuahua and Sonora, large tracts of Durango, the whole of Arizona, and a very considerable part of New Mexico, were laid waste, ravished, destroyed by this man and his followers. A strip of country twice as large as all California was rendered almost houseless, unproductive, uninhabitable by his active and uncompromising hostility. Large and flourishing towns were depopulated and ruined. Vast ranchos, such as that of Barbacomori and San Bernardino, once teem-

ing with wealth and immense herds of cattle, horses and
mules, were turned into waste places, and restored to
their pristine solitudes.   The name of Mangas Colorado
was the tocsin of terror and dismay throughout a vast
region of country, whose inhabitants existed by his suf-
ferance under penalty of supplying him with the requisite
arms and ammunition for his many and terrible raids.
He combined many attributes of real greatness with the
ferocity and brutality of the most savage savage.   The
names of his victims, by actual slaughter or by captivity,
would fill a volume, and the relation of his deeds throughout a long and merciless life would put to shame the
records of the "Newgate Calendar."   I dismiss him
with disgust and loathing, not unmingled with some
degree of respect for his abilities.

CHAPTER XV.

THE experiences of several years had not been ignored. The time which had elapsed between my first and second appearance upon the stage of Indian action had given me opportunity to reflect upon many events, and study their causes, characters, and mechanism of production. Reposing in the midst of civilized security, and altogether freed from the excitement of unseen, deadly perils to which life in the Apache countries is invariably subject, I was enabled to draw more correct conclusions than could have been arrived at on the ground, while compelled to regard personal safety as the first necessity. In this calm and undisturbed survey of the field many circumstances were accounted for which at the time appeared more the result of untoward accident than of well laid schemes founded upon a shrewd knowledge of natural instincts. The pyramidal columns of smoke, so often seen to ascend from mountain heights, had appeared to me as merely warnings of our presence in the country; the apparently casual turning over of a stone, close to the highway, never attracted attention; the breaking of a few insignificant branches in a forest did not seem to be more than accidental occurrences; but closer investigation led me to believe that all these things, and many more, had their peculiar significance; that they were neither more nor less than lithographic notices by which one party could know the force of another—the direction taken—the extent and nature of the danger which threatened, and impart the summons for a gathering. That these surmises were correct every old Indian fighter knows; but the responsibilities of my position determined me to make a study of points so essential to a successful campaign, and the safety of my command. Nevertheless, it will be found that a party, even though it be a small one, which is well armed; which *never* relaxes its vigilance; which selects clear, open ground for camping; which invariably throws out an advanced guard, and keeps its weapons always ready for use at a moment's warning, can move with safety through all portions of Arizona and New Mexico; while ten times their number, disregarding these precautions, are sure to be attacked, and if attacked about as certain to be defeated with loss. Let it be again distinctly impressed upon my readers, that the Apache never attacks unless fully convinced of an easy victory. They will watch for days, scanning your every movement, observing your every act; taking exact note of your party and all its belongings. Let no one suppose that these assaults are made upon the spur of the moment by bands accidentally encountered. Far from it; they are almost invariably the results of long watching—patient waiting—careful and rigorous observation, and anxious counsel.

Throughout nearly the whole of Arizona the traveler

encounters a succession of high mountain ridges, running northwest and southeast, overlooking intermediate, unwooded and unconcealed plains, which are from fifteen to forty miles from ridge to ridge. The sierras are not continuous or united, but occur in isolated ranges of from twenty to fifty miles in extent, with smooth and clear prairie lands between them. These intervals extend from one to five miles; but as they afford neither wood nor water, are never traveled except by very small parties, which can move quickly and are too weak to risk the dangerous mountain passes and cañons. But even this cannot be effected in some places without making a detour of many miles from the direct road, and it is often indispensable to run all risks rather than lose time, or suffer the inconveniences of such a round-about and wretchedly provided march, where one is likely to perish from the want of water.

The land along the Gila is excessively alkaline and unproductive in its present condition, although in many places the willow, cotton-wood and mesquit flourish luxuriantly. In wet weather the soil becomes a soft, deep and tenacious muck, which almost wholly impedes wagon travel, and during the dry season the roads are so deeply covered with a fine, almost impassable and light dust, that every footfall throws up clouds of it yards above the traveler's head, completely shutting out from sight all objects more than three yards distant. To such an extent does this prevail in some localities, that I have been unable to distinguish the man or his horse at my side, and within reach of my arm, on a fine moonlight night.

In the immediate neighborhood of Tucson, on the table land outside of its cultivated fields, the traveler, for the first time, meets with the far-famed grama grass, but on descending from this *mesa* does not again come in

9

contact with it until he reaches Dragoon Springs. This grama grass is beyond all comparison the most nutricious herbage ever cropped by quadrupeds. It is much heavier, contains more saccharine in connection with more farinaceous and strength-giving aliment than any other grass known. At least such is my experience, and that of all other men who have had occasion to test its virtues and time to pronounce upon its merits. I give it the very first rank among all sorts of hay, believing it to be superior to clover, timothy, alfalfa, or all three together. Although I have never been able to observe any seed upon this grass, it seems to combine the qualities of grain and hay in the greatest perfection. Horses will live and do well upon it, provided they can obtain it regularly, while doing active cavalry duty, without other feed; but they must have it, as stated, regularly in abundance, and be permitted to crop it from native pastures. It bears no flower, exhibits no seed, but seems to reproduce itself from the roots by the shooting up of young, green and vigorous spires, which are at first inclosed within the sheaths of their old and dried-up predecessors, and by their growth split and cast them to earth, and occupy their places.

I am not sufficiently versed in botany to give my readers a more elaborate and scientific account of this superb grass, and if I were, it would not be my desire in a work of this character to inflict upon the general reader a series of double-barreled Greek terms which not one in a thousand could understand, and, understanding, would care about. The object is to convey some tolerable idea of that great aliment for herbivorous animals upon which the Apache races rely for the support of their horses, and which, by its singularly strength-giving properties, is capable of enabling their ponies to perform extraordinary feats of endurance.

From Dragoon Pass eastward the whole of the vast region inhabited by the Apaches is covered with this species of grass, which is more or less thick and nourishing, according to circumstances, but always in sufficient abundance to afford all the nutriment required. It is this plentiful distribution of the most strengthening grass in the world which enables the Apache to maintain his herds, make his extraordinary marches, and inflict wide-spread depredations.

A knowledge of signals, whether smokes or fires, or bent twigs and pressed grass, or of turned stones, together with the localities of water sources, the different passes through the sierras, the nature and quantity of the fodder to be had in certain districts, the capacity to distinguish tracks and state with certainty by whom made, and how long before, are absolutely indispensable to a successful campaign among those savages. To the acquirement of all these points I devoted much attention, and, without egotism, can claim such success as to privilege me in giving the result of my researches as worthy of confidence.

Smokes are of various kinds, each one significant of a particular object. A sudden puff, rising into a graceful column from the mountain heights, and almost as suddenly losing its identity by dissolving into the rarified atmosphere of those heights, simply indicates the presence of a strange party upon the plains below; but if those columns are rapidly multiplied and repeated, they serve as a warning to show that the travelers are well armed and numerous. If a steady smoke is maintained for some time, the object is to collect the scattered bands of savages at some designated point, with hostile intention, should it be practicable. These signals are made at night, in the same order, by the use of fires, which

being kindled, are either alternately exposed and
shrouded from view, or suffered to burn steadily, as occasion may require. All travelers in Arizona and New
Mexico are acquainted with the fact that if the grass be
pressed down in a certain direction during the dry season, it will retain the impress and grow daily more and
more yellow until the rainy season imparts new life and
restores it to pristine vigor and greenness. The Apaches
are so well versed in this style of signalizing that they
can tell you, by the appearance of the grass, how many
days have elapsed since it was trodden upon, whether
the party consisted of Indians or whites, about how many
there were, and, if Indians, to what particular tribe they
belonged. In order to define these points, they select
some well marked footstep, for which they hunt with
avidity, and gently pressing down the trodden grass so
as not to disturb surrounding herbage, they very carefully examine the print. The difference between the
crushing heel of a white man's boot or shoe, and the
light imprint left by an Indian's moccasin, is too striking to admit of doubt, while the different styles of moccasin used by the several divisions of the Apache tribes
are well known among them. The time which has
elapsed since the passage of the party is determined by
discoloration of the herbage and breaking off a few spires
to ascertain the approximate amount of natural juice still
left in the crushed grass. Numbers are arrived at by
the multiplicity of tracks. Signalizing by bent twigs,
broken branches and blazed trees, is too well known to
deserve special mention here. In these respects the
Apaches do not differ from other Indian tribes of this
continent.

If a mounted party has been on the road, their numbers, quality and time of passage are determined with

exactitude, as well as the precise sex and species of the animals ridden. The moment such a trail is fallen in with, they follow it eagerly, having nothing else to do, until they find some of the dung, which is immediately broken open, and from its moisture and other properties, the date of travel is arrived at nearly to a certainty, while the constituents almost invariably declare the region from which the party came. This last point depends upon whether the dung is composed of grama grass, barley and grass, corn, bunch grass, buffalo grass, sacaton, or any of the well known grasses of the country, for as they are chiefly produced in different districts, the fact of their presence in the dung shows precisely from what district the animal last came. When barley is discovered the Apaches have reason to believe that Americans have been over the route, and when maize is found they feel confident that the travelers were either Mexicans or people from that country. These remarks apply only to unshod horses, for iron prints speak for themselves. The difference in sexes is easily told by the attitude each assumes while urinating—the male stretching himself and ejecting his urine forward of his hind feet, while the female ejects to the rear of the hind prints.

Signalizing by stones is much more difficult to comprehend, and very few have ever arrived at even a distant knowledge of this art. Perhaps the most skillful detecter of such notices was "Kit Carson," as he was generally termed, and it would be very strange if he were not. No man in the United States has had greater experience, and no man possessed a keener natural instinct to detect Indian signs. I must confess my inability to do this part of the subject full justice, but will give the result of my observations. The traveler is often surprised to notice a number of stones on one side the road, lying apparently without any set arrangement, when he can observe no others within reach of his eye. A careful observation will convince him that they never *grew* in that region, but were brought from some considerable distance. This translation was certainly neither the work of Americans nor Mexicans, but of Indians, and evidently for some fixed purpose. A closer examination will show that these stones are regularly arranged, and that the majority point to some special point of the compass, while the number of those who planted them is designated by some concerted placement of each stone. For instance, no one need be told that in wild countries like Arizona, where deluges of rain pour down during the rainy season, the heaviest side of a stone will, in course of time, find itself underneath, and when this order is reversed, especially under the circumstances above cited, there is good reason to believe that it has been purposely done. This belief becomes certainty on seeing that each one of the group, or parcel, is precisely the same way. Besides, a stone which has been long lying on one particular side, soon contracts a quantity of clay or soil on its nether surface, while its upper one has been washed clean. If it be turned over, or partly over, the difference becomes easily discoverable. If one stone be placed on end so as to rest against another, it means that the party so placing it require aid and assistance. If turned completely over, it indicates disaster during some raid; and if only partly turned, that the expedition has been a failure. Success is noted by the stones being left in a natural position, heaviest side down, but so arranged as to be nearly in line. I am not sufficiently expert in this style of signalizing to give any further explanations, and I doubt if any one but "Kit Carson" was capable of fully decyphering this kind of Apache warnings.

These remarks have seemed necessary to the full development of the Apache character, as they, in some sort, serve to account for the clear and explicit understanding which undoubtedly exists among the many detached fragments of that race. Without some such codes of signals, they would be comparatively incapable of the terrible devastations and outrages they have perpetrated. Neither could they collect their scattered bands for any occasion requiring numbers without great loss of time and trouble. Having no reliable means for subsistence beyond what they obtain by marauding excursions, they are wholly incapable of maintaining any considerable number for more than a few days at a time, and they, therefore, depend upon their signals as the means of warning each other, and consolidating whenever the "game is worth the candle." The Apaches brought their system to wonderful perfection, and from this arises their capacity to act conjointly with celerity, vigor and effect, although the operating bodies may not actually meet until just before the time for action arrives. It is to this system that the Apache bands of fives, tens and twenties, separated from each other by twenty, thirty and forty miles, feel that they are operating always in concert, and manage to maintain a rigid police espionage over the vast region they inhabit.

When will the white man ever become wise, and, instead of treating the Indian with scornful indifference, give him credit for his intelligence, his quick and remarkable instincts, his powers of reflection and organization, and his inveterate opposition to all innovation? We have been too much in the habit of treating them with contempt, and underrating our savage enemies. This has been a serious blunder, the rock upon which so many millions of money and so many precious lives have

been wrecked. Is it not time to accept a new policy in
their regard? Will civilized people never learn that they
are quite as obtuse to comprehend real Indian nature as
the Indians to understand their civilization? Can they
not see that their hauteur, self-sufficiency and overbear-
ing conceit, are quite as reprehensible as the Indian's ignorance, distrust and superstition? The savage is par-
donable in his mental darkness, but the white man is
inexcusable in his light. Semi-idiotic people believe
that the Apache of to-day is like his ancestor of half a
century ago; that he fights with bow and stone-headed
arrows; that he has learned nothing from experience;
that he is a biped brute who is as easily killed as a wolf;
that he possesses no power of organization, combination,
judgment, skill, strategy or reflection; but the truth is,
that he possesses them all in an eminent degree. When
the popular mind shall have been disabused of such
heresy, it will have accomplished the first step toward
that long-wanted result, the domination and consequent
pacification of the Indian tribes of the North American
continent.

Let it be well understood that the Apache of to-day is
armed with the best kind of rifle, with Colt's six-shooters
and with knives, and that, in addition to these, he is
never without his silent, death-dealing bow and quiver
full of iron-headed arrows. While adopting our improved weapons, whenever occasion offers, they never
abandon those of their sires. The reasons for this are
fourfold: First, the bow and arrow in the hands of skillful warriors proves very deadly; it makes no noise, and
for night attacks or the taking off of sentinels, is far superior to the gun. Secondly, it is the best weapon that
can be used in the chase, or, more properly, on the
hunt, as half a dozen animals may be slain in a herd be-

fore their comrades are made aware of the fact. Thirdly, they are so light that they can be worn without the slightest sense of encumbrance. Fourthly, they can always be relied on, at close quarters, when other weapons fail, or ammunition, of which they possess limited supplies, gives out. It is, therefore, not strange that the Apache will invariably add his bow and arrows to his personal armament, although he may be the owner of a Spencer rifle and a couple of Colt's revolvers, with ammunition to suit. Whenever they design entering one of our military camps they invariably conceal, at some distance, firearms; so that they may appear innocent of designed enmity or their possession, but should occasion serve, they quickly manage to re-possess themselves of all their weapons.

Let it also be understood that the Apache has as perfect a knowledge of the assimilation of colors as the most experienced Paris *modiste*. By means of his acumen in this respect, he can conceal his swart body amidst the green grass, behind brown shrubs, or gray rocks, with so much address and judgment that any but the experienced would pass him by without detection at the distance of three or four yards. Sometimes they will envelop themselves in a gray blanket, and by an artistic sprinkling of earth, will so resemble a granite boulder as to be passed within near range without suspicion. At others, they will cover their persons with freshly gathered grass, and lying prostrate, appear as a natural portion of the field. Again, they will plant themselves among the yuccas, and so closely imitate the appearance of that tree as to pass for one of its species. These exact imitations of natural objects which are continually present to the traveler, tend to disarm suspicion; yet, I would not advise the wayfarer to examine each suspected

9*

bush, tree or rock, but simply to maintain a cautious system of marching—never, for a moment, relaxing his watchfulness, and invariably keeping his weapons ready for immediate use. Whenever these precautions are observed, the Apache is slow to attack, even at monstrous odds in his favor.

The selfishness inherent in the human race crops out with intensity among these Indians; yet their hatred and animosity toward all other races is even stronger, and is the matrix of the cohesive principle by which they have been kept together, and which has proved their safeguard against all outside corrupting influences. Under no circumstances will one Apache risk anything for another, unless it is manifestly to his interest. The most refined civilization could not advance him in this respect. He appreciates self just as well as those who have been the habitues of Wall street, the Stock Exchange, or the Parisian Boulevards. If the height of good breeding consists in being perfectly impassive, and disregardful of the events which attend on fellow men, then the Apache has arrived at the apex of good breeding, and lordlings may take lessons from his school of manners. Their great natural intelligence makes them comprehend that "in union is strength," and their desire to exhibit that strength is ever prevalent. They delight to manifest their numerical power, for the reason that opportunities for such exhibition are very rare, and whatever is of common occurrence ceases to interest; and also because such combinations tend to inflict additional dread upon their enemies, and the inculcation of this sentiment is a chief cause of security to each Apache.

In all our dealings with Indian tribes we have quite underrated their abilities, and in this we have demonstrated our own stupidity. The vanity and self-conceit of civilized and educated men are never more stilted than when brought in contact with savage races. Such persons are prone to address the Indian with a smirk or patronizing air which is very offensive, and would never be used toward an equal. No allowance is made for the fact that the proud savage does consider himself not only the equal, but the superior of his white brother. It seems never to have been understood that considerable deference should be paid to his very ignorance, because that ignorance is his sufficient excuse for crediting himself with superior intelligence. The conceit of the educated white man is fully equaled by that of the savage, and the lower he is in the scale of mental ability the greater will be his pretension to superiority. The fact that a wise man knows himself to be ignorant, while an ignorant man believes himself to be wise, is fully exemplified in our intercourse with the Apaches, but it is a question in my mind whether the Apaches have not had the best end of the argument, when the character and acts of their agents, and others, who have been appointed to treat with them, are known and considered.

To arrive at a successful arrangement with these Indians they must be approached in the first place as equals. This will flatter their inordinate vanity, and minister to their excessive selfishness. After a few interviews for the purpose of establishing amicable understanding, the agent, or treating party, or traveler, should carefully introduce some cheap natural effects, the employment of which would be ridiculed in ordinary civilized life, but present astounding revelations to the wild Indian. The use of a double convexed lens, as a magnifier, or as a burning-glass; the employment of a strong field glass; exhibiting the powers and qualities of a strong magnet; showing the wonders of the magic lantern, and other

like simple demonstrations, will invariably impress them
with something of respect and regard toward the oper-
ator, provided he is exceedingly careful in his first attempts not to alarm their pride and suspicion by any
boastful or vain expression or demeanor. These things
should be done as if with the intention of asking from
them an exhibition of their skill in return for your efforts
to please. They should never be permitted to infer that
they are the results of boastful superiority. In this manner a feeling of mutual regard can be engendered which
is the first step toward the establishment of durable
amity. They should be asked to exhibit their address
in shooting, riding, hunting and other pursuits of like
character, in which they are expert. The white man
should evince a desire to learn as well as teach; but so
long as we continue to approach them with hauteur and
with patronizing airs, they will resist our efforts and employ all their cunning to overreach and leave us worse
off than ever. As they cannot rise to our level we must
descend to theirs to understand and appreciate their true
character.

But even under the most favorable circumstances, and
with the employment of every resource within our power,
only very meagre and unsatisfactory results can be obtained. The labors and experiences of two hundred
and fifty years have failed utterly to create any favorable impression upon our Indian races, with the exception of the Choctaws and Cherokees, who were actually
hemmed in by intelligent people, and had civilization
forced upon them to some extent, and scarcely one of
whom is to-day of pure Indian blood. I consider the
idea of emancipating our savage tribes from the thraldom
of their ignorance and perverse traditional hatred of the
whites as wholly utopian. Of all the tribes on our con-

tinent the Apache is the most impracticable. Their enmity toward mankind, and distrust of every word and act are ineradicable. As their whole system of life and training is to plunder, murder and deceive, they cannot comprehend opposite attributes in others. He whom we would denounce as the greatest scoundrel they regard with special esteem and honor. With no people are they on amicable terms, and never hesitate to rob from each other when it can be done with impunity. There is no sympathy among them; the quality is unknown. Should an Apache's horse escape and run past another of the tribe, close enough to catch the animal by simply reaching forth his hand, that hand will never be stretched for the purpose; but the owner must do the business for himself, if his squaw is not at hand to do it for him. Nevertheless, after a successful raid, in which they have captured many animals, and having selected the best for riding, retire to some remote fastness to feed upon the remainder so long as they last, they will freely share to the very last bit with any and all comers of their race. This seeming hospitality is, however, not the result of kindliness, but the prompting of a selfish policy, for they are aware it assists to unite them in one common band of plundering brotherhood, and to preserve those relations toward each other without which they cannot operate advantageously. Frequently when one has received a small present of tobacco, or some such article, he will divide it among all on the spot, simply because he knows that the same thing will be done to him by the others whenever occasion serves, and not from any sense of generosity, as may be seen from the fact that, if one only be present to receive a gift, he immediately hides it on some part of his person and complacently ignores its existence to all who may arrive after the event.

There is nothing of which they are so careful as ammunition. Always difficult to obtain, and indispensable in their engagements at the present day, every grain of powder is preserved with extraordinary solicitude. In their hunting excursions they never fire a gun or pistol if it can possibly be avoided, but depend entirely upon their skill in approaching the game near enough to use the bow and arrow. At an early period they understood fully the value of double sights on any weapon carrying a ball, and the old-fashioned single-barreled shot guns, a few of them possessed at that time, were invariably sawed into with a knife to the depth of one-eighth of an inch, a few inches from the breech, when the thin sliver was raised above the barrel and carefully notched to form the rear sight.

At the present writing they have a considerable number of Henry's, Spencer's and Sharp's rifles, with some of the fixed ammunition required by the two first mentioned. Every cartridge they get hold of is preserved with solicitude until it can be expended with decided advantage. These weapons have been obtained gradually by the robbery and murder of their former owners, and not a few have been bought in the frontier Mexican towns, where they were sold by immigrants to obtain food and other supplies while crossing the continent. The hostilities which raged along the northern portion of Mexico for four years also contributed to place within their reach many weapons of fair quality. That they know how to handle these arms with deadly skill has been attested on too many occasions to need particular mention in these pages. From Gila Bend to Paso del Norte is little better than a continuous grave-yard, grizzly with the rude monuments of Apache bloodthirstiness. Town after town, once containing several thousand inhabitants and even now showing the remains of fine brick churches; rancho after rancho, formerly stocked with hundreds of thousands of cattle and horses, and teeming with wealth; village after village all through the northern parts of Sonora and Chihuahua, the whole embraced in a belt five hundred miles long and from thirty to eighty wide, now exhibit one wide-spread and tenantless desolation, the work of the Apache Indians. For ninety consecutive years this ruthless warfare has been carried on against a timid, nearly unarmed and demoralized people. Thousands of lives have been destroyed, and thousands of women and children carried into a captivity worse than death, during that period; and yet the deadly, destructive and unholy work goes on with unrelaxed vigor. It is both sickening and maddening to ride through that region and witness the far-reaching ruin, to listen to the dreadful tales of unequaled atrocities, and note the despairing terror which the bare mention of the Apaches conjures up to their diseased and horrified imaginations.

Coming to the American side, we enter upon another field of destruction, but in nowise comparable to that which Mexico exhibits. The great majority of our sacrifices of life and property have been the results of want of caution, of fool-hardiness and too great self-reliance. As already stated, we are too prone to underrate the Apache in all respects, and by so doing set a trap for our own feet. But even on our side the border the traveler will encounter many fine farms abandoned, their buildings in ruins, and the products of years of industry wrested from their grasp. On every road little mounds of stones by the way-side, some with a rude cross, and others with a modest head-board, speak in silent but terribly suggestive language of the Apaches' bloody work. Scattered all over Arizona are mines of wondrous wealth utterly inapplicable to the uses of mankind so long as that tribe remains unsubdued and unconquered. Communication between any two places, if not more than a mile apart, cannot be ventured upon without absolute danger. No man can trust his animals to graze three hundred yards from the town walls without incurring the risk of losing them at high noon. Mexican women and children have been carried off during the day time, while washing in the stream, within four hundred yards of their own doors and in plain sight of their townspeople. These atrocities, and others unnecessary to mention, go on year after year; and thus far no successful result has been obtained, as might have been expected, from the puerile and ill-directed efforts made to suppress them. Wherever an intelligent and well conceived movement has been concerted within the power of the limited force in Arizona, official stupidity has invariably disconcerted and paralyzed its efficiency. This is no vague and untenable charge, as will be seen in succeeding pages. There is but one opinion on the subject throughout all Arizona. The correspondence between Gov. McCormick and Gen. McDowell, some of which has been made public through the daily papers, is in itself sufficient to establish the assertion, and no doubt led to the removal of Gen. McDowell from the field of his operations. Personally, my regard for that officer as a gentleman is very sincere: but it may be doubted if the army register contains the name of another so wholly, so utterly incapable of comprehending Indian nature and the requirements of Indian warfare. As a cabinet officer he may have few equals in the service; but for Indian campaigning, it would be difficult to select another so little fitted.

CHAPTER XVI.

Condition of New Mexico and Arizona.—Active Campaign.—Californian Soldiers.
—Bosque Redondo.—More Intimate Relations with Apaches.—Site of Fort
Sumner. — Scarcity of Wood. — Climate. — Arrival of Apache Prisoners of
War.—Dog Cañon.—Apache Embassy.—Mr. Labadie.—Placed in Charge of
the Apaches.--Form a Council.—Hunting Excursion with Apaches.—Their
Mode of Killing Antelopes. — Learn more of Indian Character. — Obtain a
Greater Share of their Confidence.

So soon as Sibley's command had been driven from
Arizona and New Mexico, Gen. Carleton devoted his attention to protect from Indian outrage the inhabitants
of those Territories. Previous to our arrival no one had
the hardihood to venture outside the skirts of the towns
and villages, unless accompanied by a force respectable
in numbers, if in nothing else. The whole country was
a theater of desolation. What the Confederates failed
to appropriate, the Apaches destroyed. The inhabitants
were literally starving and utterly demoralized. Instead
of being able to furnish us supplies, we were compelled
to afford them occasional assistance. This state of affairs
had been foreseen by Carleton, to some extent, and we
were consequently in a condition to be independent until such protection could be granted as would induce the
resident population to re-commence farming operations.

Soon after our advent, Gen. Canby was recalled, and
the chief command invested in Carleton. From that time
a series of active and energetic campaigns against the
Apache and Navajo tribes was inaugurated, which had
the effect of completely humiliating those leading na-

tions and re-establishing the peace, security and produc-
tiveness of the two Territories. After much deliberation, and years subsequent to the incidents narrated, it
is my conviction that the many signal triumphs obtained
over the Apaches and Navajoes could only have been
achieved by Californian soldiers, who seem gifted in a
special manner with the address and ability to contend
advantageously against them. This assertion has been
so frequently admitted by the resident populations that
it is not deemed necessary to dilate further than mention
the names of such men as Roberts, McCleave, Fritz,
Shirland, the two Greens, Tidball, Whitlock, Thayer,
Pettis, and many others, who rendered good service and
compassed the security and peace of the two Territories
during their term of service. With the retirement of
the Californian troops another series of robberies and
massacres was instituted by the Indians, and maintained
until the present time without apparent hindrance.

In the winter of 1862–3, I was ordered from Albu-
querque to join Capt. Updegraff, commanding company
A, Fifth United States Infantry, and to proceed to the
Bosque Redondo, somewhere on the Pecos river, over
two hundred and fifty miles to the eastward—outside the
bounds of all human habitation, and ninety miles from
the nearest civilized inhabitant. Capt. Updegraff was
instructed to examine the Bosque Redondo, and select
a site for the construction of a large fort, with the view
of establishing an extensive Indian Reservation in its immediate neighborhood. This sort of exile was anything
but displeasing to me, for I much preferred being from
under the nose of a commanding General, whose unscru-
pulous ambition and exclusive selfishness had passed into
a proverb, despite his acknowledged ability and apparent zeal. But it is not my task to discuss matters of

this nature; and the reference is only to show by what means I again became intimately acquainted with renowned Apaches and acquired their language, together with a knowledge of those traits, customs and organizations, which has enabled me to write with confidence and understanding upon these and kindred points.

Capt. Updegraff was ordered to make a reconnoissance of the Bosque Redondo, and select a site for the future post and reservation; such selection to be approved or disapproved by a board of engineers, specially ordered to make a thorough survey. On arriving at the Bosque, the Captain ordered me to go ahead and select a camp ground; and in obedience thereto, I took ten men and reconnoitered the river and its banks for several miles, finally fixing on a spot formerly used as a sheep corral by Mexicans during a time of peace, many years before. This spot was chosen for the three fold reasons that it was near water, which was approachable through an open space in the woods; that it was covered with excellent pasture; and that it contained the stakes and timbers of the old corral, which were dry and made excellent fire-wood. This selection was approved, and the next day a further reconnoissance was made to fix a permanent site for the fort. This ended in confirming the first choice, and here the most beautiful Indian fort in the United States was ultimately constructed, the board of engineers having indorsed the spot as being the most eligible on the river. This fort was built almost wholly by Californian soldiers, and is beyond comparison the handsomest and most picturesque in the Union. Nevertheless, it was easy to comprehend that, should any great number of persons be assembled thereat, a scarcity of wood must ultimately occur, and as Fahrenheit's thermometer occasionally falls to eight and ten degrees be-

low zero in the winter time, wood was an object of prime
necessity.   The alamo furnished the whole supply of this
material, and the extent of the Bosque Redondo, or Round
Woods, was only sixteen miles long by half a mile wide
in the widest place, and for several miles affording only
a few scattered trees, which were by no means thick even
in the densest portions.   When we arrived the weather
was very cold, with eight inches of snow upon the ground,
and the first duty was to "hut in" the command.   This
was accomplished in a short time, after which rude but
serviceable stables were put up, a hospital, quartermas-
ter's and commissary's stores built, and the other requisite shelters erected.

Scarcely had these precautions been taken before we
received an invoice of five hundred Apaches, including
the leading warriors of the Mescalero tribe, their women
and children, and a few of the chief Jicarillas.   These
were the savages who had so long held Dog Cañon, and
defied all attempts to force a passage through that renowned stronghold.   Capt. McCleave, of company A,
First Cavalry California Volunteers, determined to
"give it a try;" and having obtained permission, soon
succeeded in routing and completely demoralizing the
savages, who fled to Fort Stanton for shelter and protection, closely pursued by McCleave and his company—so
closely, in fact, that the Apaches saw no other means of
escape from certain destruction except to deliver themselves up as prisoners of war to Col. "Kit" Carson, at
that time in charge of Fort Stanton, with four companies of infantry and one of native New Mexican cavalry.
Carson informed McCleave that the Indians had placed
themselves under his protection, subject to the disposal
of the General commanding; upon which McCleave withdrew, not over-pleased with the result, although he had
whipped them handsomely in Dog Cañon.

Soon afterward five of the leading warriors proceeded to Santa Fé, under an armed escort, to confer with the General, who exacted that they should submit to being placed upon the reservation of the Bosque Redondo. The answer of their chief spokesman, named Cadete by the Mexicans, but whose Apache appellation is Gian-nah-tah, or "Always Ready," is indicative of the nature and character of his tribe. Having listened to the General's final determination, he answered and said:

"You are stronger than we. We have fought you so long as we had rifles and powder; but your arms are better than ours. Give us like weapons and turn us loose, we will fight you again; but we are worn-out; we have no more heart; we have no provisions, no means to live; your troops are everywhere; our springs and water holes are either occupied or overlooked by your young men. You have driven us from our last and best stronghold, and we have no more heart. Do with us as may seem good to you, but do not forget we are men and braves."

They were remanded back to Fort Stanton, and from thence sent to the Bosque Redondo, since called Fort Sumner, where they arrived after a long and painful march of one hundred and thirty miles, with short rations and much suffering. They were immediately turned over to my charge by Capt. Updegraff, although the Indian agent, Mr. Labadie, was with them, and from that moment I laid the foundation of that confidence and respect which was never alienated, and which enabled me to perfect a knowledge of their character far greater than ever arrived at by the experiences of any other white man.

In a short time their number was increased to seven hundred, and subsequently to nearly fifteen hundred.

By their own request I was authorized to take exclusive charge of their affairs. In so far as military movements were concerned, they appointed me their Nantanh-in-jah, or Chief Captain, and submitted to my arbitration all their social and tribal difficulties, my decision being final. I soon formed a council of their principal men, and lost no opportunity to make myself acquainted with their views, manners, habits, customs, religious and social observances, language, and, in fine, whatever tended to unfold their characteristics. My council consisted of Gian-nah-tah, or Always Ready; Na-tanh, or the Corn Flower; Too-ah-yay-say, or the Strong Swimmer; Natch-in-ilk-kisn, or the Colored Beads; Nah-kah-yen, or the Keen Sighted; Para-dee-ah-tran, or the Contented; Klosen, or the Hair Rope; and a Jicarilla man of note, whose Indian name has escaped my memory, but the meaning of which was the Kicking Horse. The renown of these warriors was too well established in the tribe to admit of doubt, and, whatever they said, was submitted to without question. How this control was obtained over these grim savages is worthy of mention, as indicative of their profound respect for personal adventure.

Five days after their arrival in camp, Mr. Labadie came to me and said: "These Indians are in great destitution. They consumed their rations two days ago, and have nothing to eat. There are many women and children among them, and two days more must elapse before rations are again distributed. Their warriors have asked that they be allowed to go hunting. The plains close by are filled with herds of antelopes, which may easily be taken. I have been to Capt. Updegraff, but he will not hearken to the proposition; please try and see what you can do, for otherwise they may attempt to escape from the Reservation."

I immediately sought the post commander and said to him: "Captain, the Apaches have asked your permission to go on a grand hunt, which you have refused; allow me to say that they are starving, that you have their wives and children as hostages for their return, and if you will recall your determination, I will volunteer to go out with them and be answerable for their safe return within forty-eight hours."

Capt. Updegraff peered at me through his black, intelligent eyes for a moment or two, and then replied: "Very well, Captain; if you choose to trust yourself with these unmitigated red devils and make yourself responsible for their return, and give me official assurance in writing, that it is indispensably necessary, you can start with them to-morrow morning at daylight; but do not remain away longer than forty-eight hours."

This resolution was forthwith conveyed to Mr. Labadie, who spread it among the Apaches, taking care to inform them by what means the favor had been granted.

Next morning, at seven o'clock, we sallied forth, the party numbering one hundred and ten Apaches, ninety-five of whom were warriors and fifteen women—the only person present, not an Apache, being myself. I had four Colt's six-shooters, two in my saddle-holsters and two in my belt, with a large bowie knife, but my horse was infinitely superior to anything they could boast in that line. They were all armed with bows and arrows—all who possessed rifles or pistols having left them in camp.

In the field, whether for warlike purposes or for hunting, the Apache is very reticent, and by no means given to talking. Conversation is only indulged while in camp, and amidst friends during a period of apparent security. But upon this occasion they gave full vent to their joy

and satisfaction, and offered me a number of little atten-
tions. We rode on for five miles until the top of a hill
was reached, from which we could obtain a fair view of
the surrounding country. Here a short consultation was
held among them, during which I smoked a cigarito,
giving several to those close in my neighborhood. A
certain direction having been selected as the field of operations, we again started, and after having progressed
about two miles, the band formed into two lines, the
first being about six hundred yards in advance of the
second. These two bodies then prolonged their lines so
that no two individuals were nearer than forty or fifty
yards, which stretched each line to the distance of two
thousand five hundred or three thousand yards, sweeping a large surface of territory, and yet close enough
to prevent the escape of an antelope through the two
human barriers, or between the huntsmen in each. In
this formation we progressed until a herd was seen about
half a mile in advance. Instantly the two wings of the
first line rode forward at full speed, and succeeded in
cutting off the retreat of the doomed animals by com-
pleting a circle; at the same time the gaps were rapidly
closed up, and the circle narrowed with amazing celerity
and dexterity. The terror-stricken antelopes turned to
flee, but on every side they met an inexorable and keenly
watchful enemy. Bewildered, panting with agony and
fear, inclosed on all sides, they soon became incapable
of continuing the unequal contest, and were killed with
perfect ease. The few which contrived to break through
the first line were sure to meet death at the hands of the
second. Not one in fifty escaped, and their preservation
seemed almost miraculous. In this way we managed to
destroy eighty-seven antelopes on that expedition, and
it was my good fortune to kill five, being two more than

were bagged by any other hunter on the field. These I gave the Apaches, reserving only a hind quarter for myself. Within thirty-six hours I had the satisfaction of reporting to Capt. Updegraff, and relating to him the complete success of our hunting excursion, at which he was so well pleased that I never afterward met any objection from that gallant and good officer when a like expedition was to be undertaken.

After this event the Apaches seemingly gave me more of their confidence than ever, but I was still far from the point ultimately reached, although I then thought I had achieved it nearly all. This fact should warn us never to arrive at hasty conclusions, especially when dealing with a people which have studiously endeavored to mislead and cozen all with whom they come in contact. I had rendered them an important service; they were grateful to me for such aid. I had trusted myself unreservedly among them, the avowed enemies of my race, and they respected me for my confidence. But I was still a white man, and they were still Apaches. While professing a certain degree of personal regard, they not only refused to admit me within the sanctum of their trust, but some of them even began to look upon me as endeavoring to gain their confidence for the purpose of betraying and using it against them should opportunity serve. Fortunately, these suspicions were allayed in the course of time, and after a year and a half of constant intercourse, during which period they and several thousand Navajoes — a branch of the great Apache race — were under my personal supervision, I was admitted to a tolerably fair knowledge of the points under consideration in this work.

10

CHAPTER XVII.

THE successful result of our hunting expedition put the Apaches in high spirits. They understood that they were not to be treated as prisoners of war, in the strict sense of that phrase, but were to be allowed the privilege of wide and extensive hunting grounds, teeming with game; were not interrupted in their social relations, only in so far as a rigid police of their camp was required to prevent disease, and could live almost as unrestrained as in their native wilds, provided they were all present or duly accounted for at the stated roll-call, which took place every evening at sunset.

Feeling that many of these privileges had been obtained through my instrumentality, they sought my tent daily in great numbers, and seemed inclined to regard me as their protector and best friend. As it was well known that they were in constant correspondence with those of their race who had not surrendered, and as the members of my company were always detailed for military couriers between Fort Sumner, Fort Mason, Fort Stanton, Santa Fé, and other points, I judged it prudent to gain the confidence and good will of the Apaches to the greatest possible extent, knowing that their kindness for me would extend itself to the men of my company, and this belief was afterward fully justified when roving parties of Indians happened to meet my couriers. This occurred on several occasions, when the savages were so numerous as to make resistence out of the question. They would ride up, examine the soldier attentively, find out that he belonged to my company at Fort Sumner, bid him good-by in their best manner, and ride off, without attempting to do him harm or deprive him of horse or weapons.

About six months afterward, Gian-nah-tah, commonly called Cadete by the Mexicans, told me confidentially that neither myself nor my men would be harmed by the Apaches so long as we remained in the country, as those in camp felt that they were greatly indebted to us for many little kindnesses. This promise was carried out to the letter, and convinced me that gratitude for services rendered is by no means a strange emotion in the Apache character. I, however, doubt much if any other white man ever had the opportunity, or, having it, ever did take so much pains to win the respect and confidence of those strange and suspicious people. It will be observed that I use the word "those" in the foregoing sentence, instead of "that," and simply because each is so perfectly independent in all his belongings from all other tribes that they cannot be justly classified as a conjoint or co-operative race except for purposes of plunder and mutual defense when attacked. When summoned to prosecute hostilities, unless against some marauding party of Comanches, Navajoes, or other tribes, each individual is free to join or not as he may see fit. Should the enterprise promise plenty of plunder with but little personal risk, no trouble will be found to engage all the

warriors needed; but, no matter how greatly superior
their force may be, no precaution for safety is neglected, and no means ignored which promises to secure
their object without loss of life. It is only when prompt
and immediate action is necessary that they resign their
personal independence wholly to the guidance of some
well known and selected warrior, but the occasion passed,
that same leader falls back to his original individuality,
the same as the President of the United States resumes
his plain citizenship after the expiration of his term of
office.

About this time Gen. Carleton instituted rigid inquiries
as to the quantity of provision on hand in the subsistence departments of New Mexico and Arizona, and from
the reports made to him, came to the conclusion that
there would be somewhat of a scarcity before supplies
could be received. Nearly three thousand Californian
troops had been thrown into the two Territories, nine
thousand Indians — Apaches and Navajoes — had suc-
cumbed to our arms, the country had been overrun and
devastated by Sibley's column from Texas, no industrial
nor agricultural pursuits had been re-commenced, and
absolute want stared everybody in the face. Orders
were immediately given to shorten the rations, and that
for the Indians on the Fort Sumner Reservation were to
be cut down largely. The order was issued to Capt.
Updegraff, Fifth United States Infantry, commanding
Fort Sumner, to take effect at a fixed date. Capt. Updegraff notified Mr. Labadie, the Indian Agent, of the
order; Mr. Labadie communicated the fact to me, and I
immediately waited upon Capt. Updegraff and requested
him to communicate with the General commanding, and
state the following arguments: There were nearly nine
thousand Indians on that one Reservation. They had

been subdued by the Californian troops after great exertions, and the Territory rendered comparatively free from those terrible Indian raids that for so many years had laid it waste from one end to the other; that so long as those raids continued the industry of the people would be suppressed and crushed out, and that the best guaranty which could be given the inhabitants would be to retain the savages on the Reservation. This could be done so long as they had sufficient to eat. There were large numbers of women and children who could neither hunt nor obtain their livelihoods by any means except through the Government rations, so long as they remained in semi-captivity; that the Reservation farm was not yet in a condition to yield the requisite support, and that if their rations were diminished, a spirit of intense dissatisfaction would display itself in the escape of thousands whom it would be impossible to restrain with our very limited force, and that the escaping parties would immediately betake themselves to plunder, assassination and destructive inroads. I, therefore, begged Capt. Updegraff to represent these and other cogent arguments to the General, with a view of having the full ration continued to the Indians.

These arguments had weight with the Post Commander, and were by him urged on the attention of the General, who immediately perceived their truthfulness, and ordered the full ration continued until such time as he could make personal investigation. Fortunately an opportunity soon occurred, and the General visited Fort Sumner with several officers and the Rt. Rev. Bishop Lamy, Bishop of New Mexico.

Next day Capt. Updegraff candidly informed the General that I had prompted his letter, and I was summoned to the interview which followed. After a careful inquiry

and examination of several days, Gen. Carleton arrived
at the same opinion with myself, and the full ration was
ordered to be given as before.   Six weeks subsequently
the several Commissaries in the two Territories made
official returns of their supplies, and it was found that
their former estimates were far short of the mark.   At
the same time subsistence stores began to arrive from the
East, and the new crops were being harvested, *in peace*,
for the first time for many years.   Upon these represen-
tations, orders were issued to restore full rations to all
the troops, and abundance once more gladdened our ta-
bles.   Whether right or wrong, the savages were taught
by Mr. Labadie to believe that I was the person whose
agency had preserved them from half rations, and the
reader can well suppose how much I rose in their esti-
mation.   I was appointed grand director of their camps,
with power to decide all differences and settle all quarrels between parties.   Every grievance, real or imagined,
was submitted for my jurisdiction; and, I am proud to
add, that my administration was regarded with affectionate reverence.   Those wild and untamed sons and
daughters of the forests, the plains and the mountains,
would throng my *casita* from reveille until tattoo, asking
a thousand questions and always receiving proper attention.   Among them was a Mexican, about forty years
old, who had been a captive to their "bow and spear"
for twenty odd years.   He was taken at the age of eleven
and did not obtain his release until he was past thirty-
three.   That man, Juan Cojo, spoke their language as
fluently as themselves, and had been engaged as interpreter.   Juan and I soon became good friends, although
I must confess that his Apache education had somewhat
unfitted him to be the most moral character of my acquaintance.   Nevertheless, his services were indispensa-

ble, and I induced Gen. Carleton to appropriate fifty dollars per month additional pay to Juan, to teach me the Apache language. The fellow worked faithfully with me for nearly three months, during which time I compiled the only vocabulary of the Apache language in existence, and forwarded the result of my labors to Gen. Carleton, with the view of having it published for general use at the different posts in New Mexico and Arizona. The General sent the manuscript to the Smithsonian Institution, and it was placed in the hands of Prof. George Gibbs for publication in an exhaustive work on Ethnology, to be issued under the auspices of the Institution. I have waited several years for its appearance, but have not yet seen anything of the kind. Perhaps it will some day come to light. In the meantime, I received from the Institution an acknowledgment of my labors, the chief credit being given to Gen. Carleton — probably because he was General, and I only a Captain, subject to his orders. Let that be as it may, I felt both pride and pleasure in acquiring a language never before spoken by a white man, and I took much pains to systematize it as far as practicable, or my abilities could go. In order to be certain about the reliability of my novel acquirement, I every day submitted what I had learned the day previous to the criticism of the leading warriors of the tribe. They expressed much delight at my desire to learn and communicate with them in their own tongue, and manifested zeal in putting me right on all occasions. Nothing was committed to final record until it had been fully tested four or five times, and I believe the work to be as nearly perfect as could be got up under the circumstances.

This zeal on my part enhanced the favorable opinion the Apaches already held toward me, and rendered them

unusually communicative. So soon as they found that
I was anxious to converse with them in their own language, and had labored to acquire it, their confidence
and regard increased in geometrical progression. It was
not unusual with them, when asking a favor, another
officer being present, to address me in Apache, and their
little secrets were never betrayed. The reader will have
no difficulty to comprehend how, under such circumstances, the writer should have gained an ascendancy
over this most untamable and intensely suspicious of all
our Indian tribes. It was not the work of a month nor
of a year, but the experience of several years, aided by
events which may never happen again. Many of them
had seen and known me while interpreter of the Boundary Commission under the Hon. John R. Bartlett.
Some of them were present and took part in that terrific
chase along the Jornada del Muerto, and they reminded
me of the event, after they became convinced that I was
their best friend and harbored no vindictive feelings
against the parties. While conversing on this matter
one day, a warrior led to me an old squaw, her two
daughters and one son, all grown up, the oldest being
about twenty-two, and informed me that they were the
wife and children of the man who led the chase against
me thirteen years before. I received them kindly, and
asked if they did not think it better for them that I
should be alive to do them kindness then, than to have
been murdered by their relatives in 1850. They replied
by saying, "Yes, much better," laughing and asking me
to give them some vermilion—a color very highly prized
by the Apaches.

On the Reservation were one or two who happened to
be at the Copper Mines at the time that Inez Gonzales
and the two Mexican boys were rescued, as related in

preceding chapters, but they never could be made to comprehend the justice of those rescues, until I asked them—"You took those people captive by force, did you not?"

"Yes; we took them because we were stronger and more expert than they."

"Well, I took them from you for the same reasons. We were stronger and more expert than you, and we deprived you of your spoil. Suppose you were to meet a small band of Comanches with two or three hundred horses which they had stolen from Mexican owners, and your party were the stronger of the two, would you not take their spoil?"

"Certainly, because they would do so to us under like circumstances."

"Very well; you would have taken two American lads and an American girl, if you had met them unprotected, I know, because you have done it; and we took not your people, but those you had reduced to captivity, and restored them to their relatives. We did not keep them for our servants and slaves; but, they being our friends, we released them from your grasp when we found them in distress. The same rule you apply to the Comanches and all other peoples we applied to you; were we not right?"

The justice and pertinence of these remarks were admitted with reluctance, for the untutored Apache mind, like that of what is called high civilization and refinement, is eminently selfish and obtuse to moral conviction. Extremes meet.

It was, nevertheless, pleasant to recall the many times I had escaped their well-laid plans to deprive me and my associates of life or property, and the as many occasions in which they had been foiled in their benevolent

10*

intentions. The sanguinary deaths of Mangas Colorado, of Cuchillo Negro, of Ponce, of Delgadito, of Amarillo, and other renowned warriors, were cited in proof of the futility of their efforts to combat successfully against the white men. Their then dependence, as prisoners of war, their defenseless condition on the Reservation, their rapidly decreasing numbers, their disintegrating forces, and other like examples, were also pointed out and emphasized, and had momentary effect; but the next day, after admitting the severe lessons of history, they would resume their hauteur and exclaim, "that if they possessed as good weapons as ours, they could whip us out of the country they claimed as exclusively their own."

The teachings of experience are lost upon the Apache. He believes himself the superior being, and frequent adversities are accounted for in so many and plausible ways that his self-love and inordinate vanity are always appeased. He has shown himself more than a match for other barbarous tribes, and for the semi-civilized natives of New Mexico and Arizona. He infers that because we inhabit the houses of the last mentioned, and consort with them freely, in the absence of other society, that we are of the same general stamp and character. He admits the superior gallantry and prowess of the American race, but attributes them to our confidence in the superiority of our weapons. The result is that he uses more precaution in approaching the American than the Mexican; but this renders his attacks more to be dreaded and guarded against, although he never loses sight of subtlety and careful consideration in all his movements, no matter against whom directed. This is a distinguishing feature of the Apache. If fifty of them were to approach a single armed traveler they would do so with caution.

Like all other savages they highly prize physical strength and personal courage, but are severe critics in reference to the latter quality. When Lord Cardigan led the famous charge of the six hundred at Balaklava, it was carefully observed by the French Marshal, Pelissier, who exclaimed: "*C'est beau, c'est grande, mais, c'est né pas de la guerre.*" In like manner, the Apache regards our reckless onsets as vain and foolish. He is in the habit of saying: "The Americans are brave, but they lack astuteness. They build a great fire which throws out so much heat that they cannot approach it to warm themselves, and when they hear a gun fired they are absurd enough to rush to the spot. But it is not so with us; we build small fires in secluded nooks which cannot be seen by persons unless close by, and we gather near to them so as to obtain the warmth, and when we hear a gun fired we get away as soon as possible to some place from which we can ascertain the cause." They regard our daring as folly, and think "discretion the better part of valor." I am not so sure but that they are correct in this idea, as well as in several others.

There is nothing which an Apache holds in greater detestation than labor or work of any kind. All occupations unconnected with war or plunder are esteemed altogether beneath his dignity and attention. He will patiently and industriously manufacture his bow and quiver full of arrows, his spear and other arms; but he disdains all other kinds of employment. He will suffer the pangs of hunger before engaging in the chase, and absolutely refuses to cultivate the ground, even at the cost of simply sowing the seed; but he is ever ready to take the war-path, and will undergo indescribable sufferings and hardships for the hope of a little plunder.

Herein lies his credit and fame as a warrior; upon his
success in such undertakings rests his whole celebrity
and standing among the squaws whom he affects to treat
with indifference, but whose smiles and favors are, after
all, the greatest incentives to his acts. It is a grand
mistake to suppose that because the Apaches are seemingly indifferent to the condition of their women—that,
because like other savage tribes, they force the burden
of hard labor upon them, they are not elated by their
praises or humbled by their censures. On the contrary,
they are keenly alive to such sensations, and under the
mask of apparent indifference and assumed superiority
are quite as susceptible to the blandishments of the female sex, and to their opinions as regards merits, as the
most civilized and enlightened of their fellow countrymen—white Americans. After a successful raid they are
received with songs and rejoicings. Their deeds are rehearsed with many eulogiums, and they become great,
in their own estimations, for a while. But if unsuccess-
ful, they meet with jeers and insults. The women turn
away from them with assumed indifference and contempt. They are upbraided as cowards, or for want of
skill and tact, and are told that such men should not
have wives, because they do not know how to provide
for their wants. When so reproached, the warriors hang
their heads and offer no excuse for failure. To do so
would only subject them to more ridicule and objurga-
tion; but, Indian-like, they bide their time, in the hope
of finally making their peace by some successful raid.
When it is understood that the Apaches neither sow nor
plant, that they do not cultivate the ground, that they
manufacture nothing except their arms, that they depend altogether upon their wars for plunder as a means
of livelihood with the exceptional occasions of hunting,

that their women collect all the mescal for food and intoxicating drink, that they dig all the roots, gather all
the seeds, and make them into food, there will be no
difficulty in perceiving that the women are their real
supporters.

In some branches of the great tribe, residing on the
head-waters of the Gila, and among the Mescaleros and
Jicarillas, a very limited amount of planting is done, extending mainly to maize, pumpkins, squashes and beans.
Their great dependence is on mescal, the roots of which
are collected in quantity and placed in a large hole dug
in the ground and highly heated. The mescal roots,
being deposited, are then covered with green leaves and
grass, which is in turn overlaid with earth, and a steady
fire kept burning on top for a whole day. After allow-
ing the mass to remain in this impromptu oven for three
days, it is unearthed, pared and eaten with great zest.
It has a sweetish taste, not unlike the beet; but it is not
so tender, and possesses remarkable anti-scorbutic properties. In order to make an intoxicating beverage of
the mescal, the roasted root is macerated in a propor-
tionable quantity of water, which is allowed to stand
several days, when it ferments rapidly. The liquor is
boiled down and produces a strongly intoxicating fluid.

CHAPTER XVIII.

AMONG the Apaches under my charge were a number highly renowned as hunters. Those men seemed to possess a peculiar sagacity for this business, and whenever I indulged in a hunt I invariably took one or more of them with me. The Pecos for twenty-five miles about the Bosque Redondo is fringed for a half mile in depth, on both sides, with gigantic cotton-wood trees, or rather it was, for I have since learned that they were nearly all destroyed in furnishing fuel to the numerous body of Indians collected at Fort Sumner, and for the garrison at that place; and in consequence of the scarcity now existing, the fort and Reservation have either been abandoned by this time, or soon will be, as the Indian Department has already taken steps to locate the Reservation on a more favorable location.

The cotton-woods and the dense undergrowth of shrubbery, which produced many kinds of wild berries, and large fields of wild sun-flowers, abounding with nutricious seeds, render the Bosque Redondo a favorite abode with wild turkeys, which existed there in great numbers, and were exceedingly fat and fine flavored. My Apache friends kept my larder lavishly supplied with turkeys, grouse, deer, bear and antelope hams, and a species of very superior turtle, which is abundant in that part of the Pecos river. I have had as many as seven live wild turkeys in my corral at one time, and quite as many dead ones dressed and hanging up. On public days, such as New Year, Christmas, Fourth of July, and sometimes on Sundays, my company were fully supplied with good things from my private larder. But hunting was somewhat of a dangerous pastime in that vicinity. Prowling bands of hostile Apaches, Navajoes and Comanches were at any time liable to be met, and it was safe practice, when double-barreled guns were used, to place a dozen well-fitting balls in one's pouch and a goodly quantity of heavy buck-shot. Besides, what are known as Californian lions, were very plentiful, while catamounts, panthers, grizzly bears, and even jaguars were by no means uncommon. The Apaches never ventured out unless in sufficient force to resist an ordinary attack, until they had resided there some time and had made themselves perfect masters of the situation. On the other hand, the Comanches, with whom the Bosque Redondo had formerly been a chosen hunting ground, gradually but reluctantly withdrew, when they found out that the Apaches were numerous and would be protected by our troops.

Soon after our first arrival at that spot—then a howling wilderness, ninety miles distant from the nearest habitation—a commission of engineers, headed by Col. A. L. Anderson, was sent down to the Bosque, for the purpose of selecting a site for a permanent fort, to be called Fort Sumner, with the view of establishing a large Indian Reservation there, and erecting a valuable advance post on the line of approach from Texas. Among our visitors was Dr. J. M. McNulty, then Medical Director for New Mexico and Arizona, and probably the

most popular officer in the "Column from California."
The Doctor and myself had long been acquainted, and I
was proud to have the privilege of showing him some
little attention; but his visit came near being attended
with fatal results, to him at least. When we left Albu-
querque for the Bosque Redondo, Gen. Carleton supplied us with five semi-civilized Indians from a town
about eighteen miles distant from Santa Fé, the name
of which has escaped my memory. The chief of the
tribe was named Don Carlos, a man about fifty-five years
of age—short, thick-set and resolute. He had visited
Washington, New York, Philadelphia, and other Eastern cities, and had an exalted opinion of the American people. Dr. McNulty, learning that wild turkeys
abounded in the immediate vicinity, determined to go
on a hunt for some of those delicate birds, and took one
of Don Carlos' Indians as a guide. As the distance to
be traveled was not more than a mile and a half, they
waited until within half an hour of sundown, and then
repaired to the roosting place. The birds were fast
gathering upon the tree, and the Doctor determined to
wait a little until they got quiet, when he perceived that
a band of hostile Indians were as eagerly watching him
as he the turkeys. His guide also became cognizant of
the fact about the same time, and both turned their
horses to recross the river and gain our side—for, be it
known, that the banks of the Pecos are from ten to
twenty-five feet perpendicular descent, and that cross-
ings are only found at rare intervals—and the Doctor,
having crossed, was compelled to seek the same ford for
his return. The Apaches, for they were of that tribe,
perceiving his intention, made a bold and concerted
effort to cut him off, but the Doctor succeeded in foiling
their plan, and returned safely to camp much faster

than he had gone. His ardor to obtain wild turkeys of his own killing at the Bosque Redondo was considerably cooled by this adventure.

Another more serious, but very laughable, adventure occurred on a turkey hunt a few days afterward. My First Lieutenant, Mr. Descourtis, was exceedingly fond of the chase, and he joined me about that time, after nearly nine months absence from his company, in obedience to very strict orders from Gen. Carleton. One evening he determined to go and shoot some wild turkeys, and engaged one of the Indians of Don Carlos. About an hour after their departure the guide came back howling with pain, and declared that Descourtis had shot him. Upon examination it was found that his posteriors were fully pitted with small shot, and upon the return of Mr. Descourtis, which occurred about five minutes later, that officer stated that his gun had gone off accidentally and shot the Indian. The wounds were painful, but by no means dangerous, and under the skillful treatment of Dr. Gwyther, Post Surgeon, were healed in a few days. The Indian subsequently said, that on arriving at the ground he perceived a band of hostile Apaches or Navajoes, and warned Mr. Descourtis of their presence; but he failed to discover them. The guide then told him that he would not risk his life for a turkey or two, and started to leave him, when Mr. Descourtis became enraged and shot him. I cannot pretend to decide between the two, but it is certain that Mr. Descourtis brought back no turkeys, and the Indian fetched a whole load of shot in his carcass, and both came home as fast as their horses would carry them; but the Indian's animal having received a liberal supply of the same pellets in his rear, came much the quicker. This event greatly disgusted Don Carlos and his people, and it was

only with infinite trouble, during the time that the guide
was under surgical treatment, that I could persuade
the old man to remain and fulfill his contract. None
of them could ever be induced to approach Descourtis
again.

Among the Apaches was one who particularly out-
shone the rest in the chase. He was a young man of
about twenty-seven years, named Nah-kah-yen, or the
"Keen Sighted," a reputation to which he was fully entitled. This man's knowledge of woodcraft, and the
habits of animals, was really wonderful. He could not
only perceive an object so distant as to be almost invisible, but could distinguish the particular species.
Nah-kah-yen was of medium height, well formed and as
active as a panther. He was a sort of dandy among
them, being always the best dressed, and paid great attention to his hair, which was always kept well combed
and oiled. His long scalp lock was an especial object
of attention, and highly ornamented with small silver
plates, made into little round shields—buttons, beads,
feathers and tinsel. Another of my most trusted favor-
ites was a grim old warrior named Nah-tanh, or the
"Corn Flower," commonly called Chato by the Mexicans, on account of his large nose which had been broken
and flattened by the kick of a horse. Nah-tanh was much
esteemed in his tribe, both as a warrior and judicious
counselor. He was about forty years old, weighed about
two hundred pounds; broad and deep-chested, very powerful and very grave — scarcely ever deigning to smile.
His decision in reference to the qualities of a horse or a
weapon was considered final. He had been one of the
most dreaded scourges in the country, but having surrendered he professed his determination to abide by his
promise, and during the whole term of my service in

New Mexico he kept his word faithfully. His imperturbable coolness and profound sagacity, especially on a bear or lion hunt, proved very serviceable.

After killing an animal I would give the skin to the Apaches to have it dressed for me, and they turned me out some elegant deer, lion and beaver skins, softly dressed, with the fur perfectly preserved. Having discovered the tracks of a very large lion along the riverbottom, I summoned Nah-kah-yen and Nah-tanh to accompany me on the hunt for his majesty. Both were eager, and we started about ten o'clock A. M. I showed them the trail, which they examined carefully for a few moments, and then concluded that the animal had a haunt in a jungle about five miles below. Without pretending to follow up the tracks we struck off into the clear prairie, and went down stream until opposite the jungle, when we separated, each one taking a side of what we supposed to be the animal's lair, and at a signal we approached together. At that place the Pecos is about eight feet deep for a couple of hundred yards, when it shoals again to one, two and three feet, the river being much wider. The jungle was neared with caution, and it being about midday, there was good reason to suppose that the lion was taking his rest after a night's rambles. One large cotton-wood tree flung its branches out wider than the rest, while its top overlooked its surrounding comrades. It grew on the very bank of the river, and overhung the jungle. Nah-tanh dismounted from his horse, which was left free, and being perfectly broken, remained quiet where he was left; he then climbed the tree referred to and crawled out on a large limb, until he was directly over the water and could get a fair view of the supposed lair.

The Californian lion and the panther are both cowardly animals, and will rarely stand at bay, even when wounded; but there are exceptional cases, and sometimes they will become the attacking parties. While Nah-tanh was endeavoring to penetrate the secrets of the thicket, he was summoned by Nah-kah-yen to look out for himself, and gazing in the direction pointed out, we saw a large panther crouching on another limb, not more than fifteen feet from Nah-tanh, and evidently bent on trying titles with my friend. In an instant Nah-kah-yen raised his rifle and took a rapid shot at the beast, but the ball only inflicted a slight flesh wound and made him hasten his motions, for in another moment he made his spring toward Nah-tanh. That wary Apache was not to be so easily caught, for the instant that the panther left the limb on which he had been crouching Nah-tanh dropped from his into the water some thirty feet, and disappeared under the surface, nor did he rise again until he had reached the friendly shelter of the bank, out of his enemy's sight. The panther landed on the spot so suddenly vacated, and gazed anxiously down into the depths below, cracking his tail against his sides and clawing great pieces of the bark from the limb. By this time Nah-kah-yen had reloaded, and I had come up with my breech-loading carbine and two heavy Colt's revolvers. We both took good aim and brought the beast from his high perch. We soon hauled his carcass to land and stripped him of his hide. It was an enormous specimen, measuring nearly seven feet from the tip of his tail to the end of his nose. I brought his skin to California with me as a souvenir of the occurrence, and subsequently made it a present to Philip Martinetti. When Nah-tanh surveyed the lifeless body of his late antagonist, he smiled grimly and said: " *Tagoon-ya-dah; shis Inday to-dah ishan;*" which means — "Fool; an Apache is no food for you."

We were about to return home, when our attention
was attracted by a terrible noise in a rocky cañon, about
four hundred yards lower down the river. Hastily re-
mounting, we galloped to the place, and after having
dismounted, approached the cañon with caution. Suddenly we came upon a very exciting and interesting
scene. A very large lion, probably the one of which we
were in pursuit, was engaged in deadly conflict with a
well-developed brown bear. The lion was crouched
down about twelve feet from bruin, and the bear was
standing erect on his hind legs, his forearms protruded,
and his back against a large rock. His cries were pierc-
ing, and to them we owed the pleasure of being present
at the combat, which quickly began. The lion watched
his adversary with intense gaze, his long and sinewy tail
working and twisting like a large wounded serpent. His
formidable claws occasionally grappled the rocks and
gravel, and every now and then he would exhibit his
terrible teeth and utter a low but significant growl.
Having reached the sticking point, the lion leaped forward with a fearful rush and grappled the bear. Then
commenced the most frightful cries from both—fur, dust
and blood flew from each combatant in quantities; biting,
tearing and hugging were indulged without stint. After
about two minutes of this terrific strife, the lion suddenly released himself and sprang away. Each animal
then commenced to lick its wounds, the lion having re-
occupied his former position in front of the bear, and
evidently bent on "fighting it out on that line if it took
all summer." The bear was decidedly anxious to get
away, but did not dare turn his back on his more agile
adversary. After some ten minutes spent in licking
their wounds and repairing damages, the lion reassumed
the offensive, and the bear again placed himself on the

defensive. The same scene was repeated, but this time the lion had succeeded in tearing open the bear's back and drawing his vitals through the gap. The bear fell dead, and the lion hauled off once more to lick his wounds. Having taken breath, he leisurely proceeded to haul the bear's carcass down into the cañon and bury it with leaves, sand and other debris. Just then I heard the crack of a rifle, and the late conqueror tumbled over on his side dead, beside the body of his late foe, having received a rifle ball just back of the ear from the weapon of Nah-tanh, who had by no means forgotten his own recent encounter. This beast measured seven feet seven inches and a half from the end of his nose to the tip of his tail. His skin I also preserved, and afterward presented it to Major (now General) H. D. Whalen, then commanding Fort Sumner. As we had more than we could carry, Nah-kah-yen was dispatched to the Apache camp to bring some pack horses, and squaws to cut up the meat and take it to camp, for the Apaches are rather fond of lion and panther meat, but seldom touch that of the bear. This was sport enough for one day, and after discovering a couple of fine turkey roosts, we returned home, quite elated with the result of our hunt.

Beavers were quite plentiful on the Pecos, about Fort Sumner, and we used to enjoy shooting them on fine moonlight nights. The Apaches have a great regard for the beaver, which they aver to be by far the most sagacious and intelligent of animals. The Pecos beavers are very large, and in midwinter have an unusually thick, heavy and soft fur. Their tails, roasted in ashes, make a capital dish, and are much esteemed, but rather too fat and musky for most stomachs. The Apaches brought me quite a number of young ones, about a week old, but milk was difficult to obtain, and I only succeeded in

raising one until it got to be three months old and able
to care for itself, when I released the poor thing by returning it to its tribe. It had become quite a pet, and
would perform several little tricks with ease. As it was
brought up among human beings, it possessed none of
the native fear of man which is so strongly characteristic
of its race, and it is quite probable that the poor little
fellow subsequently fell a victim to misplaced confidence,
although I carried it six miles below camp, where there
was a large beaver dam, before restoring it to freedom.

The quality of mercy is unknown among the Apaches.
They frequently take birds and animals alive, but invariably give them to their children to torture. A warrior
is seized with delight when his son exhibits superior skill
in this way. He looks on approvingly and makes occasional suggestions to the aspiring youth. The squaws
are especially pleased with the precociousness of their
children in the art of torturing. Even their horses are
not spared, and their dogs may truly be said to lead
''dogs' lives.'' What we call chivalry is also unknown to
the Apache, who regards it as sheer folly and useless
risk of life; yet there are instances of self-sacrifice and
heroic devotion which would be second to none recorded
in history, were it not for the fact that in each case the
hero was mortally wounded before he displayed remarkable bravery for the safety of others. A badly wounded
Indian is much more dangerous than one who is not.
Feeling that he cannot escape, his first object is to kill
as many of his foes as possible, and protect his own
people to the last gasp. I have seen a single Apache,
stationed at the narrow entrance to a defile, receive four
carbine balls through the breast before he sank on his
knees, and every time the cavalry charged that man
would keep back the horses by dashing a red blanket in

their faces.   By this heroism and wonderful tenacity of
life he saved some sixty or seventy of his people, who
gained time to retreat amidst inaccessible rocks.   He
was only finished by receiving a pistol ball through the
brain, and continued fighting, single-handed, until finally dispatched.   His bow and quiver of arrows are now
in the rooms of the California Pioneers.

CHAPTER XIX.

AMONG the many unique incidents which occurred at
Fort Sumner may be mentioned one, which had a great
effect among the Indians gathered at that place. The
Navajoes, who had become captives to the "pioneers"
of the Column from California, numbered over nine
thousand, including well known chiefs and distinguished warriors, women and children. The Apaches
proper, who were in like condition, amounted to nearly
fifteen hundred. This disparity is sufficient to prove the
superior warlike character of the latter tribe; their in-
vincible determination to "fight it out on that line," and
their utter intractability. Capt. H. B. Bristol, Fifth
United States Infantry, was one of those genial, kind-
hearted and educated gentlemen who have the happy
faculty of attaching all within the sphere of their acquaintance. A strict disciplinarian, and imbued with a
deep-seated love for his profession, he possessed the tact
of gaining the affections and confidence of his men, as
well as their implicit obedience to order. The *suaviter in
modo et fortiter in re*, for which he became distinguished
in the command, gradually spread its influence among
the Indians, who are ever ready to appreciate and recog-

11

nize those characteristics which influence other men. In a short time his cabin became a popular resort among the nomads, who were delighted with his generosity, while he experienced a pleasure in studying their various attributes. Capt. Bristol frequently amused his friends by sticking pins and needles in various parts of his person, driving them in full length without appearing to suffer a particle of inconvenience. One afternoon, while his cabin was full of savages, he proceeded to peg his pantaloons fast to his thighs with pins, until an hundred or more were imbedded in his flesh, without drawing blood, or provoking any evidence of distress. The Apaches and Navajoes were filled with surprise and admiration, while the officers present pretended to be afflicted with anxiety. Having succeeded so far, Bristol deliberately opened his penknife, and thrust the blade alongside of the pins. He then invited the Indians to plunge their knives into his body, assuring them that it could do him no harm. This last *coup de jonglerie* completely upset all their doubts, and with one accord, they voted him to be a "great medicine." From that date his influence was very considerable, as they believed that he could not be slain by ordinary means. All this was done without ostentation, and in a purely natural manner. No attempt was made to impress the savage visitors with an idea of superiority, and they accorded their full homage and respect to the act. Had they been led to understand that some extraordinary ability of the white man was to be exhibited; had they been told that something was to be done in the "medicine" line excelling what they could do, they would have regarded the affair with distrust, suspicion and aversion; but it was so *impromptu* and unaffected that their confidence was won, and their belief fixed.

Quite a number of other innocent devices were resorted to for the purpose of quietly infiltrating the Apache mind with a sense of our superiority, but always most carefully guarding against any appearance of seeking to contrast American attainment with savage ignorance. Their bigotry and self-conceit could not be rudely assailed without exciting their natural distrust and alarm. They were ready to perceive a "nigger in every fence," and were ever on the alert to detect the slightest approximation to deceit, or effort to mislead by the assumption of higher intelligence. A person once discovered in the attempt to make them believe that in which he himself had no faith, is immediately and forever tabooed. No subsequent acts or promises of his could restore their confidence. It was after I had acquired a very fair knowledge of their language that these traits became fully apparent, and I made it my study to conduct myself in such a manner as to allay all doubts.

I possessed a very good microscope, which I had purchased from a French priest, and also an excellent sun-dial, with several other instruments, such as burning-glass, field-glass, compass, several maps of New Mexico, etc. The anxiety to show the wonders of these instruments to my untutored visitors was very great, but I felt the imprudence of so doing until occasion could serve, when it would appear the result of their application, and not of my ostentation.

One day, while receiving instruction from Juan Cojo, my preceptor in the Apache language, I suddenly pretended that it was necessary for me to examine a minute object whose conformation was somewhat indistinguishable to the naked eye. Juan watched me with intense interest as I uncased the microscope and placed beneath its focus the body of a common flea. I was careful not to ask him to view the object, feeling convinced that his own curiosity would induce him to make the request. After I had gazed attentively for a few seconds, Juan asked what I was looking at, and I told him that I had an instrument which made a flea look as large as a mule and showed me his whole conformation. He immediately expressed a desire to see this monster, and after being accorded a good, long look, he exclaimed: *"Madre de Dios, que cosa tan hororosa!"*—which means, mother of God, what a horrible thing. In this manner we went through half a dozen objects, each of which elicited expressions of unbounded surprise from Juan, who commenced to regard me as a magician of power and influence. In this way the train was laid for further confidence on the part of the savages, to whom Juan related the whole affair, because I had never employed such means to assert claims to their respect, and had apparently striven to keep my possession of them from their knowledge. They seemed to have got their information by accident, and I allowed them to press me frequently before I yielded to their request for a look through the wonderful instrument of which they had heard from Juan. Their admiration was also excited by the burning-glass, field-glass, etc.; and when I took out the maps and explained to them all about portions of the country which they knew well, but I had never visited, they began to think that nothing was hidden from our knowledge if we only took the pains to consult our magical instruments.

During all the time of our intimate relations, I was as great an inquirer into their funds of information as they were into that which I possessed. I was regularly inducted into their modes of hunting, and taught where and when the desired game might be expected. The art of tracking was also sedulously shown me, but this requires very long and constant practice. Their code of signals by smokes, stones, broken branches, etc., was explained with apparent delight, in the conviction that the white man could learn something from them.

The force at Fort Sumner was so ludicrously small, in comparison with the number of Indians to be controlled and guarded, that I am convinced the savages would never have remained so long as they did had it not been for the extreme vigilance employed, and the peculiar policy adopted. In fact, within six months after my departure, Ojo Blanco, a famous Apache, took French leave of Fort Sumner, after having induced a goodly number of others to keep him company, and it was not long before nearly all the rest of his tribe followed the example.

Nothing can induce the Apaches to remain an hour in the place where one of them has died from disease, and they give a wide berth to all localities where Apaches have been known to give up the ghost from any cause.

The nearest town was Anton Chico, nearly ninety miles distant, and there were quite a number of well-known villages ranging from one hundred to one hundred and thirty miles northwest, west and southwest from the fort. The influenza was raging in the settlements, and had become epidemic. A great many children and quite a number of adults in the Mexican towns fell victims to the disease, which had assumed a malignant type. It soon made its appearance among the Apaches, but Dr. Gwyther, assisted by myself as interpreter, was unremitting in his attention, and by timely and judicious efforts, prevented the disease from being fatal in a single case, although nearly all were more or less affected. A wily and rascally old Apache, who had wielded great influence among them as a medicine man, seized upon the occasion to sow disaffection and discontent. He upbraided them for their servile obedience to the whites, covered them with reproach for having yielded their absolute independence, and taunted them in every conceivable way. These things were told me by Gian-nah-tah, Nah-tanh, Natch-in-ilk-kisn, and Nah-kah-yen, but the fact of their telling me was sufficient to prove that the prophet was not to be feared, and I counseled them to keep quiet and let me know all that passed, but on no account to acquaint their comrades with the secret of their having told me anything about such proceedings.

One day Gian-nah-tah stated that the prophet had held a great gathering the evening before, at which he had explained a vision. The time selected was about midnight. The Apaches sat in a dense circle, in the center of which stood the prophet dressed in the savage decorations of his sacred office. His eager auditors were informed that he had been blessed with a vision in which he saw a black cloud about the size of his blanket. The cloud rose gradually from the west and increased as it rose in darkness and magnitude, until it covered a large space. Its course was directed toward the Apache camp, over which it hovered and then descended until the camp was completely enveloped within its Cimmerian folds. The interpretation of this vision was that the black cloud represented the anger of the Great Spirit, and that he had sent it among the Apaches to slay them with disease for having remained captive to the Americans. He threatened that if they did not all leave at the earliest possible opportunity, not one would be saved from the anger of the Great Spirit. It may well be supposed that such an announcement from their most noted medicine man at a time when a terrific epidemic was raging, would have an immense influence among those savage and extremely superstitious people.

My determination what to do was immediately taken, and without intimating to Gian-nah-tah what my intention was, I bade him convoke the whole camp on the following night, as near midnight as possible. The moon was very brilliant, and the air clear and perfectly still. I placed a couple of six-shooters and my knife in my belt, and cutting a hole for my head in the center of a sheet, invested myself with that article as if it were a toga. When the Apaches were all assembled, and wondering why they were got together, I suddenly made my appearance among them, and taking position in the center, addressed them to the following effect. I told them that I had been favored with a vision, full of importance to them, and as they had appointed me their "Tata," or Governor, it had been imparted to me for their benefit. I said that two nights previous their prophet had seen a black cloud, which grew larger and blacker as it approached the Apache camp, over which it settled until it was concealed from sight; but that a lying spirit had been put into his mouth, and the true meaning of the vision had been withheld from his knowledge. In my capacity as their Tata, it had been revealed to me, with directions to impart it to the tribe.

They knew, I added, that the Angel of Death had been very busy among the Mexican towns and villages, cutting off the men, women and children, and sparing neither age nor condition. But who among you, said I, have died? Where is the wife that mourns for her husband, or the mother for the child, or the warrior for those that are dear to him? Not one of your number is missing, and all of you are now well or nearly well from the attacks of this infirmity which has killed so many.

Now, the true rendering of the vision is this: The Great Spirit has seen with satisfaction that you have kept your promise, that you no longer exist by robbery, that you do not murder the incautious traveler, that you live here happily and well supplied with every comfort, and are cared for by skillful medicine men when you are sick; and in reward for your excellent conduct, the Good Spirit said—I have sent the Angel of Death abroad in the land and he knows nothing but to destroy, for that is his mission. My Apache people have done well and must be preserved, and to shield them from the vision of the Destroying Angel, I will wrap them in a dark cloud which his eyes cannot penetrate; then will he pass them by, and they shall live because they have kept their promise to the Americans. This, I added, is the true rendering of the vision seen by your prophet, and I am come here to tell you, in order that his evil counsel may not prevail and lead you to destruction.

The reader can conjecture the rage of the prophet and the profound astonishment of the whole tribe, except Gian-nah-tah. No one but he knew that I possessed any information on the subject, and, of course, not a soul, the prophet included, doubted the reality of what I had said. The contemplated hegira came to a sudden end; the Apaches returned to their allegiance with more willingness than before, and our intercourse became more harmonious than ever. For my part, I was far better satisfied with the result than if we had been compelled to use force and slay a hundred or two of the savages before again impressing them with the necessity for obedience. The prophet lost his influence, while we gained in proportion.

The foregoing incident conveys its own moral, and shows the virtue of using artifice instead of force, when artifice has to be met.

CHAPTER XX.

ELSEWHERE it has been stated that my vocabulary of the Apache language had been forwarded to the Smithsonian Institute through Gen. Carleton, and that it had been handed to Professor George Gibbs for the purpose of being incorporated in his forthcoming work on Ethnology. As it was the only copy in my possession, I am compelled to rely solely on memory for the very unsatisfactory skeleton I am able to offer in this chapter. It will, however, serve to convince the reader of the superior intelligence of the Apache Indians as compared with nearly all other tribes of American savages, while it places them at the head of races purely nomadic.

Many of the African, Australian, North and South American tribes, and those who inhabit the Pacific Oceanica, together with several of Asia, cannot count beyond ten, but the Apaches count ten thousand with as much regularity as we do. They even make use of the decimal sequences. With us the number one has no correlative. It is unique in expression as well as in meaning, but when we come to two, we say two, twelve, twenty, two hundred; with the numeral three for a starter, we say thirteen, thirty, three hundred; and again, four, fourteen, forty, four hundred, and so on up to ten, when the process is repeated by referring to the same root numeral

11*

from which the higher number derives its name. In like
manner the Apaches use a unique word to express one,
and another to mention eleven; but all the rest are derived from the root name of the numbers between one
and ten.   This will be seen from the subjoined table of
their numerals: One is called *tash-ay-ay;* two, *nah-kee;*
three, *kah-yay;* four, *tin-yay;* five, *asht-lay;* six, *host-kon-
ay;* seven, *host-ee-day;* eight, *hah-pee;* nine, *en-gost-ay;*
ten, *go-nay-nan-ay.*   But on arriving at eleven they use
an entirely different word, and say *klats-ah-tah-hay,* which
never occurs again, either in part or in whole, until they
reach eleven hundred, which is *klats-at-too-ooh.*   When
twelve is to be expressed recourse is had to the *nah-kee,*
or two, which is then enlarged into *nah-kee-sah-tah.*   In
like manner thirteen is derived from *kah-yay,* three, and
becomes *kah-yay-sah-tah.*   After ten until twenty their
numbers are named as follows: Eleven, *klats-ah-tah-hay;*
twelve, *nah-kee-sah-tah;* thirteen, *kah-yay-sah-tah;* fourteen, *tin-sah-tah-hay;* fifteen, *asht-lay-sah-tah-hay;* sixteen,
host-kon-sah-tah-hay; seventeen, *host-ee-sah-tah-hay;* eighteen, *sam-pee-sah-tah-hay;* nineteen, *en-gost-ee-sah-tah-hay;*
twenty, *nah-tin-yay.*   It will be observed that after fourteen the aspirated syllable *hay* is added, and this is for
the sake of euphony, as well as the change from *hah-pee,*
eight, to *sam-pee* in eighteen.   It will also be observed
that *nah-tin-yay,* twenty, receives its derivation, like *nah-
kee-sah-tah,* twelve, from *nah-kee,* two ; and this is regularly observed in the following numbers: For instance,
thirty is called *kah-tin-yay;* forty, *tish-tin-yay;* fifty, *asht-
tin-yay;* sixty, *host-kon-tin-yay;* seventy, *host-ee-tin-yay;*
eighty, *sam-pee-tin-yay;* ninety, *en-gost-ee-tin-yay;*   one
hundred, *too-ooh,* after which comes *nah-kee-too-ooh,* two
hundred; *kah-yay-too-ooh,* three hundred, etc., until one
thousand, which is expressed by *go-nay-nan-too-ooh,* or

ten hundred; two thousand is termed *nah-kee-go-nay-nan-too-ooh*, etc.

Here we have evidence sufficient to prove that the Apaches must have possessed objects of sufficient importance and numbers to have compelled the creation of terms by which the number could be indicated. In the absence of any other object furnished by the region they inhabit, it is fairly presumable that the numerical strength of their race was the impelling cause.

Their verbs express the past, present and future with much regularity, and have the infinitive, indicative, subjunctive and imperative moods, together with the first, second and third persons, and the singular, dual and plural numbers. Many of them are very irregular, and depend upon auxiliaries which are few. In all that relates to special individuality the language is exacting; thus, *shee* means I or me; but *shee-dah* means I myself, or me myself; *dee* means thee or thou; but *dee-dah* means you yourself especially and personally, without reference to any other being. When an Apache is relating his own personal adventures he never says *shee*, for I, because that word, in some sense, includes all who were present and took any part in the affair; but he uses the word *shee-dah*, to show that the act was wholly his own. The pronouns are: *Shee*—I; *shee-dah*—I myself; *dee*— thee or thou; *dee-dah*—thee thyself; *aghan*—it, he, her, or they. The word *to-dah* means no, and all their affirmatives are negatived by dividing this word so as to place the first syllable in front and the second in the rear of the verb to be negatived. For example, *ink-tah* means sit down, but to say, do *not* sit down, we must express it *to-ink-tah-dah*; *nuest-chee-shee*, come here; *to-nuest-chee-shee-dah*, do *not* come here; *anah-zont-tee*, begone; *to-anah-zont-tee-dah*, do *not* begone, and so on throughout the language.

The word *tats-an* means dead in Apache; but they never employ it when speaking of a dead friend, but say of him that he is *yah-ik-tee*, which means that he is not present— that he is wanting. If one goes to an Apache's camp, and inquires for him during his absence, the visitor is answered that he is *yah-ik-tee*, or gone somewhere. This usage, while speaking of their deceased friends, is not so much due to delicacy and regret for their loss as to their superstitious fears of the dead, for they entertain an implicit belief in ghosts and spirits, although I could never trace the causes for their credence. In alluding to an animal destroyed in the chase, so soon as the mortal blow is given they exclaim, *yah-tats-an*, now it is dead; but if it should only be wounded, and rise again, it is said, *to-tats-an-see-dah*, it is *not* dead.

Whenever an object is shown them for the first time, they adopt its Spanish name which is made to terminate with their favorite guttural, *hay*. Formerly they knew no difference between the values or qualities of iron, silver, copper, brass or gold. Their name for iron is *pesh*, and the several metals were distinguished by their colors. Silver was called *pesh-lickoyee*, or white iron; gold, *pesh-klitso*, or yellow iron; but after learning the difference in their values and uses, they adopted the Spanish terms, and silver became *plata-hay*, gold changed to *oro-hay*, and brass was suffered to retain the appellation of *pesh-klitso*, or yellow iron.

As the Apaches build no houses, and rarely remain more than a week in any one locality, the place of their temporary abode receives its name from their word *kunh*, which means fire; so that to express a camp, or a few twigs tied together for shelter, we must say *kunh-gan-hay*, meaning fire-place. Many of their words depend entirely upon their accent for individuality of meaning.

Kah is the word for an arrow, and also for a rabbit, but when the latter is intended, it is necessary to give a strongly aspirated sound to the *k*, rolling it from the throat with marked expression. The term *ah-han-day* means afar off, a long way; but if the speaker intends to convey the idea of great distance, he must emphasize and dwell upon the last syllable, and pronounce the word *ah-han-d-a-y*. The word *schlanh* means much, a good deal; but to represent a great deal, an unusually large quantity, we must say *schlan-go*, with the accent on the last syllable.

As it is not contemplated to insert the Apache vocabulary in this work, the foregoing illustrations must suffice to convince the reader that for a race so purely nomadic, their language is in advance of many others spoken by uncivilized races residing in villages and engaged in semi-pastoral and agricultural pursuits.

Apache warriors take their names from some marked trait of character, personal conformation, or noteworthy act. Until one of these features be developed to such extent as to be prominent, the youth is called *ish-kay-nay*, a boy. The women are named in like manner, but as they are deemed altogether inferior, many of them are without particular designation, but are addressed or spoken of as *ish-tia-nay*, or woman. The names of some of the more eminent warriors on the Fort Sumner Reservation will convey the best idea of this subject. There were *Gian-nah-tah*, which means "Always Ready," and was admirably descriptive of the man's character. The name given him by the Mexicans was *Cadete*. Then came *Nah-tanh*, or the "Corn Flower," so called from having on one occasion, while on a raid in Sonora, completely hidden himself and party in a field of corn near the large town of Ures, and succeeded in running off

two or three hundred head of horses. On one occasion
he received a kick on the nose from one of the captured
animals, which had the effect of flattening that feature
over a considerable portion of his naturally unattractive
countenance. From this accident the Mexicans dubbed
him *El Chato.* A tall, stately fellow, rejoiced in the
name of *Natch-in-ilk-kisn,* or the "Colored Beads," of
which he always wore a thickly-worked and stiff collar
around his throat, and bracelets on his wrists. *Nah-kah-
yen* means the "Keen Sighted," and was so baptized because of his wonderful powers of vision. *Too-ah-yay-
say,* the "Strong Swimmer," got his title from a narrow
escape from drowning in the Rio Grande, while endeavoring to cross it with a band of stolen horses. After a
desperate struggle, in which several of the animals were
lost, he succeeded in reaching the shore and effecting
his escape with the rest from a large pursuing party of
Mexicans, who did not dare venture into the swollen
and turbid flood. A quiet, easy-tempered and good-
natured fellow was known as *Para-ah-dee-ah-tran,* meaning the "Contented." One old sagamore received the
sobriquet of *Klo-sen,* or the "Hair Rope," for having
lassoed and killed a Comanche during a fight between
the tribes, with one of those *cabestros.* His arrows had
been expended, and possessing himself of the arms of
his slain enemy, *Klo-sen* contributed greatly toward winning the fight. *Pindah-Lickoyee,* or "White Eye," was
a noted warrior, who got the appellation from the unusually large amount of white around the small, black,
flashing pupils of his eyes. His Mexican title was *Ojo
Blanco.*

As before remarked, few of the women are ever honored with names; but there are some who have decidedly
poetical appellations. Among them was a very bright

and handsome girl of eighteen or nineteen, who had invariably refused all offers of matrimony. She was light
colored, with strictly Grecian features and exquisitely
small feet and hands. Her eyes were large, black and
lustrous, while her figure was magnificently developed,
and her carriage redolent with the grace and freedom of
the wild girl of the sierras. She was known as *Sons-ee-
ah-ray*, which means the "Morning Star." Another,
likewise indifferent to marriage, was called *Ish-kay-nay*,
the "Boy," from her tom-boy character and disposition.
There was one who received particular honor from the
other sex, but her Apache name has escaped my memory.
She was renowned as one of the most dexterous horse
thieves and horse breakers in the tribe, and seldom permitted an expedition to go on a raid without her presence. The translation of her Apache title was, the
"Dexterous Horse Thief." They do not call themselves
"Apaches," but *Shis-Inday*, or "Men of the Woods,"
probably because their winter quarters are always located amidst the forests which grow upon the sierras,
far above the plains, and while they afford fire and shelter from the wintry blasts, enable them to observe all
that passes in the vales below.

The foregoing names are somewhat suggestive of
Apache character; so much so, indeed, that it is not unusual for them to refuse giving their Apache names when
interrogated; but will endeavor to give some Mexican
appellative in its place. Before marriage the girls are
much the handsomest and most perfectly formed of any
Indian tribe I have ever seen; but after bearing children
and performing for three or four years the onerous duties
imposed upon them by their husbands, they soon wither
and shrivel up, becoming thin, muscular and wrinkled

CHAPTER XXI.

AMONG those who have enjoyed the best opportunities for judging, the award for female chastity is given to the Apaches. During a period of about two years, when hundreds of them were under our charge, and mingling freely with our troops, not a single case occurred, to the best of my knowledge, wherein an Apache woman surrendered her person to any man outside her tribe. Cases of conjugal infidelity are extremely rare among them, and the girls take no ordinary pride in guarding their purity. The art of coquetry is practiced among them with quite as much zest as among the belles of our cities, and with such delicacy and tact, that the most refined among us might possibly study at a worse school. On the other hand, the Navajoes are extremely loose and sensuous. Although of the main branch of the great Apache tree they differ in tribal organization, in their manufacture of superb blankets, in their courage and address, and in the fact that they keep large flocks of sheep, and cultivate the earth. In all other respects they are pure Apaches. Female virtue is little regarded among them, but is deemed of primary importance among the Apaches proper. When an Apache girl has reached the second year of her puberty the fact is widely circulated, and all present are invited to a grand feast and dance. She is then deemed marriageable and open to the solicitations of the young warriors. On such occasions the girl is dressed in all her finery. Small bells are hung to the skirts of her buckskin robe and along the sides of her high moccasins, which reach the knee. Bits of tinsel are profusely scattered all over her attire, until she is fairly weighed down by the quantity of her ornaments. Meat in abundance is cooked after their fashion, and the guests partake of it *ad libitum*. *Twiltkah-yee*, an intoxicating beverage, is freely distributed. A dried ox-hide is laid upon the ground, and some of the more noted musicians entertain the company with improvised songs, while others beat time upon the ox-hide with long and tough sticks. The noise of this drumming can be heard for two miles on a clear, calm night. Old warriors meet and recount their exploits; young ones ogle and court the marriageable girls; old women delight in cooking the supper and furnishing it to their hungry applicants. Suddenly a shout is raised, and a number of young men, variously attired in the skins of buffaloes, deer, cougars, bears, and other beasts, each looking as nearly natural as possible, make their appearance, and commence dancing to a regular measure around a huge central fire. The women pretend to be greatly alarmed at this irruption of beasts; the men seize their weapons and brandish them with menacing gestures, to which the human menagerie pays no sort of attention. Finding their efforts to intimidate futile, they lay aside their arms and join in the dance, which is then made more enjoyable by the intermingling of the young girls. In the meantime the one in whose honor all these rejoicings are given, remains isolated in a huge lodge, in which are assembled the sagamores and principal warriors of the tribe. She is not allowed to participate in, or even see what is going on outside; but listens patiently to the responsibilities of her marriageable condition. This feast lasts from three to five days, according to the wealth of the girl's father. After it is finished she is divested of her eyebrows, which is intended to publish the fact that she is in the matrimonial market. A month afterward the eye lashes are pulled out, one by one, until not a hair remains. The reasons for this extraordinary despoliation I have never been able to learn, and I doubt much if the Apaches themselves can assign any cause for the act beyond the exactions of custom. But this system of depilorizing the brows and eyes is not confined to the women; it is universal among the warriors, nor could any arguments of mine induce them to forego the practice. It probably arose from a desire to look unlike any other people, and to add to their ferociousness of aspect.

Marriage among the Apaches also has its singularities, and is not unworthy of special mention. The girls are wholly free in their choice of husbands. Parents never attempt to impose suitors upon their acceptance, and the natural coquetry of the sought-for bride is allowed full scope. These are their halcyon days, for after marriage "comes the deluge." Any amount of ogling, sly pressing of hands, stolen interviews, etc., is gone through with, just the same as with us, until the suitor believes his "game made," when he proceeds to test his actual standing, which is invariably done as follows: In the night time he stakes his horse in front of her roost, house, hovel, encampment, bivouac, or whatever a few slender branches, with their butt ends in the ground and their tops bound together, may be termed. The lover then retires and awaits the issue. Should the girl favor the suitor, his horse is taken by her, led to water, fed, and secured in front of his lodge; but should she decline the proffered honor, she will pay no attention to the suffering steed. Four days comprise the term allowed her for an answer in the manner related. A ready acceptance is apt to be criticised with some severity, while a tardy one is regarded as the extreme of coquetry. Scarcely any of them will lead the horse to water before the second day, as a hasty performance of that act would indicate an unusual desire to be married; nor will any suffer the fourth day to arrive without furnishing the poor animal with its requisite food and drink, provided they intend to accept the suitor, for such a course would render them liable to the charge of excessive vanity.

With us the possession of gold and silver indicates the enjoyment of wealth. Gold and silver are the recognized mediums of exchange for goods, and are called money; but with the Apaches a horse is money, and the value of any article is regulated by the number of horses which it may bring. Of course, the animal must be sound, and not over ten years of age, and no farrier among us is more skillful in these matters than they.

The lover, having been accepted, it becomes his duty to determine how many horses her parents are willing to receive for their daughter, it being mutually understood that the animals are given as a recompense for her services to the family. In exact proportion to the number of horses given, her worth and attractiveness are exalted. If a girl is sold for one animal, no matter how good, she is deemed of little account—quite plebeian, and by no means of the *bon ton*—by the rest of those present, and

I am not so sure that our expression, "a one-horse affair," did not take its rise from this Apache system of
graduated values.

On the third night of the feastings and junketings incident to the marriage, the bride and bridegroom suddenly disappear. During the whole of the time mentioned, they have been constantly in the presence of the
sachems and wise squaws of the tribe, and are never permitted to even speak with each other. But love is far
more watchful than precaution, and when the old people
are overcome by drowsiness, incident upon long wake-
fulness and frequent potations, the young couple manage to make their escape, usually with the connivance of
their seniors, who pretend to be quite innocent of the
matter.

Several days prior to his marriage the bridegroom selects some beautiful and retired spot, from three to five
miles from the main camp, and there he erects one of
the shelters already described, but festooned with wild
flowers, and generally embowered among the trees in a
place difficult to discover. Thither he retreats with his
bride, a sufficiency of provision having been laid in to
last them a week or ten days, and there they take up
their temporary abode. Their absence is expected, and
re-appearance creates no visible recognition, as it is
deemed indelicate to make any open demonstration on
such occasions. The young bride assumes the air and
pretenses of extraordinary modesty, and in the event of
meeting one of her former associates, invariably turns
her back or hides her face, and puts on all the simper
of an American girl of twenty years ago—not now-a-
days—when accused of having a lover.

In a week this seeming bashfulness gives place to the
regular and arduous duties of the Apache wife, and her

life of toil and slavish suffering commences. The warrior may at any time repudiate his conjugal companion, and her chances for a second marriage consist in her reputation as a good worker, or for her personal attractions. In either case, she experiences no difficulty in obtaining a second, and even a third or fourth husband, but her market depends upon her prominence in these respects. Should there be any children, it becomes the reputed father's duty to provide for their support, and he, in turn, imposes that responsibility upon his other wives. The women are by no means averse to sharing the affections of their lords with other wives, as the increased number lessens the work for each individual, but the place of honor is always assigned to the one who was the first married, irrespective of age.

The custom of polygamy was not always in vogue among the Apaches. A celebrated warrior, and one wise in the traditions of his people, told me that time was when only one woman was deemed the proper share of one man, but their losses by war, and other causes, had so reduced the number of the males that it was judged politic to make a change in this custom. He further added, that he thought degeneracy had been produced by its adoption, and that the individuals of the tribe had become more alienated from each other. He rejoiced in but one wife with whom he had lived twenty years, and although she had fallen into the "sere and yellow leaf," he preferred her to all the young and more attractive women. She had borne him two fine sons and a daughter, all of whom were alive and well, and she possessed the experience requisite to make him a contented husband. His oldest son was a warrior, and his father's best friend and associate. He deprecated the system of polygamy, and thought that it would eventu-

ally emasculate and destroy the independence of his
tribe. This was Nah-tanh, and his views were fully seconded by Klo-sen, and several others, but they could
not hold their own against the practices of Gian-nah-tah,
Natch-in-ilk-kisn, and other prominent and more licen-
tious men. These recitals will serve to show that the
Apaches, although the most nomadic, savage and untamed of all races, have nevertheless pondered over some
of the most abstruse and perplexing social problems of
the highest civilized races.

In respect to burials I could never succeed in discovering but very little, and that little not at all of a satisfactory character. On this point they are absolutely
unapproachable, and invariably succeeded in foiling any
scheme I planned for a more thorough knowledge on the
subject. It is certain that they abhor cremation, and
resort to interment, and their burials are all performed
at night only by a few selected warriors. I have reason
to believe that their dead are conveyed to the most con-
venient height, and deposited in the ground, care being
taken to so shroud their bodies with stones as to prevent
the wolves and coyotes from digging them up and muti-
lating their remains. Everything of which the defunct
died possessed is scrupulously placed in the grave, but
with what ceremonies, and under what observances, I
have never been able to discover. The demise of a warrior provokes an excessive demonstration of woe and
general sense of serious loss; the death of a squaw is almost unnoticed, except by her intimate friends and personal female relatives. Whatever external signs of grief
they may practice among themselves when in a state of
absolute independence and freedom, were never exhibited in presence of others while under the restraints of
subjection and obedience to our dictates, and opportu-

nity to witness them at other times was at no time vouchsafed to me or any other person I ever met. It has never
been within my power to solve the reasons for this extreme caution; and all my inquiries failed to unlock the
doors of Apache reticence on this subject. The nearest
definition I ever arrived at was given me by old Klo-sen,
the same who instituted so many questions in reference
to the earth's sphericity, the formation of clouds, the
causes for rain, etc.

This reflecting and experienced warrior told me that
the reason why they buried all the worldly goods of dead
people with their bodies, was because of a strange disease
which broke out among them several years before he was
born, and carried off great numbers. It was found that
to use the clothing or household property of the deceased, or to come in contact with such person, was almost certain to result in a like sickness to the individual
doing these things, and that the rule was adopted to
bury with him or her every single thing that the defunct
possessed at the time of death, and all that he or she
might have used or touched before that event. But he
strictly forbore from telling me anything more, although
I made every effort to draw him out. It occurred to me
that the disease alluded to was the small-pox, for there
were plenty of evidences that it had raged among the
Apaches in some past period. That they know what
this disease is, and comprehend its nature, to some extent, can be exemplified by the following incidents:

Gen. Carleton dispatched Capt. E. D. Shirland and his
company, C of the First California Cavalry Volunteers,
to retake Fort Davis, in Texas. Upon Shirland's arrival
he found the fort deserted by the Confederates; but also
discovered that they had left three men behind who had
been seized with small-pox. Those poor fellows were

abandoned to their fate; but the Confederate troops had
scarcely left the place before the Apaches arrived, and
with their usual caution they made careful inspection
before trusting themselves into the building. In the
course of their investigations they discovered the three
sick men, and recognizing the disease with which they
were afflicted, filled their bodies full of arrows shot from
between the iron bars of the windows; and without attempting to enter the fortress, went on their way toward
their own fastnesses. A few days afterward, Shirland,
at the head of twenty-five men, encountered over two
hundred of those same Apaches at the place known as
"Dead Man's Hole," and killed twenty-two of them
without sustaining any other loss than that of a single
carbine.

CHAPTER XXII.

SEVERAL fine opportunities were vouchsafed me to judge
of the Apaches as warriors, when compared with other
tribes.   Some ten or twelve of them made a daring raid
on the westernmost Maricopa village, just at a time when
I was passing with my company. The Maricopas and
Pimos armed themselves in great numbers, and hurried
out to punish the invaders who had sought refuge in a
dense chaparal, just at the foot of the mountain range
which creates the Great Gila Bend. Thither they were
pursued and invested on three sides. The conflict waxed
warm, and several of the allies were wounded; but not
an Apache could be seen. The brush was riddled with
balls, and after a short council of war, it was assaulted
in great force, but their wily enemies had managed to
make their escape without the loss of a man.

A gentleman of New Mexico told me that he once witnessed a fight between eighty Apaches and one hundred
and fifty Comanches, in which the former gained a decided victory. The contest was entirely on horseback,
and the parties were equally armed. It occurred on the
plain known as the Llano Estacado, or "Staked Plain,"
east of the Pecos river. Exhibitions of rare skill in

12

horsemanship occurred during this conflict which were admirable to behold.

In January, 1864, the weather at Fort Sumner was very cold, Fahrenheit's thermometer being ten degrees below zero at eight o'clock in the morning. The Apaches under our care were then encamped about three miles south of the fort, on the eastern bank of the Pecos. They possessed quite a number of horses, in which consisted their whole wealth. One night, about twelve o'clock, Major Whalen was roused by the guard, who informed him that a deputation of Apaches were present, earnestly desirous of making some communication. An audience was immediately granted, and the Apaches informed the commanding officer that their camp had just been visited by a large band of marauding Navajoes, and their stock driven off. They came for aid to recover their animals. It happened that nearly the whole of my company—the only cavalry force at the fort—were absent on a scout at the time, and only about twelve remained with some of the most used-up horses belonging to the company. Nevertheless, the men were immediately ordered to saddle up and place themselves under command of Lieut. Newbold, while a company of United States Infantry, under the command of Capt. Bristol, was ordered to follow the cavalry with all speed. These forces were assisted by twenty-five Apache warriors, under the conduct of Gian-nah-tah, that being the greatest number the Apaches could mount since the Navajo raid. The trail led due south, and about seven o'clock in the morning the cavalry and Apaches came upon the retreating Navajoes, who were all on foot except those mounted on the animals stolen from the Apaches. The band numbered about one hundred and eighty, of whom about sixty were mounted. So soon as their pursuers came into view they halted, formed, and prepared for fight. Newbold and his small party of twelve cavalrymen and twenty-five Apaches advanced rapidly toward the Navajoes until within eighty yards, when the latter opened fire all along their line. This was answered by a closely delivered volley from a dozen carbines, which knocked over nine Navajoes at the first fire. The weather was so extremely cold that although the men found no difficulty in recharging their breech-loading carbines, yet they could not place the caps upon the nipples, their fingers were so benumbed. Fortunately, the Navajoes were in the same dilemma. The order to draw pistols and charge was given, and the allies went down among the Navajoes like a small tornado. In less than ten minutes their line was broken, and the enemy in full retreat.

The Apaches had likewise abandoned the use of their rifles, and betook themselves to their bows and arrows, and lances. The retreat soon became a rout. Each trooper had two first-class Colt's six-shooters, and used them with terrific effect. The moment a Navajo fell he was pierced full of arrows by the Apaches, and never suffered to rise again. The whites took the lead, but their savage allies seconded them with great courage and undaunted gallantry. For an engagement in which so few were present, the slaughter was terrific. No less than ninety Navajoes were stretched dead upon the ground, and so many others wounded that some of the party who afterward surrendered and placed themselves upon the Reservation, informed me that only twenty of the whole Navajo force ever arrived safely in their country. In this very remarkable engagement, neither our troops nor the Apaches lost man nor horse. Sixty-five of the stolen animals were recovered and restored to their owners.

It subsequently appeared that the Navajoes were greatly incensed at the Apaches on the Reservation for having surrendered themselves, and entered into peaceful understanding with the Americans, and the raid had been undertaken in revenge for this apparent perfidy. Our allies were highly elated at their triumph, and also conceived a more positive idea of the gallantry and prowess of Californian cavalry, for whom they had always entertained a high respect, coupled with a wholesome dread. As I was absent on a scout with the remainder of my company, I took no part in this affair, but arrived at the fort the day after its occurrence, and heard the same reports from all concerned. A visit to the battle-field, only fifteen miles off, satisfied me as to the number of slain Navajoes, and the subsequent relation of the survivors corroborated the narratives of the victorious parties.

Among the assailants were Mr. Labadie, the Indian Agent, and a man named Carillo, the *major-domo* of the Indian farm at Fort Sumner. Both these men were eminently courageous, and both did splendid service. Carillo had been a captive among the Navajoes, years before, and spoke their language, the same as the Apaches, with tolerable fluency. During the fight he hailed a retreating Navajo, and said to him: "Halt, and surrender. I do not wish to kill you. Here are numbers of your people in our camp, who have given themselves up, and are now living in peace and comfort, with plenty to eat." The Navajo replied: "Am I not a man as well as you? If you can kill me do so; if not, I will try to kill you. Surrender I never will." At this response Carillo raised his rifle and fired, putting a half ounce ball through his foe; but the fellow staggered on at considerable speed, until his rifle was reloaded, when he whirled about and let fly at Carillo, the ball passing in close proximity to his head. Having re-charged his rifle, Carillo again cried out: "Did I not tell you; will you now halt or must I shoot you again?" The Navajo made no other answer than to again raise his gun and shoot at Carillo, who, being untouched, again sent a ball through his foe. This second shot brought him to a halt, when he sat down, and throwing away his rifle, commenced to use his bow and arrows. At this juncture a soldier rode up and sped a six-shooter ball through the Indian's breast, which did not kill him, but had the effect of distracting his attention from Carillo, who slipped round behind the savage, and seizing him by the hair, plunged a large bowie-knife in his heart. While in the death agony this warrior said to his slayer, *tu no vale nada*, meaning, "you are good for nothing." This incident, and another related elsewhere, demonstrate the extreme tenacity of life possessed by the Apaches and Navajoes, and I doubt not, by most of our American savages. This engagement was signalized by many acts of valor and cool courage on the part of our men. Privates McGrew and Porter followed the retreating savages for ten miles, killing fifteen more of them. McGrew himself slew no less than thirteen Navajoes that day.

It may as well be mentioned here, that the Apaches do not scalp all their enemies. After a considerable engagement they will select one or two scalps for the performance of a ceremony somewhat allied to the "scalp dance" of other tribes, but in most respects totally different. With them it is a strictly religious ceremony, growing out of their superstitions; while among other races it is observed as a grand rejoicing, a triumphal jubilee. Four days after the fight above narrated the Apaches were observed to be dressed in their greatest

finery. About eighty of their most noted warriors were
mounted, and each was armed with a lance, from which
streamed a small red pennon. Every member of this
party was enveloped in a red blanket, given by the Government a short time previous, and they were formed in
close column of twenty men front and four ranks deep.
After going through a variety of manœuvres, they rode
directly toward the fort, and halted a few yards in front
of the commandant's residence. That officer, Major
Whalen, requested me to inquire into their wishes,
which I did, and was answered by Gian-nah-tah that
they desired permission to visit the field of the late battle
for the purpose of obtaining a Navajo scalp, in order to
perform some religious rites imposed upon them by their
prophet, who, by the by, was the same wily rascal that
had attempted to lead them astray by his pretended
vision of the black cloud. To this request Major Whalen
bade me reply, that it was entirely impossible to accede;
that they had behaved like brave men during the fight,
and that they should not tarnish their gallant deeds by
acts of intense barbarism. He further added, that their
enemies, being defunct, were past all sensation, and that
stripping them of their scalps was an act of atrocious
cowardice, of which he had not believed his Apache
friends susceptible. He had given them credit for gallantry; but if they persisted in their demand, he, and
all of us, would be coerced into the conviction that they
were not animated by true courage. He would, therefore, forbid them from visiting the battle ground for the
purpose named.

This reply evoked the extreme anger of the prophet,
who immediately informed the band that, unless the
ceremony took place, they and their people would be
visited with the vengeance of the Great Spirit. At this

they became much excited, and reiterated their request, stating that but one scalp was required to fulfill their obligations to the Most High. Major Whalen remained immovable, and gave me orders to get my company in readiness immediately to frustrate any such attempt on the part of the Apaches, at the same time instructing me to inform them of this order. They heard me through with Indian patience, and then, with undisguised expressions of hate against the commanding officer, rode down the river in solid square until they arrived at a point about three miles below the fort, where the ceremonies, I am about to relate, were solemnized.

My company had been got ready, pursuant to order; but were kept in waiting, at the fort, until it should become certain that the Apaches were determined to visit the battle ground. Accompanied by two chosen men I kept about four hundred yards in their rear, but never intruded upon their privacy. Having reached a point where the bank of the Pecos descended gradually toward the stream—a very rare occurrence in that river—they wheeled to the right, and having reached the water, formed line, the right toward the south, while the prophet, dismounting from his horse, entered the stream, about knee deep, and commenced a series of incantations, the warriors preserving profound silence. Having performed the rite of ablution upon his own person and arms, he proceeded to the warrior at the southernmost end of the line, and received from him the weapons he had used in the fight above mentioned. The lance blade, the knife and the arrow heads were bathed in the stream, and then dried with a cloth, after which they were pointed upward, and the prophet, with a strong expiration, blew upon their respective blades, beginning at the hilts and ending at the points, at the same time muttering a series

of incantations, accompanied by the groans and apparent
contrition of the owner of the weapons. This system of
purgation was gone through with every warrior present
who had been in the conflict. When the ceremony came
to an end the band separated into four distinct parties,
and went through a sort of sham fight, which lasted half
an hour. They then reformed in the order they came
and returned peaceably to camp.

I subsequently inquired of several of their more prominent men the objects contemplated in these ceremonials,
and was told that the spirits of the dead would haunt
them unless wafted away by the breath of the prophet.
The blood shed by them was supposed to be washed off
only by the power of their medicine man; but the ghosts
of the slain were laid by blowing them away from the
weapons by which they had died. This power was vested
solely in the prophet, but the ceremony was incomplete,
because they had no scalp. It was necessary to have
one, from which each warrior should take a few hairs
and burn them, in order that the fumes might purify the
atmosphere of the battle ground and prevent it from
being pestilential to the Apaches. Having been denied
the privilege by Maj. Whalen, they could no more hunt
in the direction of the field where the Navajoes had
fallen without jeopardizing their personal safety, either
from disease or other causes.

This incident confirmed my opinions in regard to the
superstitious ideas of the Apaches, and induced me to
make many inquiries on the subject, but they were never
advanced as if from mere motives of curiosity, but rather
as being desirous to learn something which might be
beneficial. On no occasion did I ever permit myself to
intrude an innate sense of American superiority over
their savage ignorance, but approached them as a seeker

after knowledge which they alone could impart. This course flattered their vanity and opened to me sources of information which I might otherwise have sought in vain. Nothing was lost by this seeming dependence. They knew as well as I that they were no match for Americans, but nothing could bring them to confess the fact. They perfectly understood and appreciated the difference between us, but it was beyond human nature to think that they would acknowledge that difference. That an American officer, placed in charge of their camp, should seek information from them—should endeavor to comprehend their laws, nature, habits, language, manners, religion, and other ceremonies—was something so new and unexpected, that they involuntarily opened their hearts and laid them comparatively bare, but never for a moment did they forget to exercise caution and reserve, even while accepting these advances. They invariably apply a test of acts, and refuse to put faith in words which are systematically used by them to cover their designs; but the ordeal passed, they are prepared to give limited credence to promises.

12*

CHAPTER XXIII.

Ojo Blanco Wounded.—Apache Doctoring.—Dr. Gwyther's Treatment.—Results.
—Ojo Blanco Killed in Battle.—Religious Creed of the Apaches.—Policy in
their Religion. — The Deluge. — Apaches Ignorant of their Origin. — Their
Ideas in Reference to Women. — Mexican Women as Wives of Apaches. —
Character of their Children.—Horrible Spectacle in Cooke's Cañon.—A few
Suggestions.—Their Respect for Traditions Upset.

ONE day, while conversing with Dr. Gwyther, information was brought us from the Apache camp that Ojo
Blanco had been desperately wounded in a personal
quarrel with another Apache. We immediately proceeded to the camp, where I arrested the assailant and
sent him to the guard house, while the Doctor visited
the wounded man, where I soon joined him. Ojo Blanco,
or Pin-dah-lickoyee, meaning the "White Eye," was
surrounded by a dozen or more of his mourning acquaint-
ances, who were keeping up a concerted howl or chant,
in obedience to the directions of their prophet. The
Doctor, seeing that perfect repose and quiet were indispensable to the patient, requested me to order his friends
away, with instructions not to return. To rudely break
through the traditions of their tribe and superciliously
set aside the dictates of their "great medicine," was a
delicate task, so I directed the orderly in attendance to
send me, from my company, ten well armed and well
mounted soldiers, with a Sergeant and a Corporal. In
fifteen minutes the Sergeant reported and requested his
orders, which were to keep vigilant guard over the sheltered cabin of Ojo Blanco, and under no pretense to al-

low an Apache to enter, or permit one to make a noise in the vicinity, but to admit only the hospital nurse who would be sent to tend on the wounded man. Having given these orders, and seen the guard properly disposed, I told the Apache mourners to quit the place, and not to come back until permitted by the doctor. They had noticed the arrival of the troops, and knew that something unusual was brewing, and when this mandate was given them they left, very reluctantly and with sad foreboding, but quietly and in order. In a few days Ojo Blanco gave evidence of improved condition, and his former mourners were admitted to see him, but commanded to make no unusual demonstration. Three weeks subsequently the wounded man was again walking around the camp, an object of wonder to his people.

The reasons for these extraordinary precautions arose from the fact that the injured person was one of the most celebrated warriors of his tribe, and exercised very great influence. His was also the first case of the kind that had come under our cognizance; moreover, I suspected that the rascally prophet would use his death, had it occurred, to stir up the dissatisfaction of his people on the Reservation, and induce their fugitive departure, to engage again in their accustomed depredations. It also afforded an opportunity to exhibit the white man's skill and his interest in the Apaches, for Dr. Gwyther, after examining the wound, pronounced it severe, but not necessarily mortal. It will be seen that with proper precaution and judicious nursing, we had the whole thing in our hands, with the opportunity of further increasing Apache confidence and respect.

It is due to Ojo Blanco to say that his first visit, after his recovery, was paid to Dr. Gwyther and myself, expressing to each his fervent acknowledgments. In less than six weeks after my recall from New Mexico, this noted warrior fled from the Reservation at Fort Sumner, accompanied by over two hundred other men, women and children. I learned that he was subsequently killed in a battle with the Californian Volunteers.

My conversations with prominent warriors and saga- mores on the subject of religion were very frequent and protracted. The Apaches believe in the immortality of the soul, but they also place credence in two divinities, the one of Good and the other of Evil, between whom power is so evenly balanced that it is beyond the faculty of man to determine which is the greater, although the ultimate superiority is credited, without hesitation, to the Good Spirit, but they modify this superiority in so far as we are concerned, by curtailing the activity and interest which the Good Spirit takes in our behalf; while the Spirit of Evil is represented as being infinitely watch- ful and interested in the affairs of the Apache people. The Spirit of Good is in the distant future; but the Spirit of Evil takes part in our daily and hourly affairs. The result is that while they look up to the God of Good with extreme reverence and ultimate trust, their orisons, or usual petitions, are made to the divinity which they suppose to shape their earthly ends. This may be called the excess of barbarism and heathenish mythology; but, permit me to ask, is there any difference between the untutored and savage Apache and the apparently chris- tianized, civilized, and refined man of the world? Does not the latter put off his worship of Jehovah and take to that of Mammon quite as fully and steadfastly as the Apache endeavors to conciliate the spirit which he be- lieves will yield the most immediate and material re- sponse to his prayers? It is not mine to answer this question; let men's consciences — those who have any — respond for themselves.

The Apaches have no tradition whatever of the flood. They are quite ignorant of their origin, and unhesitatingly state that they have always lived in the same country, and been the same unmixed people. They pride themselves on the purity of their blood, and although they admit that many of their wives have been captured from Mexico, yet they affirm that it is not the woman, but the man, who bequeathes tone, character and speciality to the child. In addition to which they assert that no Mexican woman who has become the wife of an Apache, and remained so until she has borne him children, ever desires to renew her former life. That this last assertion is true, experience has sufficiently proved to my comprehension; but the reasons are clear.

In the first place, there is but a modicum of difference between the actual condition of the women in the northern frontiers of Mexico and that of the Apaches. In each case it is she who does all the work, and undergoes all the servitude to which women are condemned among semi-civilized races. In the second place, after having born children for an Apache her affections are concentrated upon her offspring more than upon the savage author of their birth, and she will not abandon them under almost any circumstances. In the third place, she knows that her restrained and protracted residence among the Apaches would subject her to rude, inhuman and opprobrious comments among her fellow countrywomen—should she return—although their own lives may be the exemplars of all that is vile and prostituted. It is not, therefore, difficult to conceive that the captive Mexican woman, the wife of a noted warrior, should cling to family relations of her own conception, whether forced or not, in preference to those which may have formerly occupied her attention as being natural.

People everywhere, and of all stages of refinement, accommodate themselves to the circumstances by which they are surrounded, and it is not ungenerous to permit the same privilege to the ignorant, docile and demoralized Mexican women of the lower classes. "Let him who is without sin cast the first stone." But it is proverbially true that from this mixture of races arise the most bloody, cruel and revengeful of American savages. The genuine Apache, after having killed his foe will leave his body to be desecrated and mutilated by his half-Mexican offspring, should such be present. It is true, that he will not interfere to prevent such outrage; but he seldom takes part in it himself, unless influenced by unwonted excitement; but when he does, he proves himself the master spirit, and his treatment is carried to the extent of savage excess. Precisely as the cat or terrier dog teaches its young how to catch and torment their prey, does the Apache instruct his disciples. In their heathenism, and barbarous ignorance, the dead bodies of their enemies are mutilated, and left in localities where they are sure to be found, to convey a sense of dread rather than from any innate disposition to deface that which they know to be insensible to their acts.

Their philosophy and treatment of the captive is entirely different. In such a case their savage and bloodthirsty natures experience a real pleasure in tormenting their victim. Every expression of pain or agony is hailed with delight, and the one whose inventive genius can devise the most excruciating kind of death is deemed worthy of honor. One of the most cruel spectacles ever presented to my gaze occurred in Cooke's Cañon, about twenty-eight miles east of the Mimbres river. A party of eight well armed Mexicans, accompanied by their families, and having seven wagons with eight mules to each wagon, were on their way from Sonora to California. They had some money, and expected to convert their mules and wagons into cash upon their arrival. They had already traversed the more dangerous portions of the Apache country, and had commenced to felicitate themselves, when they were set upon by nearly two hundred savages in Cooke's Cañon. The Mexicans defended themselves with undaunted courage, which forced the Apaches to take refuge in their accustomed cunning. Suddenly ceasing their assault, they informed the Mexicans that they had no desire to destroy their lives, adding, that the Mexicans could perceive from the superior numbers of their enemies, and their vantage ground, that it would be no very difficult task to effect such an object, had it been contemplated. They then said, that if the Mexicans would surrender their arms, and give them half the number of mules attached to the wagons, they might prosecute their journey in peace with the remainder. This proposition was accepted by the inexperienced Mexicans, and so soon as their savage enemies had obtained control of their arms, each man was seized, bound to the wheel of a wagon, head downward, about eighteen inches from the ground, a fire made under them, and their brains roasted from their heads. The women and children were carried off captive, and the train with its contents became a prey to the Apaches. As I was the first to pass through Cooke's Cañon after this affair, the full horror of the torture was rendered terribly distinct. The bursted heads, the agonized contortions of the facial muscles among the dead, and the terrible destiny certain to attend the living of that ill-fated party, were horribly depicted on my mind.

It is all very well to argue that the Indian knows no better — that he merely possesses the teachings of his

race, that his cruelties are the results of untaught savage
disposition, etc.; but the real questions are: must we
continue to endure the perpetration of such atrocities,
simply because they are committed by uncivilized beings;
is it true policy that intelligent, christian people should
be sacrificed, year after year, and their massacres excused on the ground that the murderers were only Indians? Is the special plea of the self-styled humanita-
rian, who knows nothing about the matter, to set aside
the life-long experiences of other equally humane but
more practical and experienced men? Must we forever
continue to accept the wild and impracticable theories of
parlor readers on Indian character? Can we continue
to pay millions annually for the short-sighted and pernicious policy which has heretofore regulated our Indian
affairs? The American savage is no idiot. He knows
right from wrong, and is quite as cognizant of the fact
when he commits a wrong as the most instructed of our
race. If the reader should feel a particle of doubt on
this point, all he has to do is to commit a wrong upon
an Apache, and he will very soon become convinced
that the savage is quite as much aware of the fact as he
can be.

It is even criminal to contend that they do not distinguish the full difference between the two qualities.
Their dealings with each other, and their conduct toward other races, prove that they do, and to an extent
almost commensurate in this respect with our own system of morals. The capacity to discriminate between
right and wrong is not the exclusive property of christianized people. It obtains with almost equal force
among barbarians and heathens, for otherwise communities could not exist. Whenever the Apache commits
an act of atrocity, he does so with design and intention,

and not from any ignorance as to whether it is a good or bad deed. He knows all about that as well as if he had attended Sunday School all his life; but it is done with an object—a purpose—which his untutored mind cannot perceive the effect of when weighed in the balance of the instructed in letters. When an Apache mutilates the dead body of his enemy, he knows that he is doing a wrong and cowardly act; but he persists in doing it, because he judges us from his stand-point, and imagines that sight of the mutilated corpse will produce terror in the beholders. He has not arrived at that amount of information which would instruct him that disgust and anger, with a determination for redress at the earliest opportunity, are engendered instead of dread. Like the rest of mankind, he is apt to measure other people's corn by his own bushel.

In respect to traditions they are very tenacious; but an incident occurred, when I enjoyed a favorable opportunity, to demonstrate the utter uselessness of relying upon such testimony. After having acquired their language, the idea suggested itself that it would be good policy to make them an address in the Apache tongue. To this end I composed a short oration, and, to be certain of the terms used and the pronunciation, I summoned Gian-nah-tah, Nah-tanh and Klo-sen, to whom I read my speech, requesting them to make the necessary corrections, which they did with undisguised pleasure. Having everything exactly right, a meeting of the leading Apache warriors was convoked at my cabin to hear my address in their own language. It can be readily understood that such an extraordinary announcement insured a full gathering of the invited warriors; and, after some preliminary ceremonies, I read the lecture, which was listened to with earnest attention. I took particular pains to impress them with the importance of remembering what I said, as it was my intention to demand from them a repetition of my words, or their tenor, in a few days from that time. They were also requested to convey the substance of my remarks to those who were not present, as I intended to investigate for myself the value of oral tradition. Three days subsequently I collected Gian-nah-tah, Klo-sen, Nah-tanh, and one or two other leading men, and taking each one aside separately, I asked him to repeat what I had said on the occasion referred to above. Some of them came very near stating the tenor of my remarks, while others gave very erroneous versions; but when it came to questioning the parties who had received my speech second-hand from those who had heard it, I could scarcely recognize my own offspring. Having listened carefully to all their statements, I again read the original production, which was immediately acknowledged as genuine.

Now, said I, you can comprehend the unreliability of your traditions. If you cannot remember, for even three days, the substance of so short an address, and if it becomes so mangled by being related from one to another that its original meaning is entirely perverted, what faith can be placed in those traditions which you say came down to you through so many generations? This question, enforced as it had been by a notable example, was unanswerable, and it was followed up by pointing out the difference between oral and written tradition. This paper, I said, holding up the manuscript of my speech, will remain for generations exactly as it is now, and should it be preserved for a thousand years, it will read, at the expiration of that time, precisely as you have just heard it read.

My hearers were wonderfully impressed with the truth

of these words; but when I endeavored to imbue them with the necessity of learning to read and write, so that they might be able to create written history, with one accord they refused, on the ground that it was work and consequently degrading. This abhorrence is so deeply rooted in their minds as to be a part of their nature, and no efforts of ours can remove it. Wherever an Apache child has been taken captive, and converted into a servant or domestic, it is only by extreme precaution that they can be restrained from running off and leading a vagabond life, and, if possible, rejoining some portion of their tribe.

Among those who were present at the above mentioned reading was the wife of Para-dee-ah-tran, who was also the daughter of Gian-nah-tah. This woman deserves special mention. Even in the most elevated circles of refined society it would be difficult to find one who possessed more grace, dignity and elegant self-repose. She was above the medium height, and of very fair complexion, although a full blooded Apache. Every motion and posture was replete with modesty and innate good sense. She was always well and comely clad; but never indulged in the tawdry finery and tinsel so much prized by other Apache women. Her figure was lithe and symmetrical; her hair long, black and glossy, and suffered to grow without being subjected to the process of cutting even with the eye-brows, which had been ruthlessly plucked out. It was parted in the middle, and smoothed away from the brow with as much taste as could be exhibited by any of our ladies. Her eyes were very large, black and lustrous, with a decided modesty of expression.

This woman was the pet of her tribe, and possessed characteristics in harmony with her exterior superiority. She was never permitted to perform hard labor, and her

hands were delicately small and well formed. She was
several times invited, with her husband and father, to
dine with the officers, by whom she was much respected,
and invariably conducted herself with an ease and dignified propriety which astonished her hosts. Her Indian
name has escaped my memory, but its definition in English is the "Stately One." It must, however, be borne
in mind that hers was a solitary exception, and so considered by all of her own people. There were many very
handsome young girls among them, but none like the
"Stately," who, instead of being an object of envy, possessed their unbounded admiration and respect.

CHAPTER XXIV.

ALLUSION has been made to the wonderful endurance
of the Apache race, and it now remains to give some
proofs of the fact.

Having received orders to make a scout of not less
than thirty days duration, I sallied out with thirty-four
men in December, 1863. Having learned that a large
band of Navajoes and Apaches had crossed the Rio
Grande and invaded New Mexico, where they had sub-
divided into small parties of eight and ten each, in order
to carry on their operations with more security, and de-
vastate a greater range of country, it became necessary
to wait until the scattered companies had reassembled,
and were about to leave the Territory with their plunder
before operations presenting any decisive result could
be inaugurated with reasonable hope of success. It
was known that the district upon which they had entered
offered only two direct modes of egress, one or both of
which must be selected, or the band would be compelled
to make a circuit of twelve hundred miles before regain-
ing home, and a considerable portion of this extensive
march was to be passed over the Llano Estacado, which

was frequently favored with the presence of Comanche war parties, from whom no favor could be expected on any terms. Instead, then, of pursuing the scattered fragments of the invaders, our march was directed toward a point from which the two passes, that of the Alamo Gordo Viejo, and that of the Pajaro, could be watched, so as to intercept the savages when leaving with their accumulated plunder.

Our guide was the best in the country. He united an intimate knowledge of localities with an excellent sense of Indian character, and their modes of operating. The first portion of our march was over an extensive rolling prairie, deeply seamed with gulches, which compelled us to make wide *detours*. Several bands of wild horses were met on this excursion, but would bound off with great speed at our approach. On one occasion, however, a fine herd, headed by a superb black stallion, came directly toward us, nor halted until within thirty yards. They threw up their heads, snorted and seemed to regard their visitors with intense curiosity, mingled with doubt and fear. It was strictly forbidden to shoot those animals, whose presence and unexpected proceedings were a source of pleasure, and after a good survey of some five or six minutes, their leader stamped his hoofs with violence, and being followed by the herd, circled our little party several times, and then galloped off with incredible speed and grace of movement. All these signs were proofs positive that no Indians had been there for some time, for the introduction of horse-flesh as a delicate article of food is properly due to the Apaches, and not the Parisians, although the latter may have refined upon the original system of cooking.

The guide led us to a smooth hill, perfectly free from wood or brush of any sort, but richly covered with the finest grama grass. After ascending this moderate elevation we beheld, just below, and occupying the intermediate vale between it and the next height, a delightful and thick wood, no portion of which could be perceived from any other point except the opposite hill. In the the center of this wood was a never-failing spring of delicious water, easy of access, and immediately adjoining a first-rate camping ground. This spring was aptly named *Cupido*, or Cupid. Here our little party came to an anchor, nearly midway between the two passes already mentioned. The Alamo Gordo Viejo Pass was three miles south, and the Pajaro Pass five miles northwest from the Cupido. Three men were sent to watch each pass, and to give the earliest possible information of the approach of the savages.

The next day, after our arrival, was signalized by a heavy fall of snow, to the depth of eight or nine inches, and this was followed by an almost intense cold, my spirit thermometer showing twenty degrees below zero of Fahrenheit's instrument. Four days previous we were in a region where the same thermometer stood at forty degrees above freezing point, making a difference of ninety-two degrees in the short period mentioned. We had been unconsciously rising to a very elevated position, and had left the region of the cotton-wood and the vine for that of the fir and the cedar. Here we passed the New Year of 1864, anxiously waiting for the savage marauders to break cover; and as the snow laid thickly on the ground, it afforded an unfailing means by which to note their advent. Becoming dissatisfied with this state of rest, and knowing that the Pajaro Pass was badly blocked with snow, I determined to move down toward the pass of the Alamo Gordo, and occupy such a position as would afford us a sort of cut-off to any

movement through that cañon. Camp was accordingly
changed, and a fresh position, in the open plain, selected.
No man in the command had more than two blankets,
and many had only one; wood was scarce, requiring all
hands to collect enough for ordinary cooking purposes;
the snow was six inches deep, and the weather looked
threatening. In no sense could our condition be deemed
agreeable. At eight o'clock P. M. another terrible snow-
storm burst upon us. The wind howled with fury, and
the flakes covered us with such density that it was necessary to throw it from the upper blanket every half hour,
its weight being oppressive. In the meantime two men
had been stationed at the outlet of the Alamo Gordo
Pass, with strict orders to inform me the moment the
Indians should make their appearance. Snow continued
to fall, but in moderate quantities, all of the next day,
and I heard nothing from my spies. The storm rather
increased that night, which was also extremely cold,
and next morning, at five o'clock, one of my lookout
men arrived in camp with the information that the Indians had passed with a large body of sheep at daylight
of the previous morning. He and his comrade had immediately come on to inform me, but the severity of the
storm and density of the snow were so great that he
could not distinguish objects, even at a short distance;
he had lost sight of his companion; had wandered about
all night, and was nearly dead with fatigue, suffering
and exposure.

The order to saddle up was immediately given and
obeyed, without waiting for breakfast, or even a cup of
hot coffee, and the command moved in such a direction
as would enable it to cut the Indian trail without losing
ground. Our rate of traveling was at the trot, and every
little while the horses' hoofs "balled" badly, greatly im-

peding our progress. In due course of time we reached the Pecos river, which was frozen over about two inches thick. The bank on our side was about four feet perpendicular descent, but on the other it rose gradually from the river. We plunged in, breaking through the ice, and as the water was only about two feet and a half deep, no damage was sustained further than cutting the forelegs of the advance animals. Half an hour after crossing the Pecos, we struck the broad, fresh trail of the Navajoes, which gave evidence of having been passed over some hours previous, as in many places it was covered with fresh snow two inches deep. The knowledge of this fact was disheartening, especially as night had commenced to close its sable curtains about our vision; but there was such a marked distinction between the virgin snow and that which had been trampled, that there was no difficulty in following the trail, although with greatly lessened speed. The storm had ceased two hours before, leaving us comparatively relieved. About eight o'clock P. M., we were hailed by an Apache, who said: *Nejeunee, pindah lickoyee; nuestche shee* — which means, "good friend, white eyes; come here." I halted the command and bade the speaker come forward. It proved to be Nah-tanh, accompanied by Nah-kah-yen and Natch-in-ilk-kisn. Upon hearing my voice, they came up and said that the Navajoes in their march, the *evening previous*, had crossed through the camp of some herders of beef cattle, about fifteen miles above Fort Sumner, where a slight brush occurred between the vaqueros and the Indians, which was terminated by the Navajoes leaving fifteen hundred head of sheep behind, and making the most of their way with the great body of their plunder.

News was immediately conveyed to the fort, when

13

Maj. Whalen ordered out Capt. Bristol's company of
United States Infantry, while Mr. Labadie, with thirty
Apache Indians and seven men of my company, who had
been left in camp to care for the horses and company
property, immediately mounted and pursued the Navajoes.   At three o'clock P. M., they came up with the marauding band, which numbered about one hundred, and
at once engaged the enemy, who formed line and made
a stand with about two-thirds their force, while the remainder were urged forward with the sheep.   The conflict lasted about an hour, during which twenty-five Navajoes were killed, and the remainder routed in all direc-
ions.   Bent upon recovering the prey, the victorious
party pushed on, but did not succeed in overtaking the
sheep until three hours later, when the parties in charge
fled and abandoned their hard-earned plunder, which
numbered nearly fourteen thousand head.   Such was
the story told me by the Apaches.   I asked Nah-tanh
whether his people had remained with Mr. Labadie to
guard the sheep, and he replied that he did not know,
but supposed some of them had.

It seems that the Regular Infantry sent by Major
Whalen had obtained this intelligence, and believing
that the affair was ended, had retraced their steps to the
fort.   Feeling it my duty to protect Mr. Labadie and
his diminished force, we hurried on until half-past ten
o'clock P. M., when we saw a very dim fire on the plain,
toward which we directed our course, and shortly arrived in his camp, having accomplished sixty-eight miles
through a snow-storm.   It is needless to add that he
was delighted to find himself so perfectly reinforced, as
all his ammunition had been expended, and he only had
the seven men of my company and twelve Apaches with
him, and was apprehensive that the Navajoes would

make another attempt to regain their plunder and revenge the death of their slaughtered comrades. Mr. Labadie also gave me the gratifying intelligence that a soldier of my company, Peter Loser, had contributed more than any other person toward the success of his expedition, having killed five Navajoes, and being always in the front during the fight.

That night was extremely cold; the thermometer fell to twenty-two degrees below zero. We had not a particle of wood, but in that locality, strange to say, there was no snow whatever upon the ground. The earth was frozen as hard as a rock, and the keen, cold blasts swept over an unbroken expanse of plain for a hundred miles. Our sufferings were dreadful, but there was no chance for relief. In their panic and eagerness to escape death, the Navajoes had thrown away their blankets, and were literally without any protection from the exceedingly severe weather, whereas our Apache allies had gathered up these much-needed trophies and were comparatively well to do. Next morning, at daylight, an alarm was given to the effect that the Navajoes had re-assembled, and were coming down upon the camp. My command was mounted in less than five minutes, and led out at the gallop toward the point from whence the signal came, which, by the way, had been given by an Apache; but after spending two hours in the most active search, we failed to perceive any sign whatever of their presence. Convinced that there was no ground for the alarm, I returned to Mr. Labadie, and offered to escort him sufficiently far on his way to insure the safety of his command and their prize, which offer was gratefully accepted. Having seen Mr. Labadie out of danger, we directed our course toward the route that it was probable the Navajoes had taken, as it would be their first effort to reach water, but our search was in vain; not a soul of them ever came under our observation. Subsequent arrivals of Navajo prisoners at Fort Sumner contained several who had been engaged in the affair just narrated, and they told me that it had been their intention to attack Mr. Labadie the night of the engagement, but that our opportune arrival, of which they had become aware, completely changed the prospects of success, and that instead of coming back next morning, they hurried off with all possible speed, and at the time we were hunting for them they must have been at least forty miles distant. Mr. Labadie arrived safely at Fort Sumner with fourteen thousand head of re-captured sheep, which would have fallen to us, but for the fact that my sentinels at the Alamo Gordo Pass lost their way in a snow-storm for twenty-four hours after the Indians had left the pass with their plunder. His comrade did not rejoin us until I again returned to Fort Sumner, whither he had gone, after discovering that the command had left for parts unknown.

Several of my men, being quite indisposed, were sent back to the fort by this opportunity, while the remainder continued the scout. Once more our direction laid to the northeast, but with little hope of finding more Indians. After several days we arrived at the Conchas Springs, about one hundred and eighty miles east-northeast from Fort Sumner, and encountered a severity of cold surpassing anything I had ever before experienced, although a native of Maine, and a visitor to its northernmost borders in the heart of winter. In my command were nine men from the same State, and none of them had ever known anything to compare with the intensity of the cold we suffered. The deepest part of the Conchas Springs is about seven feet, and the men cut through six feet of solid ice in the vain effort to obtain water for their horses. Six hundred yards to the east was a slight elevation crowned with stunted cedar trees, from four to twelve feet high, and there I determined to pitch my camp. The snow was eighteen inches deep and frozen hard, so that it required the weight of the horses to break through. We had no grain, and the only subsistence for the animals was the hardy grama grass which laid covered with ice-bound snow to the depth mentioned. It became absolutely necessary to uncover this sole magazine of feed, and the horses were trotted about until a considerable surface was broken, enough to enable them to gather some fodder. In the meantime, a small quantity of dry wood was collected, and a goodly fire got under way, which was enlivened from time to time by the resinous branches of the green cedars and firs about us, which yielded a lively, hot, but evanescent blaze. Green branches and trunks of trees were cut down and carefully baked under the hot ashes until they became combustible, and in their turn did like service for others. On the night of January 5th, 1864, my spirit thermometer declared forty degrees below zero of Fahrenheit. No man could go three hundred yards from camp and return at an ordinary walk without having his moustache covered with icicles, and if he wore a beard in addition, the two would be frozen together. Large quantities of snow and ice were melted in the camp-kettles to provide water for the horses, but the animals were always led up to the fires, for if the water were carried to them it would freeze hard before the soldier could reach his horse.

These facts, of which many witnesses exist in California, will serve to furnish some idea of Apache capacity to endure intense cold, especially when we bear in mind that they were at that time running about with nothing on save a breech-cloth. When they succeed in stealing sheep, a warm suit is immediately improvised by stripping the skin from the animal and investing their own bodies within its fleecy folds. A few thin strings of hide serve to connect the skins and form a robe. When the rascals have time to make their arrangements, the sheep are formed in a parallelogram, the width of which never exceeds thirty feet, with a length sufficient to accommodate the flock. The strongest sheep are then selected and their horns lashed together in couples, and these couples are ranged along either side of the main flock, forming a sort of animal fence which prevents the inclosed animals from wandering, especially while running by night. Along each side of the mass are stationed a string of Apaches on foot, who preserve regular distances, and animate the sheep to maintain a regular rate of speed. Immediately in front, a small body of select warriors and keen runners lead the way, while the main body of Indians follow in the rear to push forward and urge on the plunder. In this manner the Apaches will run a flock of twenty thousand sheep from fifty to seventy miles in one day, gradually lessening the distance, until they deem themselves tolerably safe from pursuit. They have been known to accomplish the distance of fourteen or fifteen hundred miles in the manner above described. These data are sufficient to determine the Apache's capacity for endurance.

The term for our scout having nearly expired, I determined to seek the warmer region of the Pecos without delay, especially as the horses had become very weak and thin. Fort Sumner was one hundred and eighty miles distant, and for two-thirds of the road the snow averaged from one foot to one inch in depth. We reached the fort after five days marching, being at the rate of thirty-six miles per day. On arriving, my thermometer was again consulted, and showed five degrees below zero, which, although a severe cold, was nevertheless a very grateful change in temperature. I was informed that the morning previous to our arrival the thermometer at the fort stood at ten degrees below zero, and it was then that the action took place between a few troops and a small band of Apaches, on one side, and one hundred and eighty Navajoes, as already recounted. The day before our arrival we came suddenly upon a very large band of antelopes, and the men were given permission to ride in among them for a hunt. We had them fairly corraled in such a manner as to compel their passage through our line close enough to pass within pistol range. On they came, probably to the number of two thousand, and dashed by with wonderful speed. The cavalry closed upon them and opened a rapid fire, which terminated in giving us ten fine animals in less than ten minutes. The scene was very exciting, as the men were all splendid riders and excellent marksmen. Had their horses been in good condition, we might have procured many more. Just at the time of the liveliest shooting, an ambulance, containing Lieut. Newbold and another officer, escorted by four cavalrymen, hove in sight and halted on the road about four hundred yards from the theater of operations. They thought, at first, that we had engaged a body of Indians, but catching sight of the scampering herd, they rode forward and were given a fine buck, which was lashed on top the ambulance.

It was curious to remark the immense numbers of ravens which daily directed their course toward the recent battle field, below the fort. Regularly, about the time of "reveille," immense numbers of them would wend their way right over the camp toward the south, and as regularly return at the time of "retreat," flapping their wings in a sluggish manner, as if gorged with food. Curiosity impelled me to visit the ground and see these birds at their feast. The field was literally black with them, and every corpse was thickly covered with a fluttering, fighting flock of scavengers. This regular flight of crows and ravens was regarded by the Apaches with unmistakable satisfaction, which was indignantly resented by the Navajoes, and served to keep alive the feud which had arisen between them. So soon as this feeling evinced itself it was pressed into service by the Post Commander, who contrived to make the tribes mutual spies upon each other's actions. Any misdeed of an Apache was sure to be detected and exposed by a Navajo, and *vice versa;* but the trouble of keeping them in order was much simplified.

CHAPTER XXV.

OF religious ceremonies the Apaches have very few, and these are limited to the immediate concerns of life. The occasional scalp dance and its accompanying purification of weapons, the feasts made at marriages, and when the girls attain the age of puberty, and the ceremonials observed at the sepulture of noted warriors, comprise the whole among a people not overburdened with reverential ideas, or prone to self-humiliation. Their prayers for success, if any such are ever made, are addressed to the Evil Spirit, who is supposed to rule entirely over the apportionment of fortuitous or prejudicial results to the people of this world. It is greatly to be doubted whether the bump of reverence was ever discoverable in an Apache skull. It would be, as it has always proved, a sheer waste of time and labor to make any effort at inculcating sentiments which have been abjured by them from the earliest periods, and to which they have become wedded. The teachings of christianity are so diametrically opposed to all their received opinions and crystallized ideas, that they regard them with abhorrence. To tell an Apache warrior that when he is smitten on one cheek it is his duty to receive a

13*

slap on the other, is to proclaim the teacher a fool and an unworthy person, in his opinion. To instruct him that it is criminal to deprive other people of their property, is to inform him that it is his duty to starve in order that his enemy may prosper. An endeavor to explain to him that he should forgive his enemies and harbor no feelings of vengeance for their assaults, would at once convict his instructor of such unmitigated nonsense as to forever debar him from all future consideration. The most that can be effected is to enforce his submission to superior power, which being accomplished, it should be our aim to exhibit that leniency to which he is a stranger, and make a start from that point. This would be a practical demonstration enlisting his attention and homage, and specially contrasting, by acts, the teachings of one religion as compared with those of the other, or, more properly speaking, no religion at all. To inculcate just ideas of such important facts into the savage mind, it is necessary to practice as well as preach, and the practice must chaperon the preaching. But a discussion on this subject is so entirely foreign to the objects contemplated by the author, and so completely outside his sphere of remark, that it will be dropped for other and more practical considerations.

The Apaches entertain the greatest possible dread of our discoveries of mineral wealth in their country. They have had experience enough to assure them that the possession of lucre is the great incentive among us to stimulate what is termed "enterprise." They know and feel that wherever mineral wealth exists to such an extent as to render it available, the white man fastens upon it with ineradicable tenacity. The massacre of the pioneer set does not deter another company from experimenting in the same engaging field. These localities are always rendered more valuable by the proximity of wood and water, two scarce articles in Arizona. The occupation of mines involves the possession of water facilities and sufficient fuel. To occupy a water privilege in Arizona and New Mexico is tantamount to driving the Indians from their most cherished possessions, and infuriates them to the utmost extent. If one deprives them of their ill-gained plunder he is regarded as an outrageous robber; but should he seize upon one of their few water springs, he is rated a common and dangerous enemy, whose destruction it is the duty of all the tribe to compass. It may be reasonably inferred from these remarks that when an Apache voluntarily discovers a rich mine to a white man he is influenced either by kindness, or is attempting to lay a trap for his destruction, baited by cupidity.

Among those under our charge was a noted fighter named Tats-ah-das-ay-go, or the "Quick Killer." This man was feared even by the boldest of his tribe; in fact, he had acquired among them the reputation of being a "Rough," or "Bowery Boy," and, although noted for his personal courage and prowess, was severely left to the enjoyment of his own society in time of peace. He had espoused half a dozen wives, who found it impossible to live under his capricious rule, and he was, at the time of our acquaintance, a sort of tabooed individual, to whom all paid outward respect, but entertained concealed dislike. Tats-ah-das-ay-go paid little heed to these demonstrations. He lived alone, hunted his own game, received his own rations, and was seldom seen among his fellows. For some unaccountable reason this savage conceived a great personal regard for the writer, and was accustomed to freely recount his adventures in various parts of Mexico, Arizona and New Mexico. Ac-

cording to his own narrations, which were confirmed by
the testimony of his fellows, his whole life had been a
tissue of sanguinary deeds.   A rivulet of blood tracked
the course of his history.   He was a man of decided
native genius, and perfect master of all sorts of Apache
lures, wiles and deceits.   From him I learned much of
Indian character, and he seemed desirous to teach.   Tats-
ah-das-ay-go wore upon his body hair, which hung down
below the middle of his back in a broad, thick plait, a
number of silver shields, perfectly round, and with a
tongue or bar in the center of each, through which
passed the band of hair in such a manner as to display
the shields to the greatest advantage.   The first, or upper one, was the size of a common saucer, and nearly as
thick, while the next below was a little smaller, and each
succeeding one still less in size, until the last and thir-
teenth was about twice as large as a silver dollar.   Of
these he was extremely vain, and never laid them aside
except to comb and dress his long and luxuriant hair.
These ornaments I had always believed were taken from
the saddle mountings of Mexican victims, and one day
I jocularly remarked:

"Did you have a hard time to acquire those spoils?"

"You mistake, Tata," he replied; "these are not
spoils taken from Mexicans; but I found this silver and
beat it out myself."

"Where did you find it?" I asked.

"Away down in the mountains which border the Pecos,
far south from here;" adding, "I will tell you all about
it. We were in the Guadalupe Mountains, and were
going upon the Llano Estacado to hunt buffalo; but
previous to doing this a number of us climbed the sierra
to look out upon the plains and see that they were clear
of Comanches.   In ascending the mountain I took hold

of a small bush to assist my steps, when it gave way, and I saw a bright lump of something just under the roots. Picking it up, I discovered that it was very heavy and like the *pesh-lickoyee*, or *plata-hay*, with which rich Mexicans mount their saddles. I collected a quantity, and afterwards beat it out in the shape you see. This was many years ago and I have never been there since."

I had seen enough of the mineral richness of Arizona and New Mexico to convince me that there might be some truth in this narration, but determined to wait until a favorable opportunity should occur to permit exploration. Three or four months afterward orders were received from Gen. Carleton, ordering me to "keep the country clear of Indians for the space of *three hundred miles* around the post." Such an order had never before been issued to an officer in the service. It was unparalleled and altogether unique; but in obedience thereto a scout was ordered under my command, and I determined to make an exploration in the region mentioned by Tatsah-das-ay-go, and to take him with me. In due season the party left Fort Sumner, thirty-five strong, and traveled in a zig-zag direction for several days until the Guadalupe Mountains were reached. On the succeeding day Quick Killer informed me that we were near the cañon where he had found the silver, and that he would direct us to it next morning, which he did about ten o'clock the following day.

Having arrived at the cañon, I left the command under the charge of the First Sergeant, and proceeded with Quick Killer for about a mile and a quarter, when he dismounted and hitched his horse to a tree, requesting me to do the same, which I did, keeping my carbine ready and placing my holster pistols in my belt. We then ascended about three hundred feet until we reached a bold and unmistakable mineral ledge, thickly shrouded with underbrush and stunted trees. Quick Killer stopped a moment, examined the place well, and proceeded directly to a spot, which he unearthed for a few inches and displayed several magnificent specimens of virgin silver. I was satisfied, and possessing myself of a goodly lump, we retraced our steps to the command, none of whom were ever made cognizant of these occurrences. Wood, water and grass abound in the locality, which is in western Texas, on the Pecos river; but so long as the country is held by the Apaches, this valuable region must remain entirely useless for all practical purposes. This is but one of many experiences demonstrating the vast mineral resources of Arizona, New Mexico and Western Texas. Sonora, Chihuahua and portions of Durango are also extensively endowed with mineral wealth, but they are unavailable under present circumstances. While crossing an extensive prairie, dotted here and there by a few shrubs and diminutive bushes, Quick Killer volunteered, while resting at noon, to show me with what dexterity an Apache could conceal himself, even where no special opportunity existed for such concealment. The offer was readily accepted, and we proceeded a short distance until we came to a small bush, hardly sufficient to hide a hare. Taking his stand behind this bush, he said: "Turn your back and wait until I give the signal." This proposition did not exactly suit my ideas of Apache character, and I said: "No, I will walk forward until you tell me to stop." This was agreed upon, and quietly drawing my pistol, keeping a furtive glance over my shoulder, I advanced; but had not gone ten steps, when Quick Killer hailed me to stop and find him. I returned to the bush, went around it three or four times, looked in every direction—there was no possible covert in sight;

the prairie was smooth and unbroken, and it seemed as if the earth had opened and swallowed up the man. Being unable to discover him, I called and bade him come forth, when, to my extreme surprise, he arose laughing and rejoiced, within two feet of the position I then occupied. With incredible activity and skill he had completely buried himself under the thick grama grass, within six feet of the bush, and had covered himself with such dexterity that one might have trodden upon him without discovering his person. I took no pains to conceal my astonishment and admiration, which delighted him exceedingly, and he informed me that their children were practiced regularly in this game of "hide and seek," until they became perfect adepts. We have far-reaching rifles and destructive weapons, but they must ever be ineffective against unseen enemies; and it is part of a soldier's duty, while engaged in Indian countries, to study all their various devices.

Another excellent illustration of their skill in concealment was given me by Nah-kah-yen. We were hunting together, when a large herd of antelopes made its appearance. Nah-kah-yen immediately tore off a small strip from an old red handkerchief and tied it to the point of a yucca stalk, at the same time handing me his rifle and saying: *Ah-han-day anah-zon-lee* — "go off a long way"—he instantly buried himself under the sand and grass with the ease and address of a mole. I at once moved away several hundred yards, and sought to creep up to the antelopes, who were evidently attracted by the piece of red rag fluttering on the yucca stalk. Not wishing to interrupt the sport of my savage comrade, and anxious to witness the upshot of his device, I remained a "looker on and a spectator" of the affair. In a little while a marked commotion was noticeable n the herd, which galloped off very rapidly for a hundred yards or so, but soon recovered their equanimity, and again approached the attractive red rag. These strang e agitations occurred several times, until the antelopes finally dashed away over the plains with wonderful speed. Nah-kah-yen then arose and beckoned me to come, which I did, and found that he had killed four of the herd. We had all the meat our horses could well pack, but the distance to camp was only five miles and soon made.

Travelers over our plains have frequently observed that the prairie dog, rattlesnake and ground owl live together in one habitation, and being unable to solve the problem myself, I asked several shrewd Apache warriors to do it for me. The rattlesnake, said they, is a very wise reptile. He permits the prairie dog to make a nice, warm nest, and then he quietly takes possession, but does not disturb the safety of the inmates, who retire and fit up another cell, quite ignorant of the snake's intention, who makes it a point never to injure the old pair, unless pressed by dire necessity; but in the most stealthy manner devours one of the young brood every now and then, leaving no evidence of his carnivorous propensity. The parents never seem to entertain any suspicion of their dangerous guest, who always puts on his best behavior in their presence, although capable of destroying them with ease. On the other hand, the snake never devoursa prairie dog when he can seize his more legitimate prey above ground, but keeps them as a sort of reserved fund. The ground owls scarcely ever descend into the depths of the hole, but burrow a separate cell close by its entrance, whither they retire for repose and to deposit and hatch their eggs. In the day time they sit nodding on top the hillocks made by the prairie dogs, and at night they hunt their prey, which consists of lizards and all sorts of bugs and beetles, after which they sleep—in the early morning—and re-appear again about eleven o'clock A. M. As I have never examined into this subject, I can only relate the Apache version.

Among nearly all other of our American tribes if one man murders another, the next warrior of kin to the slain person is entitled to the right of revenging his death by killing his murderer, after he has been tried and condemned by a council of the tribe; but this custom does not obtain among the Apaches. If one man kills another, the next of kin to the defunct individual may kill the murderer—if he can. He has the right to challenge him to single combat, which takes place before all assembled in the camp, and both must abide the result of the conflict. There is no trial, no set council, no regular examination into the crime or its causes; but the ordeal of battle settles the whole matter. Should the next of kin decline to prosecute the affair, then some other warrior of the family may shoulder the responsibility and seek retribution.

Among those who had surrendered themselves was a very old man, probably nearly a hundred years of age, for other men of fifty-five and sixty told me that he was a noted warrior when they were little children. His name was Sons-in-jah, or the " Great Star." This man's frame was of enormous proportions. His height, even at that extreme age, was six feet three inches, without moccasins. His shoulders were extremely broad, his arms of uncommon length, and his shriveled limbs exhibited a volume of bone almost equal to that of a large horse. The old man's eye-sight had begun to fail, but his hearing was keen as ever. His head was as white as snow, and he was the only gray-headed Apache I ever saw. Several of his front teeth were gone, probably lost from a blow, but his molars were almost equal to those of a horse. Heavy folds of thick skin fell over each other down his abdomen; but the muscles and cords in his legs and arms seemed to be made of steel. This old man came regularly to see me every day that I was in camp, and it delighted me to treat him with kindness, although I felt convinced that for three-quarters of a century his hands had been steeped in blood. His memory was fresh and vivid, full of recollections, and teeming with experiences of the past. He outlived his usefulness, and was neglected by the tribe. He said, that when he was a boy the hills and the valleys of his country were filled with his people. They were very numerous and dreaded by all surrounding peoples. But dissention crept in among themselves. Family feuds led to family *vendettas*, and innumerable duels; that the defeated besought the aid of the Spaniards, who afterward turned their weapons against their allies. In those days, said he, we had none but stone-headed arrows, and sharpened stakes for lances. The Mexicans were just like ourselves. The other day I was in Santa Fé and saw the Mexican women dressed in great finery, with gowns of many colors; but I remember when they wore little more than breechcloths, and were but too happy to own the very coarsest kind of vesture. By and by the Spaniards went away and left the Mexicans to themselves. At first we lived quite on good terms with each other; but then some American traders arrived, who were dreadful people, always getting drunk, and killing each other or somebody else. These men made raids upon us, and carried off our women and children whom they sold to the Mexicans. This excited our vengeance against the invaders and those

who bought their plunder, and ever since a deadly feud
has raged between them and the Apaches. You "white
eyes," added Sons-in-jah, know how to read and write;
you know how to circulate your information and ideas
from one to the other, although you may never see or
know the party: but we poor Apaches are obliged to relate what we know and have seen by means of words
only, and we never get together in large parties to remain long enough to disseminate any great amount of
information.

The foregoing incisive sentences precisely reflect the
drift of the remarks made to me by the old man on
many occasions. I am largely indebted to him for much
information on other points, which he imparted with perfect freedom, especially as he considered himself a *pro-
tegé* of mine, and received more kindness from me than
from his own people. But with all my efforts I failed to
obtain from Sons-in-jah any recital of their modes of
sepulture. On this point he was invariably reticent.
He was by no means vain-glorious; seldom referring to
his own deeds, unless extracted from him under favorable circumstances. After sunning himself on a fine
day, he would wink his bleared eyes in a knowing manner, and invite me to take a seat near him and listen to
his recitals. Deeds of violence and sanguinary outrages,
hair-breadth escapes, terrific journeys and bold robberies
were rehearsed with intense gratification to the old man;
but after relating each incident he was always particular
to give me a "reason" for his acts. In other words, he
sought to excuse the bloody record of his life by stating
the incentives. If any other argument were needed to
satisfy me that the Apache is fully cognizant of the difference between right and wrong, this old reprobate's
excuses were sufficient to remove all remaining doubts

I utilized old Sons-in-jah in a variety of ways. He was entirely nude, with the exception of a much worn breech-cloth, and he complained bitterly that his people treated him with neglect, and robbed him of his rations. I gave him a good pair of soldier's pants of the largest size, a flannel shirt and a stout pair of shoes, which delighted him greatly. He came regularly every day for food, which he received from me whenever I was in camp, and at other times from some member of the company.

"How is it," said I, "that the Apaches contrive to live in places where there is neither game nor plunder?" The old man laughed heartily at my ignorance and simplicity, and replied:

"There is food everywhere if one only knows how to find it. Let us go down to the field below, and I will show you."

The distance was not more than six hundred yards, and we proceeded together. There appeared to be no herbage whatever on the spot. The earth was completely bare, and my inexperienced eyes could detect nothing. Stooping down he dug with his knife, about six inches deep, and soon unearthed a small root about the size of a large gooseberry. "Taste that," said he; I did, and found it excellent, somewhat resembling in flavor a raw sweet potato, but more palatable. He then pointed out to me a small dry stalk, not larger than an ordinary match, and about half as long: "Wherever you find these," he added, "you will find potatoes." This was in October, and a few days afterward the field was covered with Indians digging these roots, of which they obtained large quantities. Pursuing the subject, Sons-in-jah said: "You see that big field of sun-flowers; well, they contain much food, for we take the seeds, reduce them to flour upon our *metates* and make it into cakes, which are very nice. Again: the mescal, which you white people would pass without notice, is convertible into excellent food by the simple process of roasting. Furthermore, we know exactly when, where and how to trap and catch small animals, like the prairie dogs, foxes, raccoons and others; besides which there are many plants containing nutriment of which you know nothing, or would not eat if you did. One day an Apache woman died in camp, and I asked Gian-nah-tah if there would be much lamentation. He simply smiled at the idea, and replied: "It was a woman; her death is of no account." The Apaches are extremely reserved about letting outsiders approach their dead, and invariably bury them under the cover of night, with the most cautious secrecy; but the Navajoes were quite unreserved, and it was only by threats or promises that we could induce the nearest of kin to take a dead body out for sepulture. Cases occurred when the corpses were left wholly uncared for several days successively, and the deaths not reported, from a desire to escape the duty of performing the dreaded burial service.

CHAPTER XXVI.

THE boldness and address with which the Apaches carry out their designs, and the crafty cunning they display when desiring to mislead their enemies, can be best illustrated by stating several notable occurrences. The horses of the two companies commanded by Captains McCleave and Fritz, of the First California Cavalry, had become thin and weak from long and active service, and needed rest and refreshment. For this purpose General Carleton ordered them to the Reventon, a large rancho near the town of Tubac; but finding better grass and superior camping ground near the town of San Xavier del Bac, the companies took up temporary residence at that place. San Xavier is principally inhabited by Papago Indians, and contains about fifteen hundred souls. The Papagoes are semi-civilized, and have always been friendly; but a deadly feud exists between them and the Apaches, who seize every opportunity to annoy, rob and murder those people. The Papagoes had a large number of horses which were grazed, in the daytime, near the town, and caught up at night for fear of their being stolen by the ever vigilant foe. When McCleave and Fritz arrived with two hundred troopers, and grazed their horses by night under a strong guard, the Papagoes imagined that the force would deter the Apaches and keep them away. Under this impression they also permitted their animals to feed by night. On the other hand, the Apaches, as one of them afterward told me, foresaw precisely what happened. Those foolish Papagoes, said they, will think that because the Californian troops are so near that their property will be safe, and will relax their usual caution; now is our time to act. They did act, and to such purpose that they took nearly every horse once possessed by the Papagoes. Here was a specimen of nice judgment, founded upon a shrewd knowledge of human nature, and executed with boldness and address.

A wealthy resident of New Mexico, near Polvadera, owned a herd of superior horses of which he was extremely careful. The band numbered nearly one hundred, and were renowned for their excellence. These horses were strictly guarded every day, while grazing not far from the house, by twelve or fifteen well armed Mexicans, and at nightfall were inclosed in a large and strong corral, the walls of which were sixteen feet high and three feet thick, the only entrance being through a large and strong gate which was heavily barred and locked. Numerous attempts to steal this herd had been made by the Apaches, but invariably without success. The horses fed on a smooth, open plain, which could be easily scanned, and was so close to the corral that they could be placed in safety in a few minutes. At length one bold rascal determined either to get the herd or die attempting it. One very dark and stormy night he contrived to climb over the corral wall, and concealed himself in the hay and feed scattered about. Here he remained until the earliest dawn, when he selected the best horse in the lot, and mounting him, waited for the gates to be thrown open.

Soon afterward the herders, yet unarmed, collected with their *reatas*, each one ready to lasso a horse for that day's service, as was their custom, after which the selected horses were to be saddled, then arms taken, and the herd driven to pasture. As soon as the gate was thrown open the frolicsome horses made a rush to get out, as they always did, the Apache keeping in the rear until all were outside, when, with a yell, and the alarming sound of an instrument they use when stampeding animals, he started the frightened herd which darted off at full speed, leaving the astonished and bewildered Mexicans in distress. The scoundrel, by leaning down from the horse so he could not be seen, had escaped notice and accomplished the robbery. Comment upon this bold and desperate act is quite unnecessary; it speaks for itself.

Lieut.-Col. Ferguson, of the First California Cavalry, bought a fine American horse, for which he paid three hundred dollars. He availed himself of the escort offered by my company to proceed to Tucson. One afternoon we camped in a grove of large cotton-wood trees, without underbrush, and in a favorable position. The picket line was run from tree to tree, and at sunset the horses were fastened to it, fed, groomed, and a guard of two men, one each side, placed over them. The Colonel would not permit his horse to be tied up with those of the company, saying that he did not want him kicked nor bitten by those malicious half-breeds—and, I must say, with some reason — for there were a number of vicious animals among them. By his order, an iron stake was driven in the ground, about twenty feet from one end of the picket line, and just opposite the entrance to a narrow, rocky cañon. The moon was very brilliant, but would set behind the mountains about one o'clock A. M., and orders were given to keep a special watch over the Colonel's horse after that hour. About the time mentioned, the camp was alarmed by the report of a couple of carbines, and on inquiring the cause, found that the sentries had fired at an Apache who had gone off with the Colonel's horse. The successful robber had approached quite close to the animal without being discovered, and the moment the moon hid her light behind the hill, he cut the halter, sprang upon its back, stooped off on one side, and galloped up the cañon. The sentries heard the noise, suspected the cause, and fired in the direction of the retreating savage.

The mail service between Forts Sumner and Union, one hundred and eighty miles apart, required that the military courier should be mounted on the best horse disposable. The Reservation, at the former place, was forty miles square, and within its limits the Indians had a right to roam. On one occasion, while the courier was returning with the mails, he stopped near the entrance to a large and very crooked cañon, dotted with huge fragments of rock. At this place the grass was very fresh and fine, which induced the soldier to halt and permit his tired and hungry horse to graze for half an hour. He accordingly dismounted, and let the animal range to the extent of his *reata*, which was a remarkably fine one, and about sixty feet long. Although on the Reservation, he drew his pistol and seated himself on a fragment of the rock. While occupied in noticing the movements of his horse, he was addressed by an Apache, who had come up within four feet of him without being perceived. The Indian, who was unarmed, held out his hand in the frankest manner, and said: *Nejeunee, nejeunee;* which means, "friendly, kind." The soldier, believing him to be one of those under our charge, suffered him to approach and shake hands.

14

Soon the wily savage pretended to be delighted at the
reata, which he declared was the finest he ever saw,
and commenced to examine it with critical attention
throughout its length until he reached the horse, which
he also evidently admired.   Patting the animal, he remarked, *mucho bueno;* yes, answered the soldier, he is a
fine horse.   In the meantime, the Indian, unnoticed by
the soldier, had drawn a small knife from the leg of his
moccasin and severed the *reata* close to the horse, keeping the cut ends concealed in his left hand while patting
the horse with his right.   Suddenly he pointed behind
the soldier and shouted, *Comanche on dahl;* which means,
" the Comanches are coming."   Involuntarily the soldier
turned to see, and at the instant the Apache sprang into
the saddle, and in two bounds was behind the friendly
shelter of a huge rock, from whence he effected his escape with the horse, leaving the soldier holding the *reata*
in one hand and his pistol in the other.   I might go on
and relate many more incidents of the same character,
but as they all illustrate the same special traits, they
will be omitted.   The moral to be drawn is, that the
traveler can never exercise too much prudence while
among the Apaches, and it will never do to underrate
their boldness, skill and craftiness.

They are fond of bathing in the summer, and are all
expert swimmers; but nothing can induce them to wash
themselves in winter.   They are the most reckless of all
gamblers, risking anything they possess upon the turn
of a card.   Men, women and children indiscriminately
engage in this vice; but there are some games to which
women are never allowed access.   Among these is one
played with poles and a hoop.   The former are generally about ten feet in length, smooth and gradually ta-
pering like a lance.   It is marked with divisions through-

out its whole length, and these divisions are stained in different colors. The hoop is of wood, about six inches in diameter, and divided like the poles, of which each player has one. Only two persons can engage in this game at one time. A level place is selected, from which the grass is removed a foot in width, and for twenty-five or thirty feet in length, and the earth trodden down firmly and smoothly. One of the players rolls the hoop forward, and after it reaches a certain distance, both dart their poles after it, overtaking and throwing it down. The graduation of values is from the point of the pole toward the butt, which ranks highest, and the object is to make the hoop fall on the pole as near the butt as possible, at the same time noting the value of the part which touches the hoop. The two values are then added and placed to the credit of the player. The game usually runs up to a hundred, but the extent is arbitrary among the players. While it is going on no woman is permitted to approach within a hundred yards, and each person present is compelled to leave all his arms behind. I inquired the reason for these restrictions, and was told that they were required by tradition; but the shrewd old Sons-in-jah gave me another, and, I believe, the true version. When people gamble, said he, they become half crazy, and are very apt to quarrel. This is the most exciting game we have, and those who play it will wager all they possess. The loser is apt to get angry, and fights have ensued which resulted in the loss of many warriors. To prevent this, it was long ago determined that no warrior should be present with arms upon his person or within near reach, and this game is always played at some distance from camp. Three prominent warriors are named as judges, and from their decision there is no appeal. They are not suffered to bet while acting in that capacity. The reason why women are forbidden to be present is because they always foment troubles between the players, and create confusion by taking sides and provoking dissention. I once asked Gian-nah-tah why the Apaches were such fools as to risk all they had in gaming. "Why," said he, "what difference does it make? They never play with any but Apaches; fortune will not always stick to one person, but continually changes. What is mine to-day will belong to somebody else to-morrow, while I get another man's goods; and, in course of time, I once more own my old articles. In this manner each successively owns the property of all his fellows." To argue against this style of reasoning, by pointing out the vice and immorality of gambling, would only have subjected me to derision and contempt, and as I am not a missionary—especially one of the self-sacrificing class—I received his explanation with every mark of favor. The women have several games of their own, in which the men never mingle; but when cards are used, everybody takes a share in the business.

Racing on foot is another diversion frequently resorted to by these active, restless Indians, and the women generally manage to carry off the palm, provided the distance is not too great. The officers at the post offered a number of prizes to be competed for, the fastest runner to take the prize apportioned to the distance for which it was offered. The longest race was half a mile, the next a quarter, the third three hundred yards, and the fourth one hundred. It was open for men under forty years of age and over fifteen, and for girls from fifteen up to twenty-five. About a hundred Apaches and Navajoes entered for the prizes, and practiced every day for a week. At the appointed time everybody in camp assembled to witness the contest. Among the competitors was the Apache girl, Ish-kay-nay, a clean-limbed, handsome girl of seventeen, who had always refused marriage, and she was the favorite among the whites. Each runner was tightly girded with a broad belt, and looked like a race horse. Ten entered for the half mile stake, which was a gaudy piece of calico for a dress or shirt, as the case might be. At the word, they went off like rockets, Nah-kah-yen leading handsomely, and Ish-kay-nay bringing up the rear, but running as clean and easy as a greyhound. Within four hundred yards of the goal, she closed the gap, went by like a steam engine, and got in an easy winner, six yards ahead of all competitors. For the quarter mile race she again entered, but was ruled out by the other Indians, and their objections were allowed, it being decided that the victor in either race should not enter for another.

The second contest was won by Nah-kah-yen, but not without a desperate struggle with Manuelito, a very prominent Navajo chief. The third and fourth prizes were gained by Navajoes. Manuelito was the finest looking Indian man I ever saw. He was over six feet in height, and of the most symmetrical figure, combining ease, grace, and power and activity in a wonderful degree. He was a great dandy, and was always elaborately dressed in the finest Indian costume. His leggings were highly ornamented, and his buckskin jacket fitted without a wrinkle. A splendid bunch of many colored plumes, surmounted by two eagle's feathers, adorned his head, while his shapely feet were incased in elegantly worked moccasins. Navajo blankets have a wide and merited reputation for beauty and excellence, some of them being worth a hundred dollars a piece in the New Mexican market, and over his shoulders was one of su-

perior character, worn with the grace and dignity with
which a Roman Senator might be supposed to don his
toga.   So vain a man could not be well otherwise than
brave, and he was noted for his gallantry.   But he was
also esteemed one of the wisest counselors in his tribe,
and had headed many a bloody and destructive inroad
until compelled to yield to the Californian troops.   While
on the Reservation his conduct was proud, haughty and
decorous.   He never honored any of us with his presence except when he came on business, but never exhibited any animosity.

Although the Navajoes and Apaches are identically
one people, speaking the same language and observing
nearly the same ceremonies, yet they differ materially in
many respects, undoubtedly caused by a marked difference of climate.   The country of the Navajoes is cold
and inhospitable in winter—subject to deep snows and
long continued frosts—while that roamed over by the
Apaches is far milder, and in many portions of even tor-
rid heat.   This compels the Navajoes to erect substantial huts of an oval form, the lower portion of the hut
being excavated, and the upper composed of substantial
stakes brought together and firmly fastened at the top.
Long, slender and supple poles are then hooped closely
about the stakes, and the whole thickly covered with
mud.   These huts are sometimes quite roomy, many of
them being twelve or fourteen feet in diameter.   The
women are extremely dexterous in weaving a very superior kind of blanket, the colors of which are generally
black and white; but sometimes made of green, blue,
red, pink, purple, white, black, etc., so arranged as to
produce a very gaudy and striking effect.   These blankets
are perfectly water-proof, and very thick, but they scarcely
impart as much warmth as one of first-class California

manufacture. They last for years, retaining their beauty and colors without loss of brilliancy. This manufacture of blankets arises from the exigencies of the climate, and was originally learned from the Mexicans when the two people lived on amicable terms. The procurement of wool is one of their prime necessities, and is the inciting cause of the terrific raids they make into New Mexico, which is specially a sheep raising country. When large herds of cattle are met, the Navajoes "gobble them up" with avidity, but seldom molest them when few in number, as they cannot be driven with the rapidity of sheep; leave a broader and more marked trail, and serve only for food. These Indians live together in considerable numbers during the winter months, a village frequently containing from two hundred to eight hundred inhabitants. Such communities must necessarily be governed by a more systematic organization than obtains among the Apaches proper; hence they have regular chiefs and sub-chiefs, whose orders are obeyed, and who are charged with the government of all present; but his office is not hereditary, the chieftainship being determined by election. The fortunate candidate holds office for life, or during good behavior, and feels no little pride in his position. In all matters wherein the Navajoes differ from the Apaches, they will be found chargeable to the climatic differences of their several countries. Their ceremonies, religious views, traditions, language, and general deportment, as well as their personal appearance, are so strikingly similar as to be almost undistinguishable. If the Navajo woman is more industrious and skilled than the Apache, she is also much more loose and wanton. A very marked characteristic of the latter people is their strict chastity, while the Navajoes are quite as much noted for their utter want of virtue.

Prior to the time of Mangas Colorado, several disputes of a serious character had occurred between these two tribes, but that shrewd Indian statesman managed to bestow one of his daughters upon the most noted of the Navajo chiefs, and finally succeeded in restoring the strictest amity, which continued without cessation during his long life devoted to his people's good, and until the Navajoes, angered at the surrender of the Apaches at Fort Sumner, made a raid upon their horses, and were driven off with great slaughter. But the enmity engendered by such conflicts never extended to parties outside the Reservation. Fort Bascom, situated on a branch of the Red river, one hundred and twenty-five miles east-north-east from Fort Sumner, was frequently visited by Comanche Indians, and on one occasion a large band, numbering nearly two hundred, informed the commander at Bascom that they intended to "clean out" the Apaches located at Sumner. That officer replied: "Do not attempt so foolish a thing. There are three companies of soldiers at that place, two of which are cavalry, and so sure as you molest the Apaches under their charge they will not only fight you themselves, but will arm and place the Apaches in the field against you. Take my advice and let them alone." Shortly afterward, while out with a small party, I met this same band of Comanches, when the chief repeated his intention to me, and told me what the commander of Bascom had said. Divining the Indian's drift, I immediately replied: "You tell me nothing new. We have all heard this before, and have made preparations to give you a welcome commensurate with your fame as a warrior. My commander has sent me out with these twenty-five men to find you and conduct you to his camp. The Comanches and Americans are friends. He does not wish to molest you, nor will he permit you to molest him, or those for whose safety he is responsible; but if this thing must come off, the sooner the better. Whenever my Comanche brother wishes to move toward Fort Sumner, I am ready to accompany him." "I have no time now," was the reply, "but will come this way again after three moons, and then we will catch the Apaches, but we will not fight the Americans." He and his band then wheeled their horses and rode off into the wilderness, taking an easterly course. We never heard of them afterwards.

14*

CHAPTER XXVII.

Ignorance of Indian Character Discussed.—Political Indian Agencies.—How the
Indian Affairs Should be Managed.—Necessity of Force. — Absurd System
in Vogue.—Crushing Out Advised.—How the Apaches Should be Fought.—
Proper Method of Campaigning.—Suggestions.—Culpable Neglect of Congress.—General Deductions.—Californian Troops.—Conclusion.

THE romantic wanderings of Catlin, Schoolcraft and
some others among the Indian tribes of North America;
the delightful tales of Cooper, as developed in his "Trap-
per," "Last of the Mohicans," etc.; the stirring adventures of Captain John Smith, Daniel Boone, Chamberlin,
Carson, Hays and a host of noted pioneers, have invested
our Indian races with rare and absorbing interest.   But
they have also tended to convey false and erroneous impressions of Indian character, and have contributed to
misguide our legislation on this subject to such an extent
as to become a most serious public burden.

Since the foundation of our Government, Indian wars
have cost the American people nearly four hundred
millions of dollars, and the stream of expenditure continues with unabated volume.   When the whites were
few and the savages many, the cost of keeping them in
subjection was measurably less than it has been since the
reversal of our respective numerical conditions.   Whence
arises this anomaly?   Simply because of our strange ignorance of Indian character as it really exists, and not as
we have been taught to understand it by writers of attractive fiction, or the chroniclers of heroic deeds and romantic
adventures.   This sweeping assertion may be met with

one more plausible and popular, because more suggestive, and having the merit of being sanctioned by time. "Is it possible," exclaims the old school debater, "that we have been for more than two centuries and a half fighting, treating, and dealing with our Indian tribes without acquiring a positive knoweldge of their character !" Such an exclamation certainly seems to be staggering. It appears to possess the vital force of reason and unanswerable argument; nevertheless, it is exactly true that, as a people, we know little or nothing about this very important matter. Unfortunately, those who have been the best able, from long and careful personal experience, to give the requisite information, have also been, for the most part, deficient in educational attainments and the capacity to impart their knowledge; while others have given no evidence of entertaining a just value of its public importance. Satisfied with their own acquirements, they have not sought to publish them for the benefit of others.

The white races of the American people boast European origin, mainly that of English lineage; but how much did the British really know of Americans, even at the period of our Revolution? Is not the history of that struggle indisputable evidence of the most lamentable and inexplicable ignorance on the part of the mother country? But, worse still; after the Revolution, after we had been in strict and closest commercial and political relations with Great Britain for over sixty years, after a second and sanguinary contest with that country, we have only to read the works of some of their travelers to arrive at the superficial and wonderfully erroneous idea of American character possessed by intelligent Britons.

When the two leading commercial nations of the

globe, each claiming the highest civilization, speaking identically the same language, and governed by the same general laws, contrive to pass two centuries and a half of close intercourse with such unsatisfactory interknowledgable results, is it strange that a like ignorance should exist between the American people and the nomadic races of this continent?

Causes similar to those which operated as a bar to English knowledge of the American character have interposed against our acquisition of precise information relative to the leading traits of Indian nature. Without being captious, it is assumed that British tourists have, for the most part, approached us with something of an intolerant and pre-occupied spirit. They came prepared to encounter ill-bred, semi-educated, uncouth and braggart provincials, rendered more unendurable by their democratic form of government, and political hostility to the time honored institutions of their own country. Reference can as emphatically be made to the course pursued by the British in India, the Spaniards in Mexico and Peru, the French in Africa and Cochin China. The conquering race seldom care to inform themselves minutely about the condition and characteristics of the conquered, and the results have been renewed sanguinary struggles and immensely increased expenditures. Our own dealings with the nomads of North America have been but so many chapters of the same record. What has our Government ever done, in a concerted, intelligent and liberal spirit, to acquire a definite knowledge of Indian character, as it exists among the tribes which wander over more than one-half the public domain?

The Indian Bureau, with its army of political camp-followers, bent upon improving their short and precarious official positions to "turn an honest penny," can scarcely be quoted as evidence of our search for the needed information. Tales of violence and wrong, of outrage and devilish malignity, committed by Indians, are rife all along our frontiers; but who ever hears the other side? Who chronicles the inciting causes, the long, unbroken series of injuries perpetrated by the semi-civilized white savages who, like Cain, fled from the retributive justice of outraged humanity, and sought refuge among the copper-colored savages of the woods and the plains? Naturally ferocious, warlike, revengeful and treacherous as were the aborigines of America, we have educated them to a pitch of refinement in cruelty, deceit and villainy far beyond their normal standard. If the white man has come to be regarded as his natural enemy, it may be set down as the result of long and murderous schooling. The inherent disposition of the American nomad inclined him to hospitality; but that inclination has been completely blotted out, and its opposite engrafted on his nature. Legends and traditions of white men's ingratitude have been handed down through so many generations, and the experiences of the living have been in such direct accordance with them, that they have become prime articles of their creed. Keenly alive to a sense of the inferiority of their armament, incapable of subsisting large bodies of men for any considerable period, and perpetually engaged in the work of exterminating each other, the several tribes have been reduced to the necessity of employing deceit against force, cunning against courage, artifice against honesty.

One of the most serious obstacles in the way of a settled and satisfactory arrangement with our Indian tribes results from our own form of government, which requires a change of the whole working department of the Indian Bureau whenever a change of administration takes place. Nor can this evil be remedied so long as the Indian Bureau continues to be a political machine. The savages cannot comprehend why it is that every few years imposes upon their acceptance new and un-tried Agents to regulate matters between them and their "Great Father" at Washington, nor why the new Agents should institute a policy different from that of their pre-decessors. Time, patience, zeal, great experience and conscientious discharge of duty are indispensably requi-site for the proper and just management of our Indian relations, and even then they will be found delicate and difficult under peculiar circumstances which are con-stantly presenting themselves. The first great object should be a total and sweeping reform in this respect. The Department of Indian Affairs, as it is now organ-ized, should be abolished as a costly and unnecessary adjunct to a Government already overburdened with political patronage. We have a large number of meri-torious and highly educated officers of the army on the retired list. Many of them have acquired considerable insight into Indian character during the course of their campaigns in our Territories and on our frontiers. They are drawing pay from the Government without render-ing effective service. Their own high sense of honor makes many of them feel as if they had been laid upon the shelf as being no longer useful, and they would be but too happy to prove that their capacity to serve their country in this line is quite as great as it ever was in their former field of operations. By appointing such men, and merging the Indian Bureau into the War Department, a regular, systematic policy would be pur-sued, upon which our savage tribes could place reliance, and which would ultimately gain their confidence and respect.

Why persist in maintaining a Department not only unnecessary, but which has always imposed enormous expenditures upon the people, and has frequently plunged us into costly Indian wars? What can a political camp-follower, who has done party service in our cities, and been appointed Indian Agent as reward for such services, possibly know of Indian character? And being profoundly ignorant of all that pertains to the people whose affairs he is about to manage, how can he conduct them with any degree of justice toward these people? It has been the writer's lot to be present at many meetings between Indian Agents and their constituencies; and he has always been shocked at the insolent, intolerant and supercilious manner of the Agents. It is as necessary to use common intelligence and prudence in our intercourse with savages as in the performance of any other act. If a man were required to move an object, his first business would be to ascertain the weight and character of that object, with a view to applying the proper motive power in a rational manner; but in our dealings with Indian tribes this common sense and practical style of operation is completely ignored. We have not even condescended to apply the rules of every day life to a subject of such extensive interest. Is the savage to be blamed because he becomes provoked at such intolerable folly? Is it to be wondered at that he should lose all confidence in people who, while claiming to be his superiors, display such despicable disregard of decency and good faith? And when he does evince anger and disgust, after his fashion — the only one he comprehends — straightway the worthy Agent shouts "stop thief," to conceal his own avarice and rascality, while he precipitates another costly conflict. Until this pernicious system be utterly swept away, and the management of Indian affairs confided to intelligent and educated men appointed for life, or during good behavior, from the ranks of our meritorious retired officers, we may hope in vain for any better condition of our relations with the tribes.

In the foregoing pages the attentive reader will have found some food for reflection. He will have perceived that the Apaches are not fools and idiots. He will have learned that they reflect, and argue with a great deal of logical acumen. He will have understood that there is much about them which can be studied with good results. He will have comprehended the impossibility of making a durable treaty with a tribe, each individual of which is sovereign in his own right, and disavows the authority of any one to treat for him. There can be but one policy pursued toward these Indians with any chance of satisfactory result. They must be subdued by force of arms, and after submission, they must be removed from their country. It will cost much to effect these objects, but the expense will be a mere "drop in the bucket," compared with that which must be disbursed to maintain the miserable little guerrilla warfare heretofore pursued, and which has only imbued them with contempt for our much vaunted power. It will require a force of seven or eight thousand men to effectually subdue the Apache race in Arizona and New Mexico; but with such a force, properly officered and appointed, the work can be done in less than one year.

Let it be understood, however, that the troops will be required for constant, active and arduous service in the field, and not to build forts, which are abandoned a year or so after construction; nor to till the earth, nor cultivate fine gardens, nor spend their time in dress parades and burnishing weapons which are never used. The men selected for this service should be picked, and entirely reliable. The rations of coffee, sugar, tea, and everything but hard bread, the best of jerked beef, and tobacco, should be stopped while on duty in the field, and their pay should be increased in proportion. All the troops employed in active service must be cavalry, and their accoutrements should be simplified to the greatest possible extent. A trooper's horse should not be cumbered with a useless valise, holsters, and a ridiculous amount of harness for display. The soldier should be equipped with two Colt's belt pistols, a first-class Spencer carbine, and a large knife. All posts should be kept and guarded by the infantry, aided by a small detachment of cavalry to act as herders, and at each post there should not be less than from fifty to seventy-five good horses, which may be rendered immediately available by any scouting party whose animals are beginning to tire. At each post the Commissary should be required to keep constantly on hand and baled in raw-hide covers, packages of bread and meat of not more than sixty pounds in each bale, and enough in quantity to equal ten days' rations for fifty men. There should also be a sufficient number of pack mules and *aparejos* to pack this amount of provision, and no mule should be laden with more than two packs. With these precautions, a pursuing party could replenish their stores and receive fresh horses and mules without the unnecessary and vexatious delays which have proved so fatal to success in our Indian campaigns in the Territories named.

Three thousand men, divided into companies of fifty each, would place sixty such companies in the field at one time, and this force could sweep Arizona from end to end in six months. Extreme care should be taken to prevent the Apaches from escaping into Northern Mexico, and operations should commence from the southern and eastern frontiers. The same system should be applied to New Mexico at the same time, commencing at the northern and western frontiers. The men, while on scout, should take only one pair of socks, one shirt and one pair of drawers with them, in addition to those they wear. All blankets and other baggage should be conveyed by pack mules so lightly laden that they may be able to keep up with the horses. In winter the clothing should consist of thick buckskin pants and jacket, lined with flannel, and in summer of the usual cavalry dress, but without trimmings, except the chevrons for non-commissioned officers. Marching by day should be avoided as much as possible, unless when following a trail. No fires should be allowed for cooking purposes; and when the state of the weather required them, they should be concealed as much as the ground might permit. The rations of coffee and sugar should be allowed in winter. The course of operations in the field would suggest itself to each officer in command of a company, and he should be allowed discretionary power.

It will be perceived that, although these suggestions require some space for their explanation, yet they present a far more simple system than any ever put in practice, although susceptible of very great modifications and improvements, which must be suggested by the circumstances which may present themselves from time to time. It is, however, clear that a great change must be made in our mode of dealing with the Apache race. Twenty years of unceasing warfare, without any other result than the loss of many lives, much property, the expenditure of enormous sums; the devastation of a large extent of country; the unavailability of one of the richest mineral regions in the Union, and the continuance of the perils to which immigrants are exposed while crossing it, should have sufficed to teach us that we have been suffering from an inadequate system of warfare. It is time that something more rigorous were tried. Matters can scarcely be worse than they have been and are.

Forty or fifty infantry at a post, which has its Commissary and Quarter-Master's establishments, with their various belongings; its hospital with its corps of nurses, cooks and attendants; its Adjutant's office with his clerks; the Commander's orderly, the company clerk, and other modes of occupying the troops, can scarcely be deemed a very effective force in an Apache country. Nevertheless, such is the style of warfare which has been carried on—occasionally varied by a small squad of cavalry making a scout with great lumbering army wagons, marching by day, and following the highways. Let no one imagine that these remarks are in any way intended to reflect on the officers and men doing duty in Arizona and New Mexico. All such idea is emphatically disavowed. They do the very best that can be done under the circumstances. No man can be expected to fight advantageously with both hands tied behind him. They can't help themselves; but are placed in an awkward and embarrassing position from which there seems to be no escape.

While Congress has been voting millions for various improvements, would it not have been wise to appropriate a small amount for the purification of two immensely rich and extensive Territories in the very heart of the country? If Alaska be worth seven millions, Arizona and New Mexico are worth one hundred. It has been

suggested by one high in authority, that an appropriation of three millions to assist the Sutro Tunnel project
would be an act of wisdom, as it would enormously in-
crease the yield of the Comstock lode; but it seems never
to have suggested itself to the minds of our legislators,
that the region withheld from our occupation by the
Apache race contains more mineral wealth than twenty
Comstock lodes.   We are floundering under a great na-
tional debt, and financiers are puzzling their wits to determine how it shall be extinguished; but they never
dream of the untold wealth buried in the mountains
which form the stronghold of the Apaches.   We have
behaved with the most Christian spirit of forbearance
toward that people.   Every time they have smitten us
on one cheek we have turned the other to receive an additional slap, which they were by no means loth to bestow.   Is it not almost time to put our "Quaker" one
side and perform what we have so long threatened? Is
our Government aware that the people of those Territories could present a bill for over fifty millions of dollars
for damages suffered at the hands of those Indians during the past twenty years?

It matters not by what process or method of schooling
the Apache has become the most treacherous, bloodthirsty, villainous and unmitigated rascal upon earth;
it is quite sufficient that he is so, and that he is incapable of improvement.   Kindness and generosity provoke
his contempt, and he regards them as weaknesses.   Chas-
tisement does not procure his vengeance with any more
certainty than want of caution.   The man who deems it
the highest achievement to become a dexterous robber is
scarcely an object in whom to repose confidence.   Whatever regard they exhibited toward myself was more induced by the conviction that I was serviceable to them,

while their respect was enforced through their dread of
my troopers. Nevertheless, when I was ordered home
from Fort Sumner, they all mounted their horses and
rode with us for two hours, and appeared quite sorry at
our departure. This would seem to express some sense
of gratitude, and so I imagined it, until subsequent intelligence disclosed the fact that they were never more
elated.

From the time of their last conflict with the Navajoes,
in which ninety of the latter were slain outright, within
fifteen miles of the Reservation, where their dead bodies
were seen by the other Navajoes under our charge, the
two people had never lived comfortably together. Their
camps were located four miles apart, but little feuds and
disputes were constantly arising which occupied much of
my time to arrange. At length the matter became un-
bearable to the Apaches, who were outnumbered nine to
one, and they applied to Gen. Carleton to be placed on
a separate Reservation. This was refused, and they resolved to leave by the first good opportunity. The only
bar to this was the presence of my company, of which
they entertained a most salutary dread, although constantly receiving little presents and kind treatment from
all the men. The Apaches had frequently witnessed
their target practice with carbine and pistol, in both of
which arms they had acquired wonderful perfection, and
they were also struck with the easy and bold riding of
my troopers. Gian-nah-tah, being angry one day, told
Capt. Updegraff, who had denied them a favor he had
no right to grant—"You think we care for you and your
men; not a bit of it, we are only restrained by those Californians." When they saw those Californians depart,
they were actually delighted, and in less than two
months afterward, the great body of them decamped to
parts unknown.

As an example of the precision to which my men had arrived in the use of their fire-arms, the following incident will suffice. While passing the "Caves" on the road to the San Bernardino river, whither we had been to settle a little difficulty with the Piutes, we were passed by a fine antelope buck, about one hundred yards distant, and going at speed. There were fourteen men in single file behind me, and I cried out, "Fire at that antelope." At the word each man checked his horse, raised his carbine and fired. The animal fell, and upon examination, it was found that every ball had struck him.

The information which I received from Mr. Labadie relative to the Apache hegira from Fort Sumner, only added to my former conviction that they are incapable of any enduring sense of gratitude. Their intense selfishness precludes any hope from that quarter, while the long and close experience I had with them, established the conviction in my mind that their intensified proclivity to commit outrage can only be suppressed by force of arms, in a vigorous and not too merciful campaign, prosecuted with an overwhelming force, and brought to a sudden and decisive end by occupying many portions of their country at the same time, and keeping the forces in the field until the object be accomplished.

In the foregoing work only such personal adventures have been recited as served to exemplify some trait of Indian character; and if any of my readers have received either pleasure or profit from its perusal, or if these experiences should serve in any way to modify or better our Indian policy, the author will not have written in vain.

FINIS.